Monica Larner

Working and Living
FRANCE

guides

Contents

Author's acknowledgements

My most sincere thanks go to the editors, copy-editors, graphic designers, photo scanners, typesetters and printers who put the pieces of this complicated choreography together and did a wonderful job of it. Very special thanks go to Rupert Wheeler of Navigator Guides, the 'ringmaster', who deserves a long vacation and without whom none of this would have been possible.

I would also like to thank my profoundly Francophile parents, Stevan and Christine Larner, for introducing me to France and for reading over this manuscript. More thanks go to the friends I have found along the way: Andrea Coll, Renata Ivankovic, John Moretti and the summer gang of rue Plus Basse. A special salute goes to Stéphane Duchiron and that summer morning in the Bois de Boulogne.

Publisher's acknowledgements

Navigator Guides would sincerely like to thank Monica Larner for all her hard work, plus Georgina Palffy and Jacqueline Chnéour for their invaluable contributions. A big thanks also goes to Linda McQueen who has helped pull this new series together.

About the author

Monica Larner has always divided her life between the USA, France and Italy, and she is currently restoring a 13th century home in Biot, a hilltop village near Antibes. A travel and food journalist and photographer, she is a contributing writer with *Wine Enthusiast* and author of four guidebooks. Each fall, she can be found with pruning shears in hand at Larner Vineyard near Santa Barbara, California. You can write to her at monica@monicalarner.com, or visit www.monicalarner.com.

Conceived and produced for Cadogan Guides by:

Navigator Guides Ltd
The Old Post Office, Swanton Novers,
Melton Constable, Norfolk NR24 2AJ
www.navigatorguides.com
info@navigatorguides.com

Cadogan Guides
165 The Broadway, London SW19 1NE
info@cadoganguides.co.uk
www.cadoganguides.com

The Globe Pequot Press
246 Goose Lane, PO Box 480, Guilford,
Connecticut 06437-0480

Copyright © Cadogan Guides 2004
"THE SUNDAY TIMES" is a registered trade mark
of Times Newspapers Limited

Cover design: Sarah Rianhard-Gardner
Cover and photo essay photographs
© Monica Larner and © Corbis
Photo essay design: Smith, Cowan & Wilkinson
Maps © Cadogan Guides,
drawn by Map Creation Ltd
Editor: Jane Belford
Series Editor: Linda McQueen
Proofreading: Susannah Wight
Indexing: Isobel McLean

Printed in Italy by Legoprint
A catalogue record for this book is available
from the British Library
ISBN 1-86011-128-9

The author and publishers have made every effort to ensure the accuracy of the information in this book at the time of going to press. However, they cannot accept any responsibility for any loss, injury or inconvenience resulting from the use of information contained in this guide.

Please help us to keep this guide up to date. We have done our best to ensure that the information in this guide is correct at the time of going to press. But places and facilities are constantly changing, and standards and prices in hotels and restaurants fluctuate. We would be delighted to receive any comments concerning existing entries or omissions. Authors of the best letters will receive a copy of the Cadogan Guide of their choice.

Introduction

Ask almost anyone and they will say that at some point in their life life they dreamed of living in France. Snapshots of lazy afternoons dedicated to *apéritifs* and smart conversation at an outdoor café in Paris, or of leisurely strolls past retirees in tank tops and sandals playing *pétanque* on the bowling strip in Cannes, or weekend wine-touring in the Loire, loom large in the traveller's memory diary. France is a country of epic natural beauty, of sophistication and civilization, and of creative expression that has shaped our very defini-tion of who we are. Thomas Jefferson put it more simply: 'Every man has two countries, his own and France.'

It is that infectious universal appeal that drives so many foreigners to make France their home. But what was once a trickle has recently become a torrent, especially where the British are concerned. Within the past 10 years, and even more so within the past two, sun-seekers and Brie-eaters are streaming across the Channel to live and work in France. Consider foreign property purchases: in 2002, they rose by three per cent, but British purchases in France soared 40 per cent. Why now? The reasons behind the sudden boom are not entirely clear, but surely have to do with new prosperity, and new mobility sparked by budget airlines. They also have to do with the fact that today there are more resources available than ever before for making the transition abroad.

This book is one of those resources. More than a guide, *Working and Living in France* is a friendly companion written by an author who has had first-hand experience. Packed with essential information – from logistical considerations to fiscal implications – it will direct you step-by-step on your life in France. But it is anything but a standard 'how-to' manual. The book includes a detailed regional breakdown to help you choose between the urban allure of the City of Light and the rural comforts of the wine country. It addresses the needs of those who want to work in France, study, buy property or open a business. Thinking about investing your money in a 15th-century farmhouse? The housing chapter will tell you the right questions to ask. Dreaming of opening a bed & breakfast? The section on 'Starting Your Own Business' explains your options. Need to know where English-language schools are for your children? The 'Living in France' chapter details the intricacies of life in a new country.

Throughout the book are personal anecdotes from seasoned experts who have long since settled into their new life. Their stories – sometimes humorous, sometimes less so – have been selected to highlight common pitfalls and misunderstandings. They also communicate just how rewarding living and working in France can be. The book is structured to supply the information you need, to accompany you through bureaucratic procedures, and to expose basic cultural curiosities. Most importantly, it should nudge you along so that you ask the right questions and make the right decisions. If you are ready to move, or are still dreaming about it, let us accompany you on this exciting journey.

01

Getting to Know France

There are many emotions that come with moving abroad, but the one that overrides them all is excitement. It is probably a safe bet to assume you have a working knowledge of French culture, history, art and food. Familiarity with France is a part of every person's basic intellectual scope. Moving to France to live or work means you will soon know it better than most. You will embark on a new learning process, and if things go according to plan you will broaden your horizons, change your outlook, find new stimuli and be provoked by unexpected situations. You will become a little less British and little more French. More exciting is the realization you will undoubtedly have – as all integrated expatriates eventually do – that, no matter how well you think you know your new country, there is more to learn.

The aim of this first chapter is to paint a general picture of the country's geography, climate and language and provide a thumbnail sketch of its history. France's population is almost 60 million people strong and more than half those people live in towns of 50,000 inhabitants and up. Some 10 million people live in the metropolitan Paris area alone and Lille, Lyon and Marseille each count about 1.2 million inhabitants. One per cent of the world's population is French and France is the world's biggest tourist destination. Each year it accommodates 65 million tourists – more than the number of French citizens. Of those, 15 million are British and Eire residents. Almost one million Britons spend more than three months each year living outside their country and more than half a million have purchased property in France. And the British expat community is growing faster now than ever before.

It's your turn to follow in their footsteps and know France.

Climate and Geography

France is truly blessed in both these departments. Protected by mountains to the northeast and flanked by two different bodies of water, the country occupies one of the most beautiful and fertile corners of the European continent. The so-called Hexagon, an expression used to describe the French territory, spans 543,965 sq km, making it the largest country in Western Europe, accounting for one-fifth of the European Union. Its borders include the English Channel to the northwest, Belgium and Luxembourg to the northeast, Germany and Switzerland to the east, Italy and Monaco to the southeast, and Spain to the southwest. On the western side is the Atlantic and on the southeastern side is the Mediterranean. The island of Corsica, one of the biggest in the Mediterranean, is French.

There are 3,427km of coastline including 644km of Corsica coast, meaning that France has the third largest coastal area in the world after the United States and the United Kingdom.

Mistral Madness

There's an old saying in the south of France: 'The winds of the Mistral could pull the tail off a donkey.' These chilly northwesterly winds come howling southward, gaining velocity as they funnel through the tight Rhône Valley and overwhelm low pressure areas in Provence. They cause serious crop damage, and squat homes in windswept areas have roofs weighed down with rocks. The winds have forced their way into the nooks and crannies of the southern territory and folklore and the Mistral has also left its mark on the human spirit. Winds in general are a metaphor for change, impending doom and madness. And this is exactly what the Mistral brought to one of the most important modern art personalities. We all recognize Vincent van Gogh as the troubled genius who during one of his frequent bouts of despair cut off his ear. He shot himself and died two years later in 1890. We also know that his suicide was somehow linked to the torment he suffered because of the maddening Mistral. Van Gogh and his buddy Paul Gauguin lodged themselves in a charming yellow house near Arles to paint together and keep each other company. Yet the relationship between the two friends was tumultuous. The infamous ear-cutting episode occurred the night before Gauguin finally left because Van Gogh threatened him with a razor: 'I had to leave Arles, he was so bizarre that I couldn't take it,' Gauguin said to a fellow painter. Shortly after, Van Gogh painted his disturbing self-portrait with a bandaged ear and dedicated it to Gauguin.

Van Gogh was born on 30 March 1853 in Groot-Zundert, son of a Dutch Protestant minister. He was deeply spiritual and was an evangelist before becoming a painter. Today he is remembered for *The Starry Night*, *Sunflowers*, *The Bedroom* and *Irises*, and other works painted in his trademark thick, swirling brushstrokes and brilliant colours. He sold only one painting during his lifetime and worked furiously and steadily in and out of spells of madness and violent seizures, which after his death were diagnosed as epilepsy. He painted some of his famous flower paintings by tying the legs of his easel to pegs in the ground so that it wouldn't get knocked down by the Mistral winds.

France fits this vast space with a landscape that has inspired the most creative artists and poets. To the north and west are rolling hills, flat plains and forests. Mountainous terrain rises dramatically from the Mediterranean to the Alps, the Pyrenees at the border with Spain, the Massif Central and the Vosges. In the southeast corner is the Rhône river delta and France's highest mountain, Mont Blanc (4,807 metres). The territory is crisscrossed by an elaborate network of rivers – the Rhône, the Seine, the Loire, the Gironde, the Garonne and the Rhine – and hundreds of smaller tributaries. The basins left by these rivers support the agriculture that fuelled much of the prosperity and influence that France enjoys today.

In addition to 96 metropolitan departments of the Hexagon, France has four overseas departments: Guadeloupe, Martinique, French Guiana and Reunion. Its four overseas territories are: New Caledonia, French Polynesia, the French Southern and Antarctic lands, and Wallis and Futuna Islands. Lastly, France has 'territorial collectivities' and these are Mayotte and St Pierre-et-Miquelon.

France has one of the most moderate **climates** in the world but, because of the size of the country and its varying altitudes, the climate can vary considerably from one region to the next. Mountain areas such as the Alps and Jura mountains have heavy snows in winter months. The north enjoys a temperate climate and northeastern areas have a continental climate – with wider temperature extremes between summer and winter. The Atlantic gives the coastal and inland areas from the Loire to the Basque region their hot and sunny summers. The Riviera, Provence and Roussillon have a Mediterranean climate with mild weather most of the year and beach-perfect summers. Yet inland from here, in Auvergne, Burgundy and the Rhône Valley, strong Mistral winds (see p.9) force the thermometer down.

Provence is hit by hot winds off the Sahara known as *sirocco* – which carry grains of sand from Africa that blanket parked cars and gardens. France is generally subjected to maritime influences, particularly low fronts from the Atlantic. Much of the nation experiences thunderstorms at the end of August, marking the beginning of autumn. More rain comes in October, November, March and April, and the seasons are distinct everywhere in the country. For a regional temperature and rainfall chart, *see* 'Regional Climate and Rainfall Chart', p.279.

Historical Overview

It all started here. **Cro-Magnon** is the name of a man from Magnon, France, who was almost indistinguishable from modern man (unlike Neanderthal man, who also roamed this part of the world) and who lived some 40,000 thousand years before our time. Cro-Magnon is different from us only in that his body mass was 20 per cent larger. But those extra kilos can be attributed to a strenuous lifestyle and probably had little to do with genetics. Cro-Magnon was also a prolific painter, decorating cave walls such as the Grotte de Lascaux, which has been dubbed the 'Sistine Chapel of Prehistoric Art'. It's no surprise that the French have been so handy with a brush ever since. Early forms of mankind made France home up to one million years ago, and the upper Palaeolithic cultures called the Perigordian (from Périgord), the Aurignacian (from Aurignac) and the Magdalenian (from a cave in the Tarn) were Cro-Magnon's ancestors and ancient neighbours.

Carnac in Brittany was particularly popular with the **Neolithic man** who chose this area for his mysterious megaliths erected some time between 4500 BC and

2000 BC. The two structures of megalithic architecture are the menhirs (a veritable 'army' of 3,000 upright stones that form perfect lines of up to one kilometre in length and may have been astronomical in nature, aligned with the sun or the moon in some way, although this is not clear) along with dolmens and tumulus, or burial structures. These mysterious archaeological remains point to the world's very first civilization and are the most famous stone markings after Stonehenge.

At about 1000 BC, with the beginnings of the '**Iron Age**', it is thought that tribes of Celts arrived in southern Europe. Their first trading centres (*oppida*) traced the outlines of France's cities today. One such centre, named Lutetia, has since evolved into the city we know as Paris.

This sun-drenched and fertile land caught the attention of other ancient wanderers. Various tribes including the Iberians and the Basques (whose name comes from the Roman term for them, 'Vascones', and whose language may be the oldest in Europe) came, as did the Ligurians from what is today Italy. But France really got its start as a frontier land of economic potential with the Greeks. They founded many trading colonies on France's Mediterranean coast, such as Marseille and Nice. They were also the first to introduce the grapevine to France. Vine genetics suggest a link between syrah, the grape widely planted throughout the Rhône Valley, and grapes from the Persian city of Shiraz in what is today Iran.

The **Romans** made wine a global business, and ancient terracotta amphorae found across the Mediterranean basin suggest that they planted their favourite varieties all over Europe, including the territory they called Gallia. The markings on amphorae found in France suggest they originated in Italy. That points to a blossoming wine trade between the two lands. Despite the fact that the natives of Gaul were attached to their own beer-like brew, they were prepared to pay a steep price for wine. One contemporary writer remarked of the Gauls, 'They will give you a slave for an amphora of wine, thus exchanging the cup-bearer for the cup.'

Starting with Julius Caesar, the Romans invested heavily in the territory because it represented a crucial link between the Iberian peninsula and northern Europe. The city of Lyon (Lugdunum) was located at a military and economic crossroads and the Roman 'provinces' (Provence being one of the most important) grew strong. The Romans also left behind their language, Latin, which was manipulated and polluted over the centuries to become French. The various Gallic tribes had put up resistance against the Romans, united under Vercingétorix, but were defeated at the siege of Alésia (today Alise-Ste-Reine in Burgundy). France is home some of the most beautiful Roman ruins outside the Italian peninsula. Theatres and ruins in Orange, Arles and Vaison-la-Romaine are awe-inspiring examples.

The Beginnings of France

The glory days of Rome came to an end and waiting in the wings, poised to pick at the bones of the fallen empire, were groups of Germanic tribes on the other side of the Rhine River. By the third century, the Franks and the Alemanni had broken through. In AD 406, the Rhine frontier had collapsed and more tribes such as the Burgundians and the Visigoths came pouring in, as a result of greater pressure further north from bat-swinging Huns. Post-Roman Gaul was a patchwork of tribes of different people and religions in great disarray. The ambiguous situation called for a dominant power, and that finally came with the Franks and Christianity.

Clovis, King of the Franks, converted to Christianity to marry the Burgundian princess Clotilda. The move proved a brilliant political one because by doing so he gained a strong ally in the Roman church. Clovis managed to rid Gaul of many of the tribes that had been a nuisance (he pushed the Visigoths into Spain and conquered the southwest) and he based his government in Paris and called his territory Francia. The dialect spoken became known as Francien.

More troubles arose on the horizon. The succession of Merovingian kings that started with Clovis became weaker, and more tribes of different ethnic hues found refuge in Francia. These included refugees from Britain who settled in Brittany, and the Gascons, who reclaimed land between the Pyrenees and the Garonne. The Arabs, who had been trawling the waters of the Mediterranean and taking advantage of their perceived *droit de seigneur* with local brides, made an attempt at Francia but were gallantly stopped at Poitiers in AD 732.

The Merovingian dynasty, with rulers identified by ancient hippy hairdos, had trouble reproducing strong heirs, and eventually Pepin the Short anointed himself king. He established the principle of rule by divine right – the belief that a king was chosen by God. His son, who ironically towered at over seven feet, became known as Charlemagne.

Charlemagne, or 'Charles the Great', became one of Europe's strongest leaders. His Carolingian empire ruled France for half a century and within that time expanded the boundaries of his kingdom across much of Western Europe. Only the southern extremes of Italy, Spain and the British Isles were beyond his control.

But troubles continued brewing between foreign tribes, who were attracted to this land like magnets. To make matters worse, Charlemagne's territory was eventually divided into three among his three grandsons after his death. Raiding Vikings, known as 'north men', were eventually bought off with a swath of land that would become Normandy for 'Normans'. More independent states such as Aquitaine, Provence, Burgundy and Toulouse were formed. The **Dark Ages** descended on France and fighting factions and micro-countries eventually evolved into outright feudalism. **Hugues Capet** became king, although his territory had been whittled down since the time of Charlemagne to a tiny strip of land between Paris and Orléans. The Capetian dynasty ruled for eight centuries over a fragmented territory. Indeed, it was **William, Duke of Normandy** who conquered England in 1066, not **King Philip I**. The Normans also founded a kingdom for themselves in the sunny island of Sicily in southern Italy.

The Middle Ages

The new millennium opened with the **Crusades**, the first of which was proclaimed in 1095 in Clermont-Ferrand (not Rome) by Pope Urban II, specifically with the intention of rousing the attention of brave French knights. With a common goal – to seize Palestine away from Muslim rule – the hope was that they would stop making trouble back home. The tactic worked: French knights were among the most enthusiastic crusaders.

This was also a time of acrobatic artistic aspirations, and Gothic cathedrals sprang up across France like mushrooms. Architecture, art and philosophy flourished. Thanks to its university and intellectual fervour, Paris grew to become the biggest city in Europe by the 12th century. Beyond the capital, fragments of France still suffered from in-fighting. In an effort to consolidate territory, Louis VI arranged the marriage of his son Louis VII to Eleanor of Aquitaine, heiress of the biggest state in France. But, in a shocking about-face that only matters of the heart can explain, she divorced in 1152 and fell for Henry Plantagenet, Duke of Normandy and soon to be King Henry II of England. Louis VII's heir, Philippe Auguste (with blood ties to Charlemagne), fought the battle Louis VII never did. He antagonized Henry II, then took issue with his sons, Richard the Lionheart and John, and eventually beat them in the Battle of the Bouvines in 1214.

In a few swift moves, **Philippe Auguste** had gained Normandy, Touraine, Poitou and Brittany. He became the first to be known as the '**King of France**', as opposed to the 'King of the Franks'. This period represents the consolidation of French royal power within the French national territory. Yet his influence stayed in the northern half of France. The south of the country, or the Occitan, was an unruly patchwork of political and religious sects that had very little in common with northern France. The language and culture of the two spheres were entirely different. In 1209, thanks to the Albigensian Crusades, much of the south was conquered. Philippe's son Louis IX (Saint-Louis) continued to consolidate power, and his grandson, Philippe IV le Bel, designed the foundations of a modern state with the creation of the Estates-General, or parliament. His influence grew over the Church to the extent that Pope Clement V fled Rome and the papacy was installed in Avignon from 1307 to 1377.

Unresolved tensions with England gave rise to the infamous **Hundred Years' War** (although it lasted longer than a century, from 1337 to 1453). The fighting lasted too long, carried on through a succession of kings, and lacked the decisive battles that would determine a winner. This uncertainty and the dreadful length of the war caused enormous hardship back in France. Trade routes and commercial hubs had been removed and the nation suffered a debilitating loss of morale. If war wasn't bad enough, the Black Death picked off many of those who only just survived the battlefield. One-third of the population of France was killed by the plague.

This darkest chapter of history ends with a heroine. **Joan of Arc**, a teenage shepherd girl from Lorraine with visions and a holy mandate, did more than anyone else to stop a century of relentless violence. She vowed to push the English back over the Channel and put the dauphin Charles on the French throne. Her lofty ambitions won her horsemen and foot soldiers. In 1429, she succeeded in chasing the English out of Orléans, but she was captured before she could continue her campaign. Joan of Arc was eventually given to the English, who burned her at the stake for witchcraft and heresy in Rouen. But the momentum she had initiated was strong, and by 1453 the English had completely lost their footing in France, except for Calais, which would be liberated shortly after.

The Rebirth of a Nation

A new spirit of optimism washed over France, and Charles' son Louis XI started an ambitious rebuilding and recovery programme that delivered France into the Renaissance. His successors, **Louis XII** and **Francois Ier**, ruled during a spell of prosperity and peace. The music, clothing and poetry of Renaissance Italy spilled over into France and the tradition of the lavish, decadent, over-the-top court was inaugurated.

In 1559, France even got an Italian queen. After Henri II's death, **Catherine de' Medici** ruled briefly, reportedly with the help of sorcery and Nostradamus. She had three sons who proved to be nothing more than footnotes in history, and continued to exercise her influence behind the scenes.

The 16th century marked a return to violence, this time because of rising religious conflict. The Reformation kicked off thanks to French-born **Jean Calvin**, who fled Paris, moved to Geneva and invited other exiled Protestants to follow. Meanwhile, back home, Protestant villages were being burned and people were slaughtered. The nation split into two warring sides: the Catholics under the Duc de Guise, and the Protestants, also known as the **Huguenots**.

Charles IX made attempts at peace, but his 1560 amnesty for Protestants failed and tempers flared again. When Henri III was assassinated in 1589 (he had already ordered the execution of troublemaker de Guise), **Henri IV** claimed the throne. In a curious twist of fate, France's new king was Henri de Navarre, son of Antoine, and a Huguenot. The womanizing king could not commit to religious beliefs, either. He underwent numerous changes in faith, culminating with a final conversion to Catholicism in 1593. This proved a brilliant strategy for winning over both sides of the conflict, and his **Edict of Nantes** four years later (which established a truce and offered protection to Protestants) brought temporary peace, or at least he hoped it would. In 1610, he was murdered by a Catholic as he rode through Paris by carriage.

Before his death, Henri had started to rebuild French roads and towns with the help of his friend the Duc de Sully. Henri was tragically assassinated in 1610 and succeeded by his 11-year-old son, Louis XIII, under a government controlled by Louis' mother, Marie de' Medici. It took Louis till 1624 to oust Marie, with the help of the influential minister Cardinal Richelieu, Sully's political heir, and they embarked on bringing peace and order to the political scene. Richelieu also created balance of power among European nations and by the time of his death in 1642, the same year as the king, France was a model for the rest of the world.

The Sun King

The final 150 years of the French monarchy saw an intellectual flowering. It was during these glory years that science, mathematics, philosophy and art were elevated to new heights. People like Descartes, Corneille, Molière, Mansart, Lully and Rameau entered the scene and set the tone for an intellectual revival, the effects of which would last for centuries.

Louis XIV took the crown when he was just five years old, in 1643. There had been attempts at undermining the youngster ruler, but backstabbers only strengthened Louis' determination and sharpened his skills. Early in his reign, he arrested the corrupt superintendent of finances and put Jean-Baptiste Colbert in the job. Colbert increased trade, oversaw colonial expansion and implemented tax reforms. In short, he made a lot of money that Louis took it upon himself to spend. The king paid for a lavish court and indulged himself beyond reason. He had become the sun whose rays of brilliance illuminated France and the world. The pinnacle of his extravagances came in the form of a 10,000-room palace at Versailles. Unwilling – and perhaps unable – to tighten the purse strings, he allowed the economy to unravel.

The ensuing discomfort was what ultimately led to the French Revolution. The poor grew poorer and the rich richer thanks to Colbert's tax schemes. War had left the treasury empty. By the end of Louis' reign in 1715, famine and misery were common. The Edict of Nantes was revoked and Protestants suffered another round of exile and torture. Louis XIV's great-grandson (Louis XV) ascended the throne and demonstrated little talent as king. France lost the Seven Years' War in 1763, and much of its New World footing with it. His successor, **Louis XVI**, ruled over the final years of the Ancien Régime and was oblivious to two blinking neon signs. Number one was the philosophy of Voltaire, and number two was the American War of Independence, which sent ripples across the Atlantic, and placed even more of a financial burden on the French people because of the aid sent by France to help the Americans lick the British.

Liberté, Egalité and Fraternité

We know what happened next. The need to purge France of centuries of serfdom and slavery, with a 'privileged' few who greedily occupied the pinnacle of power, had reached explosive proportions. Steam was let off at Versailles in June 1789 when a breakaway group declared itself the National Assembly after the king locked them out of an Estates-General meeting. Louis XVI called in troops but his efforts came too late. Across the country, farmers, agitators and a generally peeved population took to the streets, often chanting the three words that would become the motto of a reborn country: 'Liberty, Equality and Fraternity'.

The customs house in Paris was sacked and days later, on 14 July, a rowdy crowd stormed the Bastille – for the sheer symbolism of it. Paris formed a new militia headed by the Marquis de Lafayette and the French flag was born (see **France Today**, p.67). Over the next few years, the National Assembly drafted a constitution and the *Declaration of the Rights of Man*. Meanwhile, a group of nobles, exiled abroad, were plotting to overthrow the revolutionaries and vying for a return to status quo. The king and his family attempted to flee Paris to join their cause in June 1791 (the so-called 'flight to Varennes') but were arrested instead. Those exiled nobles, backed by foreign governments, formed an army and invaded from across the Rhine, but their counter-coup failed. The French Republic was proclaimed and the king was put on trial for conspiracy. He was executed in 1793, and the upcoming months saw a glut of executions that opened the Reign of Terror, overseen by Maximilien Robespierre. Heads did roll: 20,000 people convicted of treason were guillotined in Paris, and 40,000 died by the blade elsewhere. Robespierre himself was one if its last victims, in 1794.

The government passed to a five-man executive, the Directoire, according to the new constitution. But exhaustion set in. So much had changed in so little time, and many redirected their attentions away from politics. The nascent government proved rather inexperienced, and less dramatic issues like inflation and voting rights were not properly sorted out. As a result, it failed to muster much respect. France needed someone with balls. Enter Napoleon Bonaparte.

Napoleon Bonaparte

A young artillery officer from Corsica was dispatched to quell a rowdy protest in Paris and he did so in a simple but decisive manner: He fired a cannon and frightened rioters into submission. That made an impression: the Directoire handed him control of the army and within a relatively short time Napoleon compiled a military résumé rarely seen in history. He brilliantly nabbed northern Italy from the Austrians, defeated the English at Toulon and conquered Egypt. He was on the military fast track and people back home started to get a wee bit nervous. He was summoned home for a little chat.

Napoleon did return, but with a pistol, and overthrew the Directoire. He made the move almost effortlessly thanks to collaborators, including his brother, who was already speaker of the National Legislature. Napoleon took control of France in November 1799, on the eve of a new century, and meticulously set out to give France a backbone. Proclaiming himself Emperor of France in 1804, he created new legal parameters, known as the Code Napoléon, that are still employed today; he put France on the metric system; and he created institutions of higher learning called the Grandes Ecoles.

But what do you give the man who has everything? Still energized and ambitious, Napoleon set his sights on Europe and embarked on a series of offensive strikes throughout the continent. Napoleon, a little bulldozer of determination, eventually let things get out of control. He dispatched troops to Moscow and half a million perished – many because they were unprepared for the chilly temperatures. Napoleon returned to Paris and abdicated in 1814. He was exiled to the small island of Elba off the Italian coast and Louis XVI's brother was crowned Louis XVIII.

A constitutional monarchy was restored, adding one more layer to a complicated period of French history which saw the nation juggle monarchy, empire and republic in fast succession. Napoleon returned from exile only to be defeated by the British at Waterloo and sent to another small island; this time in the Atlantic. He remained on St Helena until his death. Louis XVIII was succeeded by Charles X, who abdicated in face of a popular uprising in favour of Louis-Philippe, Duke of Orléans. He puttered forward but abdicated after another popular uprising.

After that mess France decided to focus, and the so-called Second Republic was established. France needed a president, and the person who emerged victorious from the polls was none other than Louis-Napoléon, nephew of the former emperor. Presumably unhappy with the title 'president', he masterminded a plan to shut down the troublesome National Assembly and in 1852 proclaimed himself Emperor Napoléon III.

The world was rapidly changing thanks to industrialization, and France got its first railways. Paris became the Second Empire's showcase, with grand Exhibitions, the building of the Opéra, and the replanning of the city on grand scale by Baron Haussmann. The economy flourished because of economic expansion, liberalization and the founding of strong financial institutions. It also established colonies in Algeria and Indochina, and expanded these holdings over the next decades. Last, it gained Nice and Savoy. There were glitches though. Napoléon III installed Prince Maximilian von Habsburg as emperor of Mexico, but that ended in bloodshed. In 1870, the Franco-Prussian War started and also ended in disgrace. Napoléon III was captured in battle, Paris was seized and its famished citizens were forced to eat the animals in the zoo. A humiliating peace agreement was signed and France lost Alsace and Lorraine.

Marching towards the New Millennium

France cruised into the so-called Third Republic and took a much-needed break. The usual squabbling between Catholics, bourgeoisie, peasants, nobility, radicals, conservatives and monarchists continued, but overall parliamentary power was at a peak. Trade unions were recognized. More important scientific and technological inventions helped raise the quality of life. The Suez Canal was built and become a showcase for engineering ingenuity. Education was improved and welfare acts were established. Last, the separation of Church and state formally occurred. But one blemish stirs controversy to this day and foreshadows the upcoming atrocities. Captain **Alfred Dreyfus**, a Jew, was arrested for selling military secrets to the Germans in 1894 and later convicted on forged evidence. His name was not cleared until a decade later, but the scandal polarized a nation and exposed simmering anti-Semitism.

The **First World War** hit Europe following the 1914 assassination of Austria's Archduke Franz Ferdinand in Sarajevo, and covered France in a shroud of darkness and death. France took the brunt of the war, since many of the bloodiest trench-war battles were fought on her territory. The death toll was staggering at 1.4 million, and twice that number were wounded. There is hardly a village in France today that doesn't have a sobering stone monument to honour those who perished in the Great War. You'll notice the same last name carved into stone again and again, representing brothers, cousins, fathers and uncles. Some families had the entire male line cut short. Georges Clemenceau came to power in 1917, and Allied troops under French command were victorious. That nagging thorn in the side of France – the two lost provinces of Alsace and Lorraine – were finally returned.

Once again, France made time for post-war reconstruction, and was remarkably quick to jump back on its feet. Much of the creativity and carefree optimism of the roaring 1920s came out of Paris. A café culture was born, and intellectuals from the world over, and particularly from North America, descended on the wicker chairs of the capital's pavements. But the Great Depression came, bringing with it tough economic times, inflation and unemployment, and eclipsed much of this new-found optimism. It also gave rise to empowered political forces, such as the Communists, the Socialist Party and right-wing factions. To defend the Republic, Leftist parties joined together in 1936 in the Popular Front to win elections under Léon Blum.

When **Hitler** struck in 1939, it was as if France didn't have the will to fight back. Europe's biggest army was swiftly crushed and refugees scattered aimlessly. A few months after Germany launched the Blitzkrieg, France formally surrendered. This was her most humiliating hour. The Nazis occupied all of Northern France and the Atlantic coast and 'France' was chiselled down to the centre and south. A new capital was established in **Vichy**, governed by Marshal Pétain and a band of anti-Semitic leftovers from the Dreyfus days. Jews and political opponents were readily handed over to the Nazis by the Vichy government. By 1942, the Nazis found little need for the puppet government and took all of France.

Pockets of resistance fighters were well placed throughout the country, and Général **Charles de Gaulle**, who had escaped to England, co-ordinated much of their efforts. The resistance fighters, many of whom were Communist, reluctantly accepted De Gaulle as their leader. (Looking back, it has been noted that without De Gaulle, France's position in post-war Europe, NATO and the United Nations would not be as strong today.) On 6 June 1944 Allied forces stormed the beaches at Normandy, launching the biggest amphibian attack in history, and the liberation process commenced. French General Leclerc entered Paris on 24 August and Liberation Day was fixed on 8 May, 1945. Elaborate parades on the Champs-Elysées are staged each year on this national holiday.

A new constitution was drafted and France's Fourth Republic was born. Revolving-door governments meant no one was around long enough to take care of France's foreign policy tangles. Indochina broke away and sparked an embarrassing war. The French were defeated in Vietnam in 1954 at Dien Bien Phu. Decolonization continued with Morocco and Tunisia, but one of the ugliest examples of it was Algeria. One million French people had settled and invested in Algeria and were reluctant to leave. Algerian nationalist groups had been waging a dirty guerrilla war and France installed more troops to fight them (at any cost). To this day, evidence of torture and murders of civilians by the French in Algeria is being brought to light. When the government in Paris was ready to withdraw in 1958, the military staged a near *coup d'état*. De Gaulle rewrote the constitution once again, making for a stronger presidency, and a Fifth Republic was launched in 1958. An assassination attempt on De Gaulle's life by the sinister OAS (Secret Army Organization, or the disgruntled army officers in Algeria) failed, and the French granted Algeria independence in 1962.

Marshall Plan money helped rebuild France, and the framework for the European Common Market was established with the 1957 Treaty of Rome. De Gaulle continued to introduce economic and political reforms, and a constitutional amendment established the election of the president by direct universal suffrage. The 1960s also saw a growing frustration with De Gaulle and his stubborn unwillingness to make France a more modern state. University students and left-wing activists took to the streets and in May 1968 the infamous student revolts of Paris were staged. A massive general strike brought the country to its knees and some nine million people poured through the streets. De Gaulle's government fell in 1969 after a trivial referendum failed, and he quietly retired to write his memoirs.

The right kept a firm grip on power, maintaining the presidency for a decade under Georges Pompidou and UDF (centrist) Valéry Giscard d'Estaing, but in 1981 François Mitterrand was elected, marking the first time the left had been in power since shortly after the Second World War. He served two seven-year

Chirac and the Politics of Cohabitation

In 2002, Jacques Chirac was elected Président de la République Française for a second term, on the back of the slogan 'better a crook than a fascist'. In a political earthquake that surprised everyone but its most vile protagonist, centre-Right veteran Chirac had found himself pitted against Jean-Marie Le Pen, leader of the far-Right *Front National* (*see* p.69), in the second-round run-off of the presidential elections. Goaded into action by the spectre of fascism, the French electorate rallied against Le Pen, re-electing Chirac with 82 per cent of the vote – despite weariness at the political longevity of a man dogged by scandal. The episode reflected the country's disillusionment with the merry-go-round of France's ruling élites, swapping power.

Back in 1958, after a constitutional crisis sparked by French rule in Algeria, self-styled saviour of the nation Général Charles de Gaulle had established France's Fifth Republic, replacing the series of unstable coalitions that had characterized the post-war Fourth Republic with a strongly presidential system. Post-Liberation, the Left claimed the moral victory of Resistance, but was fragmented between the diehard Stalinists of the Parti Communiste Français and Leftist factions which ultimately formed the Parti Socialiste in 1969. American opposition to Communism and lingering fear of revolution helped to keep the Left out of power for more than 20 years.

In 1981, however, François Mitterrand swept in as the Republic's first Socialist president, to jubilation in the Place de la Bastille. The PS swept into the National Assembly, too, with a manifesto of reform: industry and banks were nationalized, welfare and workers' rights boosted and a punitive wealth tax imposed to pay for it all – at a time when governments elsewhere were battening down the hatches under pressure of recession. The French economy, still weak after the 1973–4 oil crisis, went into free fall and, in a dramatic U-turn, the Socialists abandoned the reforms for an austerity package. Technocrat prime minister Laurent Fabius was wheeled in to bring the economy under control through social market reforms – a 'conversion to economic realism' which heralded the demise of the ideological Left.

While the popularity of the Socialists soon slumped, Mitterrand showed himself to be a master of political compromise, presiding over governments from across the political spectrum in a period which saw the concepts of *cohabitation* and *alternance* established. The Right won a majority in National

terms and proved that *cohabitation* (when the president and the prime minister are at opposite ends of the political spectrum) could work. Mitterrand helped to abolish the death penalty, passed decentralization laws giving more powers to regional governments, and liberalized rules governing radio and television. Yet these years are also embedded in the modern memory for corruption and general sleaze (*see* **France Today**, 'Elitism and Corruption', pp.82–4).

Assembly elections in 1986 and Jacques Chirac, founder and leader of the Rassemblement pour la République, formed a government, ushering in the first period of *cohabitation* between a president of the Left and a prime minister of the Right. Mitterrand was re-elected president in 1988 on a *'la France unie'* ticket, and the National Assembly swung back to the Left, setting a new pattern of *alternance*. After a series of uninspired premiers, including France's first woman prime minister, the gaffe-prone Edith Cresson (who called all British men gay), and in the face of unemployment that had risen to more than 10 per cent, the Left was routed in 1993 elections; the Right won more than 80 per cent of the vote. Even the prestige of Mitterrand began to look dented, as details of his chequered, collaborationist past emerged. In the French way, no one cared much about his illegitimate daughter but, at a time when France was beginning to confront the extent of its wartime collaboration (shattering the myth that all French had heroically resisted Occupation), the president's past as a Vichy civil servant and his political opportunism were embarrassing.

In 1995, Chirac was elected to the presidential palace at the Elysée. In 2002, he was re-elected president for a second term after the Socialist candidate, Lionel Jospin, fell out of the race. It was a landslide victory against Le Pen, despite allegations of corruption against the incumbent president (Chirac has been declared immune from investigation as long as he holds office). In power almost continually since 1967, as cabinet member, prime minister, mayor of Paris and now president, he has earned the nickname 'le Résident de la République'. The presidency has now been reduced from seven to five years, in a bid to bring it in line with the National Assembly and prevent the damaging 'push-me-pull-you' effect of *cohabitation*.

Although the far-Right threat got the French to the polls in 2002, apathy has become the defining feature of the political process: voters showed their dwindling interest in their rulers by a 30 per cent abstention rate at the presidential elections, and 40 per cent abstained from the subsequent National Assembly elections. In 2003 parliament approved government-backed amendments to the constitution allowing for the devolution of wide-ranging powers to the country's 22 regions and departments. This move has been widely seen as a bid to re-engage French people disillusioned by centralization and the influence of the Paris élite in the political process (*see* **France Today**, 'Elitism and Corruption', pp.82–4).

Mitterrand oversaw the acceptance of the Maastricht Treaty to open European borders, and the Treaty on European Union was ratified by referendum on 20 September 1992. Jacques Chirac was elected president in 1995 and two years later 'cohabitated' with socialist prime minister Lionel Jospin. After many reforms that took place to get France in shape for the European Monetary Union, France opened the new millennium with increased consumer confidence and lower unemployment numbers. On 1 January, 2002, the old currency, the French franc, was replaced with the euro.

For more on current social, political and economic issues, *see* **France Today**, pp.66–87).

The French Language

French is spoken by more than 200 million people around the world. It is the official language of France, Belgium, Luxembourg, Switzerland, Canada and a long list of African countries such as Zaire and Nigeria. Although English is the dominant language of the internet, French still holds its own as the language of diplomacy in the European Union, at the United Nations and on many an international level.

Latin was the language of the land ever since Julius Caesar brought the traditions of the Roman Empire to Gaul and beyond. Over the course of history, the people of France got sloppy with their Latin and allowed foreign slang to sneak into the vocabulary. Eventually, the dialect of the Franks around Paris evolved into its own proper spoken and written language known as Francien.

In AD 842, the Oath of Strasbourg, signed by Charlemagne's two grandsons Charles the Bald and Louis the German, was the first treaty to be written in the new language, although Latin continued to be spoken by scholars at the Sorbonne and in aristocratic and religious circles. Meanwhile, the streets of France were alive with exciting new sounds. A tradition of oral poetry and religious rhyme further developed the language thanks to the *jongleurs*. Two important works were written: the *Chansons de Geste* (stories of Charlemagne) and the *Chanson de Roland*.

By the early Middle Ages, France had divided into two linguistic camps. In the north, the *langue d'oïl* was spoken, and in the south, the *langue d'oc*. The measuring stick used to differentiate between the two was the word 'yes'. To indicate an affirmation, the Latin-speaking Romans used the word *hic* (which means 'thus'), and over the course of the years this was mispronounced as *oïl* in the north and *oc* in the opposite end of Gaul. Eventually, the northern version tuned into *oui*.

All regional linguistic differences were officially wiped out in 1539 with the Edict of Villars-Cotterêts that established French as the official language of the kingdom. Yet tensions brewed under the surface. Paris continued to treat the south of the country known as Occitania (a word used to describe the Provençal-Languedocien-Gascon-Aquitanien-Auvergnat culture) as foreign, and road customs houses formed a border between the two halves of the nation. Students who spoke their native Occitan language were punished. Others were charged with treason and fishing villages in Brittany were plastered with signs warning: 'no fishing, no speaking Breton'. Up until the early part

The Tongue of Oc

All over the southern part of France, you will notice what looks like a misspelling of a town's name under the familiar one by the roadside as you arrive. This custom has its origins in regional government legislation of 1982, and that apparent spelling mistake derives from the old southern tongues of 1,000 years ago. As Latin became French, two distinct languages appeared in northern and southern France. Provençal, as the southern tongue was known, is first recorded in the 10th century and came to be the language of the troubadours, with their poetry of love, satire and war. Spoken over a wide area and with no standard form, it is now better known as Occitan, from the word Languedoc. Close to the Spanish border, it is indistinguishable from Catalan and called Roussillonais. In the rest of modern Languedoc it is called Languedocien. To the north it was called Limousin and spoken as far north as Limoges. Then there is a dialect found towards the Swiss border called Franco-Provençal, which spreads into Italy. All these tongues lost their battles with French in the years since the troubadours. Frédéric Mistral (1830–1914) was the great champion of their revival and won the Nobel Prize in 1904 for his efforts. There is increasing interest in them today, but, on the whole, these languages – like those of the Celtic world – are encouraged more as a defence of regional heritage against central government and internationalization than as a means of communication.

of the 20th century, France's minority languages were dismissed as mere *patois*, or blabber.

Today, France is by no means a mono-linguistic and mono-cultural society, no matter how hard linguistic fundamentalists with the Académie Française, the celebrated institution charged with safeguarding French from contamination by foreign – namely English – words, will have you believe. In fact, the issue of France's linguistic minorities, many on the expressway to extinction, has been the focus of renewed debate.

The seven recognized minority languages of France are Provençal, Breton, Alsatian, Corsican, Catalan, Basque and Flemish. Corsican is an Italo–Roman language thanks to the long time the island was ruled by Genoa. In Brittany, a version of Celtic is spoken, as is Flemish in northern spots. Alsace is heavily influenced by German and the mysterious language of the Basque region is pre-Indo-European. Catalan and Provençal both form part of the Occitan languages, which a mix of Gallo-Roman and Ibero-Roman.

According to UNESCO's *Atlas of Endangered World Languages*, all of these (with the exception of Corsican) are among the 3,000 languages spoken on our planet that are in danger of disappearing. Although some Occitan/Provençal languages are making a comeback (you'll see the odd street sign in Provençal in small villages or hear it sung at the feasts of local patron saints), the French government is being blamed for not doing enough to protect them. A few programmes are in place to teach them as electives in state-run schools, although textbooks and dictionaries simply don't exist in many cases.

Profiles of the Regions

02

Since mythological times one theme has consistently applied to the French territory. It is the theme of abundance. Thanks to its enormous beauty, natural resources and agricultural potential, France has shaped our universal ideal of fecundity, fertility and prosperity.

The ancients were the first to celebrate the cult of abundance – personified by the Roman goddess Abundantia. She was depicted with a cornucopia, the so-called 'horn of plenty', from which she distributed grain, fruit seeds, flowers and money. Legend says the horn has the power to give the person who possesses it whatever he or she desires. Her cult spread across Gaul and, even today, tales of Lady Hobunde (from the same name) have survived in French bedtime stories and folklore. Meanwhile, according to the Celts, Cernunnos ('the Horned One'), depicted with the antlers of a stag, was the god of fertility, life, animals and wealth. His cult was also celebrated in France, where Palaeolithic cave portraits of him have been uncovered. Is it mere coincidence that these horn-toting deities – one Celtic, one Roman, one from the north and one from the south – would meet in France? It seems France has forever been the point of convergence for outsiders searching for 'abundance'. In today's language we call it 'quality of life'.

The following chapter offers a thumbnail sketch of the land shared by Abundantia and Cernunnos, divided into 15 geographical areas. From Alsace to the Basque country, facts relating to geography, history and architecture have been collected to give you a better idea of what it's like actually to live in particular areas. If you are house-hunting, this section should help you narrow your search. Or, if life in France is still a dream, we hope this section will fuel those fantasies. Whatever the case, remember that France yields abundantly to those who call it home.

Paris and the Ile de France

'England built London for its own use, but France built Paris for the world,' said Ralph Waldo Emerson. True to his words, Paris glimmers in our hearts, no matter what our nationality. The 'Ville Lumière' (City of Light) is the universal capital of sophistication, culture, gastronomy and beauty, and is at the centre stage of western civilization. It is what other cities aspire to be. Parisians are quick to remind you of that, in case you should neglect to concur. In this city, vanity is never in short supply.

Paris has reason to gloat. The urban landscape was assembled as an experiment in superhuman ideals. It was designed as a fantastical metropolis in which its buildings and public squares were calculated to reflect its inhabitants' soaring aspirations. Everything is larger than life in Paris: if you stand in the middle of Place de la Concorde and swivel on your heel, the effect is overpowering. From this enormous rectangular opening, your field of vision is assaulted on all sides: the Seine, the gardens of the Tuileries and the broad Champs-Elysées all compete for your attention.

The city was born on the Ile de la Cité as a cluster of buildings surrounding a temple to Jupiter, the first patron of Paris. The site remains a place of worship because it is where the Gothic Notre-Dame cathedral stands today. As the city swelled beyond its ancient boundaries, it succeeded in carefully accumulating – like a pernickety shopper at the greengrocer's – a collection of the most visited and recognized monuments on the planet, spread throughout its many *arrondissements*. Who doesn't immediately conjure a vision of the Arc de

The Power of Numbers

If you are in Paris to work, a neat little studio to impress your friends and hide from your relations is probably not what you need. If you're bringing a family you may even be looking towards the dormitory and neighbouring towns such as Créteil, Evry, Bobigny, St-Denis, Nanterre, St-Germain and Versailles. Beyond the city are six other *départements*: Seine-et-Marne, Essonne, Yvelines, Val-d'Oise, Hauts-de-Seine and Seine-St-Denis.

For the dedicated urbanite, however, the city proper is divided into 20 districts, or *arrondissements*, radiating from the centre in a spiral, and referred to by number: 'the Sixth' for instance, as you might say 'West One' in London.

Forget the First and Second, they are not for mere mortals. The Third to the Sixth are both central and desirable and include areas like the Latin Quarter, still an academic centre that gets its name from the medieval student ban on speaking any other language but Latin there, and the newly trendy and desirable Marais district. The Seventh (the Eiffel Tower) is very posh and very expensive. The Eighth (the Elysée Palace, the Champs-Elysées) is even more so, and potential residents would rub shoulders with the president, among others. The Ninth does have some residential properties but is mostly home to the head offices of big companies. The Tenth to the Fourteenth (with the Bois de Boulogne) tend to be less glamorous and consequently less expensive. The Fifteenth is a mixture both of reasonable and expensive and of old and new, and is residential. The Sixteenth (the Arc de Triomphe) is grand, exclusive, expensive and conservative. The Seventeenth (also running from the Arc de Triomphe) is posh, too, but more trendy and lively, with some democratic pockets. The Eighteenth, which includes Montmartre and Pigalle, is the reverse – a few fashionable pockets in an otherwise mixed and rumbustious area that includes the largely immigrant Bàrbes. The Nineteenth (Gare du Nord) is a quieter continuation of the Eighteenth. The Twentieth (around Père Lachaise cemetery) is quieter, bigger and cheaper still. Take your pick: Paris's urban transport network of métro, RER and bus is cheap, fast, reliable, and so nowhere is really very far away.

Triomphe or the Eiffel Tower at the mere utterance of the names? The encyclopaedic offerings of Paris include the Louvre, the Centre Pompidou, the Musée d'Orsay, the Palais Royal quarter, the Champs-Elysées, Montmartre's Sacré-Cœur, the café culture of St-Germain, the Palais du Luxembourg, the great department stores of Opéra, the elegant labyrinth of the Marais, the ethnic neighbourhoods at the foot of the Montparnasse skyscraper, Trocadéro, and the greenery of the Bois de Boulogne.

Fine. But what's it like to live in Paris? Like the world's two other truly cosmopolitan corners (London and New York), Paris is a city that keeps you occupied, like a full-time job, or a new lover. It is not merely a place where you make your home, it becomes part of the description of who you are. The energy levels are impossible to beat and Paris is never a boring city. Even the chronic couch potato is a respected professional here: he or she could easily be mistaken for a writer or a painter who dedicates any empty hours to some mysterious masterpiece. The inhabitants who are not artists are the bankers, entrepreneurs and specialists charged with powering the nation's economy. Parisians from all walks of life do interesting things and have interesting things to say.

The New Yorker, the Londoner and the Parisian have all been typecast according to their particular idiosyncrasies and neuroses. The average Parisian seems to exhibit higher doses of snobbery and chauvinism than most of us are accustomed to (or are willing to accommodate). On the flip side, he or she makes stimulating and informed company. Paris is a healthily competitive environment. You wouldn't want to be caught in a public place without adequate grooming, and you wouldn't want to enter a conversation without having first shaped your opinions on current events and history. Like it or not, Paris pushes you to be better – or, as some might phrase it, 'to be more Parisian'.

Outside the capital is the urban sprawl of the rest of the Ile de France region that always lies within the golden rays of Paris. Two main attractions, Versailles and Disneyland Paris, are in many ways a parody of one another. There are also great cathedrals within reach, at Beauvais, Amiens and Chartres.

Normandy

Open to the chilly waters of the Atlantic and exposed to winds from the north, Normandy has seen more than its share of violence and difficulties. This is where the fierce warriors from Scandinavia known as 'the men from the north', or the Normans, settled after unleashing a wave of terror that swept across Europe. Centuries later, Normandy was where American and Allied soldiers landed from 6 June 1944 – a date that represents a turning point in world history. Among the region's many illustrious sons and daughters, both painter Monet and writer Flaubert have captured Normandy's nostalgic side.

In Haute-Normandie, dramatic white cliffs span the entire Côte d'Albâtre, from Dieppe to the mouth of the Seine at Le Havre, and the chalky debris gives the water a milky colour. Both **Dieppe** (from the Norman word for 'deep' because of the city's profound harbour) and **Le Havre** are strategic sea ports that have too often been at the opposite end of binoculars held by incoming conquerors. Dieppe suffered repeatedly in the French and English wars, and Le Havre, France's second largest harbour after Marseille, was bombed to smithereens in the Second World War. The gateway to Normandy is further north at the charming monosyllabic town of Eu.

Before reaching its estuary, the Seine snakes its way from Paris through much of Normandy, carving out France's most important trade corridor. Merchant ships still push their way up the river past the inland port town of Rouen, loaded with goods and foods from abroad. The banks of the Seine are industrial until Lillebonne and give way to picturesque landscapes that serve as the background for a series of romantic medieval abbeys. **Rouen** is where Flaubert set much of his tale of adultery, *Madame Bovary*, and the city's Place du Vieux Marché marks the spot where Joan of Arc was burned at the stake for witchcraft and heresy on 30 May 1431. Her ashes were tossed into the Seine, but legend claims that her heart did not burn.

Down the Atlantic coast from Honfleur starts the **Côte Fleurie**, home to the seaside resorts of Deauville and Trouville, so much in vogue during the late 19th century that they were considered a Parisian *arrondissement*. Slightly inland is the **Pays d'Auge**, where the best Camembert cheese is made. Half-timbered houses, apple orchards and cow-dotted countryside make this one of the prettiest corners of Normandy. Dairy enthusiasts won't want to miss a pilgrimage to the gorgeous village of Camembert.

The **Côte de Nacre** is dotted with English names: Sword Beach, Juno Beach, Gold Beach, Omaha Beach and Utah Beach in memory of the American, British, Canadian and other Allied soldiers who participated in the D-Day campaign. Of the various landing points, the bloodshed was worst at Omaha Beach, where the Germans mowed down men as they swam to shore. The amphibious Sherman tanks were launched too far from the shore to give them cover. Once the 60 kilometres of coastline was under Allied control, an extraordinary number of men (more than two million) and war supplies flowed into Nazi-occupied France. In 1988, the moving Mémorial de la Paix was opened outside the city of **Caen**. Southern Normandy, south of Caen and Falaise to Le Mans, is home to fertile farmland and peppered with medieval castles. **Alençon** in the Sarthe Valley is a lace-making town, and **Le Mans** has a handsomely restored historic centre that sits on a spur of rock overlooking the Sarthe river. Automobile enthusiasts will know of its famous car race.

To the west is the **Cherbourg Peninsula**, capped by Cap de la Hague, which offers a succession of quaint villages and dramatic seascapes all the way to

Mont-St-Michel. The Archangel Michael had a habit of appearing to people in their sleep to instruct them to build shrines in his honour. Bishop Aubert was the recipient of one of these dreams in 708, and set out to build a grotto modelled after the Santuario di San Michele in Monte Sant'Angelo on Italy's Gargano Peninsula. Over the next few centuries the site was enlarged to include a stunning Romanesque abbey. The result is a powerful Christian symbol and one of the world's most photogenic spots. The abbey's spire pierces the sky and points to God. Its girth rests on the tiny island that is connected to the mainland by a causeway. Mont-St-Michel is the second most visited site in France after Paris.

Brittany

Most of the action in Brittany occurs on the coast, or the stretch of land that starts at Mont-St-Michel in the north and loops around south to the industrial shipbuilding hub of **St-Nazaire**. Between those two points is an infinite number of seascapes: from rocky bluffs to sandy beaches, craggy coves, offshore islands and sporadically placed lighthouses perched on the tips of promontories, often dramatically engulfed in sea mist and spume. Walk in any direction in Brittany and chances are you'll end up facing the Atlantic Ocean.

The Breton Peninsula is home to early signs of civilization, as the Neolithic drawings in Carnac and Locmariaquer testify. It was also home to the most famous Gaul of them all, and mascot of France: Astérix. But throughout its history Brittany has always been a tad different from its neighbouring regions. Thanks to linguistic purists in Paris, the Breton dialect, which is related to Welsh, is being carefully nurtured back to life after near extinction. The folklore, traditional dress, dance and crafts of Brittany are also making a long-overdue comeback.

Shortly after the bay of Mont-St-Michel is the walled city of **St-Malo** on the Clos Poulet peninsula. You can walk around the rampart walls to get a better idea of the city that was a port of call for countless merchants, explorers and sea adventurers. Nearby sand beaches make this one of France's trendiest summer holiday spots. Thick protective walls have done their share to safeguard cities like St-Malo (although it was destroyed in the Second World War and was rebuilt), but other cities, like **Rennes**, were founded inland with access to the sea by a network of rivers and tributaries for extra protection. Today Rennes, capital of Brittany, is a lively city teeming with students and cafés and offers a full schedule of music and art events.

The **Côte d'Emeraude** or Emerald Coast is also high on the list of top destinations among beachgoers. Royalty and aristocrats traditionally migrated here in the hottest months, leaving behind a trail of châteaux. Among the most impressive is Fort La Latte, built in the 14th century. Straddling the edges of the

Bay of St-Brieuc is a colourful collection of marinas and fishing villages where you can feast on delicious fish soups. The **Goëlo Coast**, including Paimpol and Bréhat, comes up next and is followed by the romantic **Côte de Granit Rose**. As its name implies, the famously beautiful coastline, which extends for some 20 kilometres between Pointe du Château to Trégastel-Plage, is composed of pink-coloured granite boulders that have been sculpted by the sea and winds.

The north coast of Finistère goes past **St-Pol-de-Léon**, named after Pol, one of the founding saints of Brittany, and extends to **Brest**, which overlooks a beautiful bay. Offshore are spatterings of marine rock formations and islets that continue to haunt the most skilled seamen. The Ile Vierge lighthouse is the tallest in Europe at 263ft – but even this towering beacon is often powerless against the mighty Atlantic. The **Crozon Peninsula** is home to hairpin roads and slate-roof villages. Long beaches line the Bay of Douarnenez, which juts out into the water towards the Ile de Sein. To the southeast is the inland city of **Quimper**, best known for its yellow and white pottery featuring men and women dressed in Breton costume.

Before the port of **St-Nazaire** is the **Morbihan** area of Brittany, where Neolithic man erected stones in perfectly aligned patterns that no one has ever been able to comprehend fully. One theory is that the rock arrangement dating to 3000 BC represents a solar or celestial calendar. The nearby Golfe du Morbihan is an inland sea dotted with dozens of tiny islands.

The Loire Valley

Home to an incredibly dense swath of beauty and charm, the Loire Valley has a perfect combination of elements: great food and wine, breathtaking touring opportunities, and more châteaux than you can shake a grapevine at. Perpendicular to the Atlantic Ocean, the Loire river slices inland towards the very core of the nation. Its unique positioning has awarded it microclimates that are ideal for viticulture, farming and a rich culinary tradition.

The Loire Valley also served as a home from home for much of France's nobility, and they left a long trail of castles and other architectural delights for us to enjoy today. Some kings, such as Charles VII, Louis XI, Charles VIII and Louis XII, actually set up shop and ruled from here. The nobility erected hundreds of châteaux, of which more than 50 are open to the public. Among them are Chenonceaux, Chaumont, Chambord, Cheverny, Amboise, Blois, Azay-le-Rideau and Villandry. Each one could occupy a page in a calendar of the world's dreamiest homes.

On the eastern side of the region, grapevines snuggle close to the town of **Sancerre**, the home of an aromatic white wine of the same name. The town of **Bourges** is dominated by an UNESCO World Heritage site Gothic cathedral, and the verdant valleys that radiate out from the town are where numerous foreigners have opted to make their homes. The Cher, Berry and Creuse Valleys are perfect destinations for weekend explorers. Nearby is the mysterious area called the **Sologne**. Thickly covered in woods, it has an abundance of deer, ducks, wild boar, birds and rabbits, and hunters flock from all over to indulge in their sport. Logically, game dishes and hearty home cooking are another irresistible attraction here.

The Loire Valley *per se* starts at Orléans and follows the Loire river, which meanders through 200 kilometres of breathtaking scenery to the ocean. **Orléans** is a lively and prosperous city that has always been an important seat of power (Joan of Arc started on her fast track to heroism here). To the north of the city is **Chartres**, a site that simply must be seen to be believed. An enormous Gothic cathedral rises unexpectedly from the fields of wheat that surround it.

The Loire river slices through the town of **Blois** and opens on to more château dreamscapes. Next is the university city of **Tours**, but before your main course make room for an architectural appetizer: the Château d'Amboise. It is among the most impressive castles of its kind. If that doesn't satisfy your hunger, head south of the Loire from Tours to **Chinon** and the heartland of France's fairy-tale châteaux.

One of the most picturesque additions to the Loire Valley is the Château de Saumur, perfectly perched on a hill so that it can be admired kilometres away. Built in the 14th century, its design includes four pointed black towers that poke at the sky like spears. The lucky inhabitants of this man-made marvel could peer down at the village below. Ironically, troglodyte cave-dwellers also made their home in this area, but they put up with less compelling interior design schemes.

The Loire's strongest panoramic punch arrives in the stretch of river between Saumur and Angers. The road here is built on a tall flood bank, giving motorists an unobstructed perspective. Limestone in the river and reflected in the air gives a creamy quality to the surroundings. And most of the homes are made of white stone, surrounded by colourful flowerbeds that add more eye-candy.

All that brilliant whiteness ends at the city of **Angers**. Dubbed 'Black Angers' because of the nearby slate mines, much of the cityscape appears to be covered in soot and grime and seems a world apart from the Loire Valley. In fact, Angers does not straddle the Loire. It is built on the banks of the Maine river and is dominated by the hilltop Cathédrale St-Maurice and the daunting military Château d'Angers.

Another impressive fortification is the château at **Nantes**, complete with a moat and bastions. Only 50 kilometres from the Atlantic Ocean, Nantes may well be France's friendliest city. But behind the smiles lies a dark past. It grew rich thanks to the slave trade, which reached such embarrassing proportions that a 1754 ordinance limited households to one *négritte* each. When slavery was abolished, Nantes fell back on the sugar refinery business, and the few surviving biscuit factories are lasting remnants of that legacy.

The Atlantic Coast

The area between the Loire and the Gironde rivers is where northern France gradually gives way to southern France. Terracotta tiles replace slate roofs, window shutters appear in brilliant pastel colours and daylight has a crisper quality. This segment of the Atlantic Coast has unspoiled beaches and two important port towns: La Rochelle and Rochefort, which are often crammed tight with yachts. This is a land that will awaken your inner Cupid. Romantics can feast on aphrodisiac oysters and mussels as they watch the setting sun dip into the ocean.

The north **Vendée** coast starts south of Nantes and is well equipped to accommodate holidaymakers. Many head over to the beaches and the quaint fishing villages on the Ile de Noirmoutier and the Ile d'Yeu. Others opt for the vast sand beaches of resort towns like **Les Sables-d'Olonne**. Beyond the modern buildings and the casino, the main attraction is the Remblai beachfront promenade. This area is remembered for the violent uprising of the 1790s, or the Guerre de Vendée, against French Revolutionary powers. The southern Vendée coast has more seaside resorts facing the **Ile de Ré** and a fairytale marshland further inland: the **Marais Poitevin**, crisscrossed by canals and dotted with poplar trees, and a haven for frogs, dragonflies and chirping birds.

The Thouet river opens a passage inland to where châteaux and Romanesque abbeys come into view. A delightful highlight here is the provincial capital of **Poitiers**. Built on the crest of a hill, both the upper and the lower town are bustling with lively streets and beautiful shops.

Back on the coast, **La Rochelle**, the **Ile de Ré** (connected to the mainland by a bridge) and **Rochefort** make up the Holy Trinity of Atlantic coast holiday spots. There are enough restaurants, portside strolls, beaches and sailing possibilities to cram your summer schedule tight. Oyster-lovers won't want to miss the fresh catch on the Ile d'Oléron.

If you don't want to live near the noise and crowds of a seaside resort town, and your heart is set on trellis-lined wine country, this area has one last ace up its sleeve. **Cognac** is surrounded by vineyards, which produce the wine that is later distilled to make world-famous brandy. The **Charente Valley** is particularly pretty countryside and is where you can visit the hilltop town of **Angoulême**.

The Southwest

The pin-up queen of French geography arouses your appetite the same way as Italy's Tuscany, with soft hills framed by rows of trees and sun-drenched farmhouses made of honey-coloured stone. If you are looking to unleash your bucolic dreams, the sumptuous southwest will probably top your list of

Case Study: Grape Expectations

Bud break? Veraison? Double cordon? Bunch rot? Phylloxera? Drip line? Rootstock? Sometimes starting a new life means learning a new vocabulary to go with it. This has certainly been the case for Patricia Atkinson.

Patricia's first professional incarnation was as a PR manager with an international bank in London. Her husband James worked as a financial consultant, and both flirted with the idea of leaving the rat race and making the transition to the French countryside.

The couple eventually bought a property outside Bergerac in the Dordogne region, of which 4.5 hectares were planted to vine. Around 40 years old at the time, Patricia and her husband hoped to make a few barrels of wine as a hobby, although they knew nothing about viticulture, and spoke only a few words of French.

Shortly thereafter James grew ill and, as the couple's savings dwindled, Patricia started to see her grape-growing hobby as a means for survival. Singlehandedly she tended to the vineyard, pruned, learned to drive a tractor and operate a sprayer, and eventually mastered the techniques to produce a quality crop. 'The French have great respect for people who work,' she says. 'It was very confusing at first and there was a steep learning curve. Learning French was essential.'

Thus marks her second professional incarnation as a *vigneron*. The couple eventually split, but Patricia's heart was too deeply rooted in the vineyard to leave what she had worked so hard to create. 'I had grown new muscles where I didn't know I had them.' She bought additional land to expand the vineyard and worked on marketing her merlot, cabernet sauvignon and cabernet franc. Her wines caught the attention of top retailers and appeared in the Waterside, London's three-star Michelin restaurant. Today, Patricia's winery, the Clos d'Yvigne (**www.cdywine.com**), produces some 70,000 bottles per year, of which two-thirds are exported to the UK market.

An inspiring story? Random House thought so. Patricia Atkinson penned her recently released book *The Ripening Sun*, describing how she reinvented herself and detailing life on her vineyard. In her third professional incarnation as an accomplished author, a new vocabulary is the fruit of an excellent harvest.

preferred destinations. But don't expect to be alone. Countless other expatriates have chosen this area as their home from home, and its popularity continues to grow.

The northern top of the region mixes rural and industrial scenery and its name, **Limousin**, inexplicably ended up being used to define the elongated black cars often seen outside movie premières. The area is also home to **Limoges**, famous for its delicately painted porcelain, and **Aubusson**, which made some of the world's most prized carpets and tapestries outside Persia. Flemish weavers are believed to have settled here in the 14th century and lent their stitching techniques to local artisans. To the south are the Vézère and Corrèze Valleys and a series of dams that have made lakes from the Dordogne river.

The idyllic countryside that has captured the expatriates' imagination doesn't start until you get to the **Dordogne** *département*, which is one of the biggest in France. Also referred to as Périgord, Dordogne is divided into quadrants and each is identified by its own colour. The northern Périgord is the green quarter thanks to its forests and lush pastures. Named after its limestone formations, white Périgord is home to the Dordogne's capital, **Périgueux**. The small city is large on charm and is famous for truffles and *foie gras* and has scatterings of Roman ruins. Thick forests into which little sunlight seeps inspired the colour for black Périgord near Sarlat, and the countryside around Bergerac is called purple Périgord thanks to a blossoming wine industry.

Dordogne highlights include the riverside town of Montignac and its world-famous **Grotte de Lascaux**, dubbed the Sistine Chapel of the prehistoric world; one hall of the cave is painted with bulls so real in detail, rendering and movement that it is impossible to think they were created 17,000 years ago. Moisture brought in since the cave was discovered in 1940 has damaged the drawings, forcing their permanent closure to the public, but you can admire a reproduction in the so-called Lascaux II. The museum in Les Eyzies-de-Tayac has more artefacts from prehistory, including buxom Venus statues.

Another highlight is the town of **Bergerac** and the surrounding wine country. Bergerac sits proudly on the Dordogne river and once had the only bridge crossing it. That fortunate asset helped the city grow rich through commerce, and today you can admire its timberwood homes and shaded parks. Ducks are the favourite pet – and many of them end up in the endless array of local dishes. For the ultimate wine village set among the vineyards, you must head to **St-Emilion**. The town and its oversized bell tower rise from the hilly landscape like a dream. St-Emilion wine is among the best in France and there are shops and tasting-rooms throughout the area.

The largest city in these parts is the extremely well positioned **Bordeaux**. On the Garonne river, Bordeaux opens on to the Atlantic and the Americas. Commerce helped it grow into an important metropolis, and sadly many of its older buildings were replaced with grander edifices in the 18th century to reflect its growing importance. Many need a sprucing-up, and in fact much of Bordeaux looks as if it needs a good scrub. Yet, this is a city with soul and nuggets of beauty.

Bordeaux's *département* is the **Gironde**, and it is in this unique climate, between Atlantic mists and southern sunshine, that some of the world's most expensive grapes are pressed into the ultimate ruby nectar. A list of nearby towns reads like an encyclopaedia of white and red wine: Médoc, Pomerol and Sauternes, to name just three. Of course the most celebrated wine comes from the banks of the Gironde estuary, north of Bordeaux. The Médoc *appellation* in the vicinity of Pauillac is the lucky home to Châteaux Latour, Mouton-Rothschild and Lafite.

The lower lip of the Gironde estuary marks the beginning of an elongated sand beach that extends to the Basque country and is known as the **Côte d'Argent**. Fishing villages along the way, such as **Arcachon**, with its sandy dunes, are popular with summertime tourists and oyster enthusiasts. In fact, the Bassin d'Arcachon is the fourth largest oyster-producer in France.

If you were to travel southeast of Bordeaux to inland Toulouse you would work your way into the **Lot-et-Garonne**. River tributaries and canals crisscross the landscape and irrigate a large parcel of fertile land that gives rise to the excellent plumes and dried prunes of **Agen**. Come in the autumn and the shops are teeming with wild mushrooms. Asparagus reigns in spring. Not far away is the Abbaye St-Pierre in **Moissac**, heralded as one of the most important buildings left to us from the Middle Ages. Another curiosity is the red brick town of **Albi** in the Tarn.

Thanks to an excellent university and its burgeoning 20-something population, **Toulouse** is one of the most exciting places to live in France. Built with rose-pink-coloured bricks and straddling the banks of the Garonne river, the distinctive city is a business and commercial centre and an important crossroads for the south. At night, its cafés and bars rock with all kinds of music – from French rap to North African pop – and a lively art crowd creates a ripe atmosphere and intellectual buzz.

Gascony, the Basque Lands and the Pyrenees

Like a carpet pressed too close to a wall, the southern French territory butts up against the Spanish border and folds over itself to form the dramatic contours of the Pyrenees. In the nooks and crannies are a wealth of tiny villages and pockets of personality shaped by a peculiar combination of elements. The area is an island of isolation within France, but it is also a crossroads, with a varied ethnic mix influenced by Spain and the Basque country. And it is where millions of pilgrims have come over the years to be healed.

Before the mountains is an expanse of former windswept swampland known as the **Landes de Gascogne**, or the moors, that was drained in the mid-1800s thanks to Napoléon III. He ordered pine trees to be planted for the resin trade, which now fuel a papermaking industry. Beyond the natural parks and the pine forests, humans found little reason to settle here. There is a scattering of villages where townsfolk dance on stilts (*tchanques*) on feast days; the stilts are a throwback to when the area's shepherds mastered the difficult task of walking and working on wooden sticks to better navigate the muddy terrain.

Between the forest and the Bay of Biscay is Europe's longest continuous sand beach. The dunes of the **Côte d'Argent** attracted hordes of sun-seekers in the early 1900s, and today the long breaking waves attract swarms of surfers. Further inland is **Mont-de-Marsan**, and the Adour riverbanks on the toes of the Pyrenees and **Dax**, a top thermal spa; seven million litres of mineral-rich water pour into its wells each day. Beyond the garlic fields of the Gers is the countryside of **Armagnac**, famous for its fine French brandy. Nicknamed *picquepoul*, for 'tingles your lips', it is thought to be the oldest distilled *eau de vie* in the world. Not far is another town with wide-reaching name-recognition: Condom, although there is little evidence linking it to the prophylactics industry. **Auch** is famous for the stained-glass windows in its Cathédrale Ste-Marie.

The **Pays Basque** is a world apart, and you'll know you are there when you see signs written in a strange language heavy with 'z's and 'x's, and red, white and green flags. The Basque country, or Euzkadi, is home to what many believe was Europe's oldest tribe; most of the information we have on them, including their otherworldly language, is shrouded in mystery. The scenery here is gorgeous: emerald hills softly undulate, dotted with whitewashed gingerbread houses.

Gascony becomes Basque country at **Bayonne**, which is a delightful city bisected by the Adour and Nive rivers. The Petite Bayonne neighbourhood is home to popular bars and outdoor restaurants. South of here is the resort town of **Biarritz** with its rags-to-riches story. A little more than a century ago it was a simple fishing village, but, as suntans came into vogue, Biarritz grew into one of the most fashionable holiday spots in France. Its heyday may have passed, but it is still a preferred destination for both high and low season breaks, with a coast as famous as Miami for rolling surf. Biarritz's pretty little sister is the bijou **St-Jean-de-Luz**, home to countless fish restaurants and romantic corners.

Pyrenean mountain magic comes into view in the **Béarn** region, which was a formerly independent state. **Pau** is the Ruritanian capital, and offers a charming network of pedestrian streets around the Renaissance King Henri's castle. The gateway to the Béarnais Pyrenees is **Oloron-Ste-Marie** and the Vallée d'Aspe. But, for many, **Lourdes** is the final stop after a long pilgrimage to the area. In 1858, a 14-year-old girl named Bernadette Soubirous wandered into a cave and had a vision of the Madonna, who guided her to find a spring with miraculous waters capable of healing the sick. Since then, people have queued in front of the cave hoping for a small piece of the miracle – although the hotels and religious souvenir shops may have got the best deal.

Tarbes is a rather drab departmental capital city that doesn't do justice to the **High Pyrenean Valleys** nearby: the Lavedan, the Vallée d'Aure and the Vallée de Louron. Verdant hills, Romanesque churches and sporting resort towns set the scene. East of the Vallée de Louron starts the Haute-Garonne, or the **Comminges**. The Upper Comminges is where you'll find the queen of the Pyrenees, **Bagnères-de-Luchon**, a calm spa town flanked by Pyrenean peaks. The

Ariège area borders Spain and tiny **Andorra** and marks the transition between Gascony and Languedoc.

The North

The northern point of the Hexagon, flanked by the English Channel and Belgium, has seen too much violence. Sticking out like a sore thumb, it has taken bashings from left and right, by sea and land. But a tough history has moulded a tough people, and a good number of towns have magically managed to outlast years of battles and bombing.

The main city, **Calais**, is last on a list of nice places to live in France. But it is first among Britons who come over the Channel for discount supermarkets and retailers. Most don't stay long and emerge on this side of the Chunnel Terminal only to get out of the area as soon as possible. Past the city is the Flanders countryside, which extends from Gravelines and Dunkerque to **Lille**. The latter has Flemish Baroque buildings and has evolved into a vibrant, growing cultural centre ever since it was put on the Eurostar grid. A short trip away are the smaller **St-Omer** and **Arras**, in the Artois, boasting the best of Flemish territory. Two jewels in the Hainaut are **Douai** and **Cambrai**. But, sadly, much of this area still has deep scars left from the First World War battles that unfolded here.

The so-called **Côte d'Opale**, which gets its name from the colour of the water, spans from Calais to Boulogne. To the south, the war cemetery at Etaples is yet another painful reminder of the bloodshed to stain these shores during the Great War. The battlefields of the **Somme** in Picardy resonate with relatives of war veterans. Fittingly, the city of **Amiens** is home to France's largest cathedral, St-Martin. On a brighter note: the Château de Chantilly, where fresh cream was reportedly first whipped up, lies on Picardy's border with the Ile de France.

The Northeast

Grouping the many faces of the northeast into one section implies that they share the same characteristics and personality, but nothing could be further from the truth. The corner of France that borders Belgium, Luxembourg and Germany is a cultural crossroads and a hotbed of diversity. Within are three distinct territories: Champagne, Lorraine and Alsace. The first produces the world's merriest beverage, and the second two were hijacked during the Franco-Prussian War, leaving a wounded France humiliated and festering with plots for their safe return. Only after the First World War did the territories revert to French control, and indeed Lorraine put up the fiercest resistance to the Germans. Alsace, on the other hand, is both French and German. Scratch that: it is Alsatian, and its fairytale landscape ensures you are in a world apart.

The three main cities of **Champagne** country are Reims, Troyes and Epernay. The biggest and the best connected of the three is **Reims**, surrounded by endless slopes planted with pinot noir and chardonnay grapes. Begun in 1221, the vertical cathedral is a UNESCO World Heritage site and an awe-inspiring vision. But it's grapes that bring much of Reims' fame today. This is the country of the big names of bubbly: Louis Roederer, Moët et Chandon, Pommery and Veuve Clicquot, who perfected the *méthode champenoise* for creating carbon dioxide during the wine's secondary fermentation. Beautiful wine country extends from Reims and **Troyes**, a treasure chest of timberframe houses and Gothic churches. **Epernay** is closely associated with bubbly wine. Many producers are based here and are open for tasting appointments.

Lorraine is the birthplace of Joan of Arc and was home to the staunchest First World War Resistance fighters. It is an area of rough beauty, pride and honour. **Verdun**'s spirit is heavy with the memory of the Great War. Long battles were orchestrated here in 1916 and it became one of the worst killing fields in the entire war; around 175,000 French soldiers and 165,000 Germans lost their lives here. There is a moving memorial site north of Verdun. If you follow the Meuse river, you will slice through several little towns, and among the prettiest of them is **Domrémy-la-Pucelle**, where Joan of Arc was born in 1412.

The city of Metz is the modern capital of Lorraine, but **Nancy** is its cultural capital. It experienced a strong spurt of wealth in the early 20th century and consequently is the most important showcase of Art Nouveau architecture in France. When Lorraine was annexed by Germany, Nancy remained French and many exiled families moved here, bringing their wealth with them. Happily, the small Art Nouveau renaissance had enough steam to leave its mark on the cityscape and leave behind a generally good vibe that is felt today more strongly than ever.

The **Vosges**, or the incredibly beautiful range of mountains composed of dazzling red sandstone, is what separates Lorraine from **Alsace**. Once inside, you can no longer rely on your cultural compass for bearings. *Sauerkraut* platters and plump sausages top menus, and the local wine gives off whiffs of crisp, clean, cold-climate aromas. The timberframe houses with brick-laid chequers and geranium-crowded windowsills are unmistakably neither French nor German. **Strasbourg** is the gorgeous regional capital, and is an important European Union headquarters whose historic centre is remarkably well preserved despite its history. Most of France's troubles have poured in from the east over the Rhine riverbanks, hitting Strasbourg first. But now this city hosts thousands of students and EU workers and is bustling with restaurants and museums. There is great touring in the wine country outside the city. Many foreigners opt to live in the corridor of trellised countryside that extends south of Strasbourg to Colmar along the Vosges and slices through a succession of timberframe villages.

Burgundy

The name alone evokes the velvety and spicy aromas of many of the world's best wines. Bourgogne (the French name for Burgundy) is a large chunk of rural central France where great attention is paid to little details. Grapes aside, this is the birthplace of a large number of culinary treats: chicken from Bresse, Charolais cattle for creams and cheese, and of course Dijon for mustard that tickles the tip of your tongue. Any way you slice it, Burgundy offers an enviable quality of life.

The northwest part of the region follows the Yonne river from **Sens** to **Auxerre** along a beautiful stretch of countryside with two oversized cathedrals at either end. Sens is home to the Gothic cathedral of St-Stephen and Auxerre pays tribute to St-Etienne with its single-towered church. More abbeys can be admired in nearby **Vézelay**, and in the Serein Valley is the enchanting town of **Chablis**, synonymous with crisp Chardonnay.

The **Morvan** is the little-known heart of Burgundy, where forests carpet the hillsides and little lakes glisten between the folds of the land. The main town here is **Château-Chinon**, where the late President Mitterrand was once mayor. **Autun** started as a Roman city and has fragments of a ruined temple of Janus to prove it. But 'Christianity shines brighter than Paganism' is the powerful message of the Romanesque-Gothic cathedral of St-Lazare.

More wooded countryside extends over western Burgundy up to the edges of the Puisaye and Nivernais areas, where little villages and random châteaux sprout up from the ground like mushrooms. **Nevers**, the largest town, is famous for its pottery and for being the resting place of the preserved body of Bernadette of Lourdes. The Bourbonnais area extends into the **Auvergne** *département*, although it looks and feels more like Burgundy. Here lies **Vichy**, the town that will forever be remembered as the capital of the Pétain puppet government under the Nazis. Otherwise, thermal waters in Vichy make for a happier and healthier connection. The Auxois area is home to the UNESCO World Heritage Fontenay Abbey, and Alésia is where Caesar conquered the Gauls in 52 BC, thus expanding the parameters of the Empire. Last is the city of **Dijon**, among the gourmet capitals of the world. Not only is it famous for wine and its namesake mustard, but Dijon's diners serve up elaborate menus that start with a mandatory *kir* (white wine coloured with a drop of *crème de cassis*), which was invented here.

Most people who come to Burgundy flock to the **Côte d'Or**. This valley, which runs for 60 kilometres south from Dijon, past Beaune, is where some of the world's best wine-makers make their home. Burgundy is known primarily for pinot noir and chardonnay, and those interested in sniffing, swirling and sipping red wine should tour the châteaux of the **Côte de Nuits**. The **Côte de Beaune**, further south, is where you can taste exceptional white wines. Because land is prohibitively expensive here, few foreigners have moved in, but almost everyone who loves France makes the pilgrimage to the Burgundy wine regions. The city of **Beaune** makes an excellent base from which to explore and visit wineries (and enjoy a memorable meal or two).

The **Côte Chalonnaise** is the natural extension of the Côte d'Or and produces cheaper versions of the expensive wines found slightly to the north. In fact, the **Mâconnais** has more land planted to vine than any other part of Burgundy. The Saône river cuts its way to the abbey of **Cluny**, the largest church in Europe throughout the Middle Ages. The last two spots in Burgundy of culinary interest are **Beaujolais**, whose young and cheap wine is making a comeback, and **Bresse**, where the most succulent chicken dishes in the world are said to be served.

The Rhône Valley and the Auvergne

The Rhône river carved a corridor of communication and commerce into the heart of France, through Paris and finally to the English Channel, that was used since antiquity. Most of anything that came from outside France – grape cuttings, spices, silks and goods – travelled along this important gateway route. As a result of the riches pouring in, the towns of the Rhône Valley prospered and invested heavily in their artistic heritage. They also often attracted unwanted attention from invaders and conquerors.

Lyon, the second largest city in France, is a sight to be seen. Its colours reflect the sun, spanning ochre, coral, orange, burgundy and yellow. Its positioning on the convergence of two rivers makes for a dramatic juxtaposition between hillside and water, which is repeated twice. Lyon's two rivers, the Rhône (the mighty male backbone of the city) and the Saône (the delicate, picturesque female) are married south of the historic centre and the end of the Presqu'île. Besides the sheer drama and beauty of Lyon's urban landscape, visitors identify Lyon as a gastronomic capital of France.

The Rhône Valley jets out from Lyon and travels southwards, eventually ending in the Rhône delta sandwiched between Montpellier and Marseille. The northern Rhône is where the valley is tightest. Famous for hearty wine, mostly made from the syrah grape, the **Côte Rôtie** produces pricey Hermitage and Condrieu wines and its terraced vineyards are draped spectacularly along steep slopes. Special farming methods were invented here to enable viticulturists to prune and harvest in near-vertical terrain. The southern Rhône is known for a blend of grapes that makes up the leathery Châteauneuf-du-Pape.

Another valley lies east of the Rhône Valley and follows the course of the Drôme, a Rhône tributary. Here, a flatter terrain that soaks up moisture is perfectly suited for fruit orchards. To the west of the Rhône Valley is the **Ardèche** region, with gently rolling hills in the north and sharp gashes in the earth to the south. The many villages nestled with within the deep gorges of the southern Ardèche, such as Vogüé, Balazuc and Ruoms, all offer a unique attraction that comes in the form of a castle, an abbey or a panoramic platform. Cave enthusiasts will find hundreds of grottoes in the area to explore.

The **Auvergne** region, to the west, was shaped by wind and fire. Ancient volcanoes beautified the area with towering chimneys, gapping craters, thermal springs and an unforgettable landscape. The man-made highlight is **Le Puy-en-Velay**. Smack in the middle of town is a statue of the Virgin perched on top of a volcanic pinnacle that points to the heavens. A nearby cathedral stands atop a seemingly infinite flight of stairs.

The **Dore Valley**, between the upper Loire and the upper Allier, offers more vertical scenery with its many towering mountain summits. **Clermont-Ferrand** is the biggest town in the area and is largely built of black stones taken from quarries in the Monts Dômes; its black cathedral with twin spires takes Gothic architecture to a whole new level of spookiness. The Monts Dômes make a fitting backdrop and showcase more peaks after which the cathedral spires are inspired. Below the nearby Monts Dore to the south is the stunning **Cantal** area, which is basically a giant extinct volcano. Streams, miniature valleys and fertile pastures round off the landscape.

The Alps and the Jura

Mountainous areas tend to safeguard isolated pockets of individuality where inhabitants often march to the beat of a different drum. This is certainly the case with the French Alps and Jura mountains. Little collectives, hidden between the jagged peaks and alpine meadows, tried various attempts at independence, and the Savoy area wasn't even officially part of France until 1860. To this day, the so-called **Franche-Comté** ('free country') enjoys degrees of regional autonomy, and the local dialects and cuisine remind you of that.

The Alps and the Jura mountains are a country within a country, and that's what gives them a magical appeal. For many French who want to get away from it all and change scenery, heading here is a natural choice. The mountain air refreshes the senses and unused muscles are quickly toned. Sporting options span the spectrum. There is downhill skiing, cross-country skiing, luge, bobsled, skating, bigfooting, ski-jumping and snowboarding. When the snow melts, endless kilometres of hiking, mountain-biking and horseback-riding trails are revealed. Some trails take several days to complete. There is ice-climbing, rock-climbing and free climbing. The Alps are also popular with wind-gliders, windsurfers and those who want to go fishing, canoeing, kayaking or sailing on the many lakes. Non-sporty types can simply lounge at one of the world-class spas located here.

Besançon, the capital of Franche-Comté that has waltzed in and out of French citizenship, dominates the northern part of the Jura mountains. Not far is the Jura wine region where grapes are pressed from some of the highest vineyards in Europe to produce a unique beverage. Jura wines, also called *vin jaune* ('yellow wine') or *vin de paille* ('straw wine'), are usually concentrated fermentations of grape odds and ends – ranging from chardonnay to unnamed mystery grapes – that are randomly thrown together. Some wines are made from raisins to ensure a high sugar content, although many connoisseurs try to avoid them. The area is also home to significant salt mines and in the past those who produced salt levied a special salt tax (*la gabelle*) that made a few producers extremely rich.

In the southern part of Franche-Comté, the lake region of the Gex is a stone's throw away from Switzerland's Geneva. In fact, France has managed to almost completely engulf **Lake Geneva** (Lac Léman). The majesty of these snow-capped peaks is captured in stunning detail in the mirror-like surface of the water.

South of here starts the territory known as **Savoy**, which once belonged to what would become Italy. Savoy is divided into Savoie to the south and Haute-Savoie to the north, and its ancient capital was **Chambéry**. Two lakes to the north, Lac du Bourget and Lac d'Annecy, are now embellished with Belle Epoque hotels, elegant casinos and thermal bath structures. Since the Romans, aristocrats have flocked here for facials, sulphur cures, mud wraps and other beauty treatments. In fact the area is home to some of France's ritziest accommodation and finest dining.

Savoie is also where ski buffs need to make frequent pilgrimages. Resorts like Mont Blanc, Chamonix and Mégève are legends among mountaineers. The second great French alpine range is the Massif de la Vanoise, which is home to **Albertville** (host of the 1992 Winter Olympics). To the far south is the last of the great skiing spots: **Grenoble** (host of the 1968 Winter Olympics). The city centre is rather nondescript, but the beauty of the surrounding mountain scenery will inspire a stream of descriptive adjectives. Near the Italian border is **Briançon**, supposedly Europe's highest town at 4,330ft, and to the south the mighty Alps take a dramatic nosedive into the Mediterranean Sea.

Provence and the Côte d'Azur

Conveniently adjacent to the winter playground is France's summer one. The ancient Greeks were the first foreigners to hit the pebble beaches of this heavenly stretch of coastline. Next came the Romans, who also bestowed particular affection on their beloved 'province'. For both, the region represented an important crossroads between the Italian and the Iberian peninsulas, and served as a point of entry for commerce and trade into France via the Rhône river. Beauty, good weather and geographic proximity to Europe: that's why the Greeks and Romans came, and that is why everyone else has put in appearances since then.

Provence and the Côte d'Azur are two very different species. Provence refers to the idyllic inland countryside in the Midi, dotted with stone farmhouses and covered in orchards and lavender fields. The Côte d'Azur, on the other hand, is the seaside world capital of glitz and glamour and home to a high-octane nightlife. Add Italy's Portofino to California's Beverly Hills and multiply the results by a thousand and this is the result.

The quietest and most genuine part of Provence is the Rhône river area, including Roman satellite towns like **Orange**. It boasts two of France's most important Roman era monuments: an ancient theatre and a triumphal arch that dates back to AD 20. The stone carvings on the arch depict the Romans' conquest of the area. South of Orange is **Châteauneuf-du-Pape**, a former papal residence synonymous with excellent wine. Every child knows **Avignon** thanks to the nursery song about its truncated bridge: the arched Pont St-Bénézet extends into the middle of the river and stops to overlook nothingness since angry waters washed away its other half. Avignon was the seat of the 14th-century papal court, which made it one of the most important and influential cities in the country. Today, with its narrow streets teeming with lively cafés and boutiques and its sun-warmed stone buildings, it is the most visited city of the area. Within close proximity are the towns of **Villeneuve lez Avignon** with its nearby abbey, and **St-Rémy-de-Provence**, which was home to a glut of historic celebrities ranging from Nostradamus to Vincent Van Gogh. The Dutch painter also put in long hours contemplating an empty canvas in **Arles**. Celebrated as one of the most intact and charming of Provence's countryside towns, it is in high regard among expatriates today. The area between the two branches of the Rhône river further to the south is known as the **Camargue**, a vast marshland where wild white horses and black longhorn cattle were long tended by cowboys called *gardians* in their distinctive black hats.

It may have a reputation as a dangerous and somewhat seedy port city, but **Marseille** is currently experiencing a renaissance of sorts. The former Greek colony flourished during the Crusades and its port eventually marked the entrance point for thousands of foreign immigrants – Algerians, Jews, Turks and Italians – who have since become part of the country's ethnic mix. But after the 18th century this mighty port city fell on hard times. An ambitious public works campaign has recently kicked off to restore hundreds of historic buildings and give the city a much-needed facelift. North of the city you return to rustic Provençal charm in **Aix-en-Provence**. Paul Cézanne grew up here, and the small city is home to a famous school for French for foreigners.

Northern Provence, the area known as the **Vaucluse**, is a house-hunter's paradise. Writer Peter Mayle picked up property here and sparked an incoming avalanche of foreign house-hunters. Although the homes can be pricey, properties in the Luberon and around the city of Apt are among the most beautiful you can buy in southern Europe. Bald Mont Ventoux marks the northern boundary of Provence, and **Vaison-la-Romaine** is home to more Roman ruins, including a bridge.

The Alpes-Maritimes descend violently to the sea, making for dizzying contrasts in scenery within a few kilometres. From craggy, grey-coloured mountain spires, the altitude literally drops to sea level like a thick wall. Indeed, the snug ribbon of land known as the Côte d'Azur that straddles the waterfront is protected against cold temperatures from the north and enjoys blissful isolation from the rest of France.

Starting from the Italian border, **Menton** is an excellent preface for what follows. There's more beauty packed with this former fishing village at the foot of the Maritime Alps than most large cities could hope for. Scooting west down the coast, you soon come to the unexpected skyscrapers of **Monaco**, which stand tall from within this tight natural harbour like a cluster of concrete cypress trees. More land was added to the Principality to accommodate its growth, casinos, car races, royal family and the lucky tax-dodgers who claim residence here, but it was still forced to sprout upwards within its confines like a mini Toronto.

The corniche roads break away from Monte-Carlo and lead west to what may be the most expensive piece of real estate in the world. **Cap Ferrat** is a pine-covered peninsula that jets out to sea between Monaco and Nice. Shaded by the massive umbrella pines are the homes of the world's richest and most famous glitterati.

A few more dramatic bends of the coastline, and suddenly the landscape opens on to **Nice**'s port and old quarter. Vieux Nice has a morning flower and vegetable market that tickles all your senses, from sight to smell to sound, and the labyrinth of tiny streets behind the market is painted in the various ruddy pastel colours of nearby Liguria. In fact, Nice was part of Italy until 1860 and its Italian heart still beats strong. The Promenade des Anglais, the beachfront walk scattered with metal chairs, is named after the many English visitors who took time off in Nice. There are very few places where you can swim in clean water just a few steps away from a bustling metropolis, and Nice is one of them.

Past the picturesque hilltop Cagnes-sur-Mer, the tourist-friendly St-Paul-de-Vence, and the glass-blowing centre Biot, is the port of **Antibes**. A favourite with the British yachting-set, Antibes is home to a wealthy and numerous expat population. The peninsula, Cap d'Antibes, is home to more lavish summer villas. **Grasse** is an inland perfume capital, with the techno-new-town of **Sophia-Antipolis** providing many jobs nearby, and **Cannes**, on the coast, is famous for its beaches, luxury shopping and the Cannes Film Festival every May.

West of Cannes, the landscape reinvents itself. The glaring white rock of the mountains suddenly gives way to iron-dyed bluffs. The **Massif des Maures** is bathed in brilliant contrasts: red rocks meet cobalt water and lush green pines round off the colour wheel. **St-Raphaël** and **Fréjus** are favourites with swimsuit- and sandal-clad visitors heading to and from the spectacular cove beaches. On the western end of the Massif des Maures is the ultimate fishing village-turned-luxury resort: **St-Tropez**. Nearby are **Hyères** and its islands and southeast still is **Toulon**. Past the modern outskirts of the city are the delightful towns of **Bandol** and **Cassis**, home to some of the best white and rosé wines in the south of France.

Languedoc-Roussillon

You get the feeling that something extraordinary is about to happening in Languedoc-Roussillon. Wine critics have praised local vintners, who shun rigid *appellation d'origine contrôlée* regulations, for being 'revolutionary' and 'innovative'. The region is now known for high quality wine, priced better than Bordeaux and the Rhône. Another example is real estate. Languedoc-Roussillon is sometimes referred to as the 'anti-Provence' because property is cheaper and the market is flooded with attractive fixer-uppers waiting for the right buyer. For the same price as a farmhouse in trendy Provence, here you can buy a house *and* a few extra hectares of land. The region is up-and-coming from a business point of view too. Nîmes and Montpellier are attracting high-end and high-tech talent and a slew of new companies are poised for almost certain success. As the allure of Provence and the Côte d'Azur wears thin with those fatigued by its traffic and exaggeratedly high prices, Languedoc-Roussillon is stepping into the limelight. Named after Occitan, or the language of the Pays d'Oc, Languedoc is a rising giant of France.

Nîmes was an ancient Celtic outpost that flourished under the Romans who created the Via Domitia trade route, connecting the Italian and Iberian peninsulas. The Roman imprint is strong and the city is home to a remarkably well-preserved amphitheatre. Not far away, past the charming town of Sommières where many foreigners have set up residence, the landscape flattens out before **Montpellier**. The self-appointed 'capital of southern Europe', Montpellier is home to a pharmaceutical industry that started in the 13th century with the founding of the *Universitas Medicorum*.

Another model city of the Pays d'Oc is **Narbonne**. Founded as a Roman trading colony, it is home to the oversized Cathédrale St-Just, visible for miles. Narbonne is an agricultural capital and the biggest city servicing the sprawling vineyards of the nearby Corbières countryside and the area's famous white bean plantations. Another nearby attraction is the tree-lined Canal du Midi, conceived with the idea of connecting the Atlantic and Mediterranean.

Immediately after Narbonne, the motorway heads inland to the walled city of **Carcassonne**. A perfect jewel of urban planning with excellent postcard potential, the bastion was erected to safeguard trade routes that crossed over to the Atlantic side. Today, it is a major tourist attraction. But don't be put off by the day-trippers. The entire Languedoc countryside and its laid-back attitude is ideal for expatriate house-hunters who want to settle in for the long term.

Roussillon is the southernmost angle of the French Hexagon and its inner soul is Catalan, not Gallic. In fact, the region spent much of its history trying to untangle itself from France. The capital city is **Perpignan**, and west of it the landscape butts against the foothills of the majestic Pyrenees.

Corsica

As if France weren't perfect enough, it has Corsica too. This Mediterranean island boasts a stunning natural beauty that spans all the geographic possibilities within a comfortably tight space. Good things do come in small packages, and Corsica has crystalline sand beaches and snow-capped mountain scenery, all within a short drive. Thanks to these valuable assets and its rich flora and fauna, La Corse is the ultimate summertime destination for the French and foreigners alike.

Scratch beneath the glossy surface depicted in brochures and Corsica is associated with a troubled past that sees occasional violent outbursts. The island's history has traditionally linked it to Italy and Corsica's Italian heart is tangible in its foods, dialect and in the faces of its people. In fact, it is closer to Tuscany (82 kilometres away) than it is to the south of France (160 kilometres). Corsica has been in French hands since 1769 when it was annexed from Genoa – months before the birth of its most famous son, Napoleon Bonaparte. The feisty general may have been the very incarnation of French pride, but a sense of national belonging did not adhere to all islanders. The ongoing independence movement is marginal but does see flare-ups of terrorist activity and occasional

The Moor's Head

Of the images associated with Corsica, one is inescapable. The Corsican flag is hoisted wherever possible and depicts a Moor's head with a white headband. The *bandiera testa mora*, as it is called in the local dialect, takes top honour on the pole in front of Ajaccio's Chamber of Commerce. Here, it is positioned above the French tricolour. According to legend, a black man saved a Corsican king from assassination. In gratitude, the king ordered that the white band, or *tortil*, be removed from his eyes. The Moor wears the band on his forehead as a symbol of Corsica's vigilance, awakening and as a promise that its inhabitants will never be blind to their past. Some associate the Moor's head flag with the Corsican separatist movement, but this is incorrect. The flag represents all Corsicans and was officially adopted by islanders in 1755 under island hero Pascuale Paoli.

assassinations. Corsica enjoys degrees of autonomy. France may have loosened its bureaucratic grip, but keeps the Corsican question on the back burner.

Since 1975, island has been divided into two departments. The southern half, **Corse-du-Sud**, is home to **Ajaccio**, Napoleon's home town, and the breathtakingly beautiful **Bonifacio**. Perched over the straits of the same name, Bonifacio represents one of the most perfect junctions between mankind and Mother Nature. Immense sand-coloured cliffs rise from a cobalt sea and are transformed into church spires, layered apartment buildings and panoramic perches. A little more than 10 kilometres away is Italy's Sardinia, where the sea's gentle massage has smoothed and shaped granite rocks into feminine shapes.

The top of the island, or **Haute-Corse**, is separated by a tall range of mountains that sees freak weather even in summer months. It is not uncommon to hear of lost hikers getting frostbite in late May or June. The main towns are **Calvi**, an important port, **Cortes** and **Bastia**. Calvi is another fortified sea-facing citadel of unforgettable beauty. The western flank of Corsica is rocky and marked by steep cliffs and tiny cove beaches, and the eastern side is flat and home to the island's only patches of agriculture and vineyard land. Corsica has 250,000 inhabitants.

France touring atlas

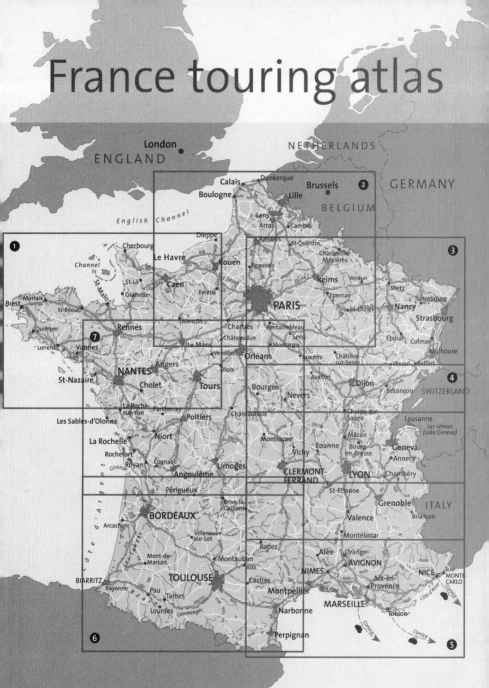

ENGLAND

NETHERLANDS

London

GERMANY

English Channel

Calais
Dunkerque
Boulogne
Brussels
Lille
BELGIUM

Lens
Arras
Cambrai
Amiens
St-Quentin

Dieppe

Cherbourg
Le Havre
Rouen
Beauvais
Charleville-
Mézières
Reims
Verdun

Channel Is
St-Lô
Caen
Evreux
PARIS
Epernay
St-Dizier
Metz
Sarrebourg
Nancy

Morlaix
Granville
Alençon
Chartres
Fontainebleau
Sens
Strasbourg

Brest
St-Brieuc
St-Malo
Rennes
Châteaudun
Montargis
Auxerre
Châtillon-
sur-Seine
Epinal
Colmar

Quimper
Le Mans
Vendôme
Orléans
Mulhouse
Vesoul
Belfort

Lorient
Vannes
Angers
Blois
Bourges
Avallon
Dijon
Besançon
SWITZERLAND

St-Nazaire
NANTES
Cholet
Tours
Nevers
Chalon-sur-
Saône
Lausanne

Les Sables-d'Olonne
Parthenay
Poitiers
Châteauroux
Mâcon
Bourg-
en-Bresse
Lac Léman
(Lake Geneva)

La Roche-
sur-Yon
Niort
Montluçon
Vichy
Roanne
Geneva
Annecy

La Rochelle
Rochefort
Cognac
Limoges
CLERMONT-
FERRAND
LYON
Chambéry

Royan
Angoulême
St-Etienne

Gironde
Périgueux
Brive-la-
Gaillarde
Grenoble
ITALY

Côte d'Argent
BORDEAUX
Valence
Briançon

Arcachon
Villeneuve-
sur-Lot
Montélimar

Mont-de-
Marsan
Montauban
Rodez
Alès
Orange
AVIGNON
NICE
MONTE
CARLO

BIARRITZ
TOULOUSE
Albi
Castres
NIMES
Aix-en-
Provence

Bayonne
Pau
Tarbes
Montpellier
MARSEILLE

Lourdes
Comminges
Narbonne
Toulon
Côte d'Azur

Perpignan
Corsica

SPAIN

Madrid

N

100 km
50 miles

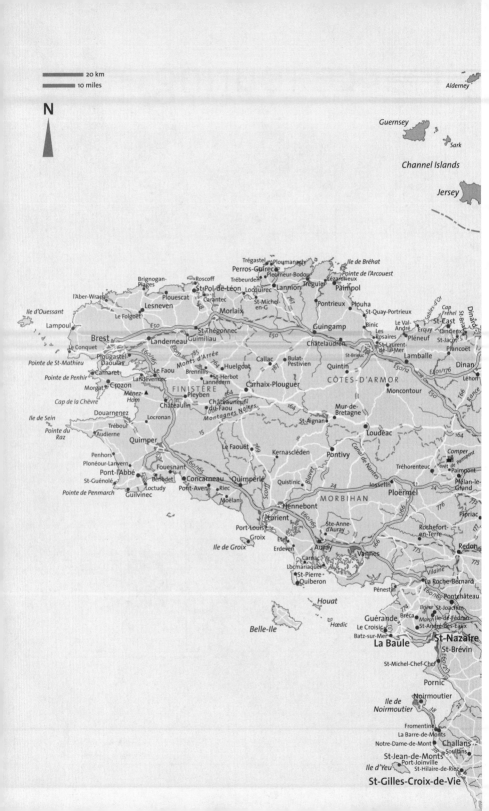

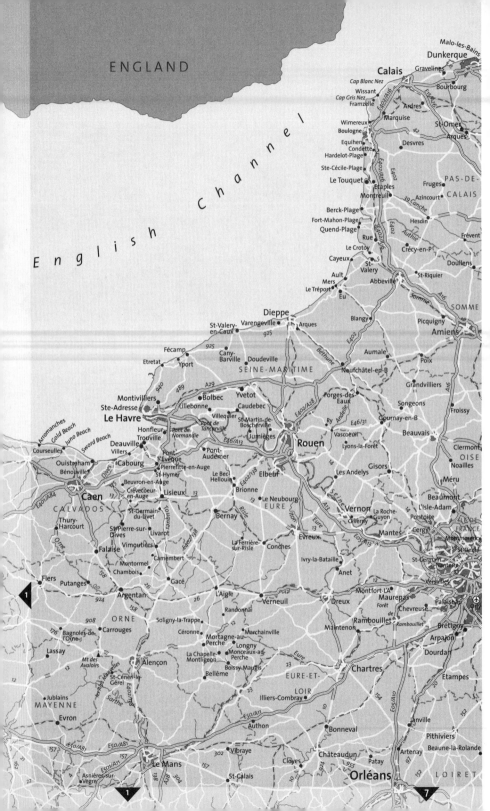

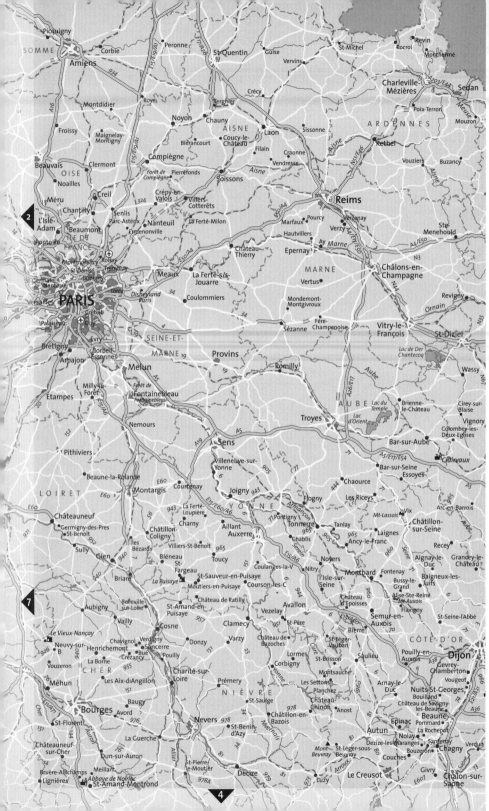

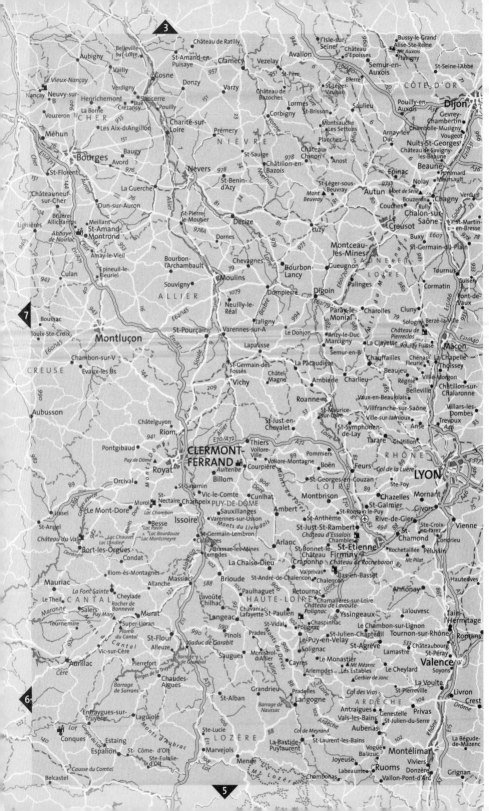

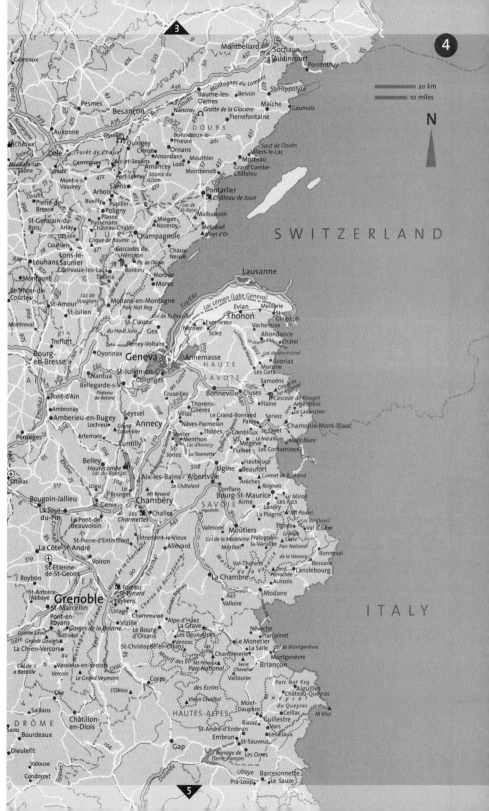

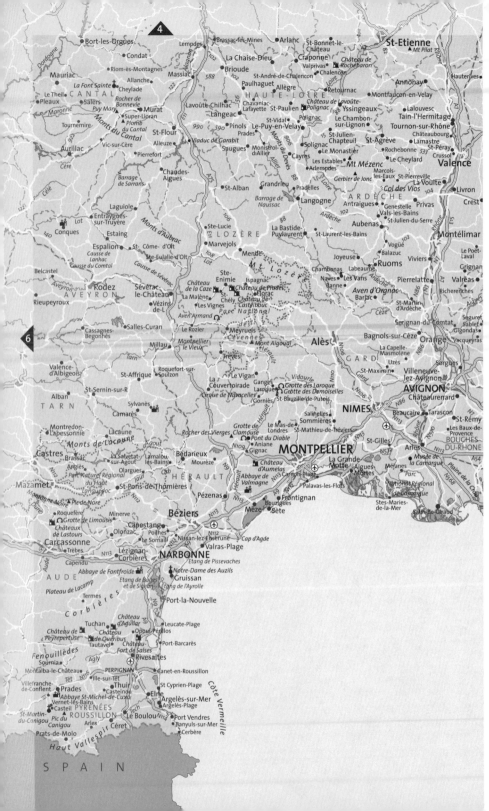

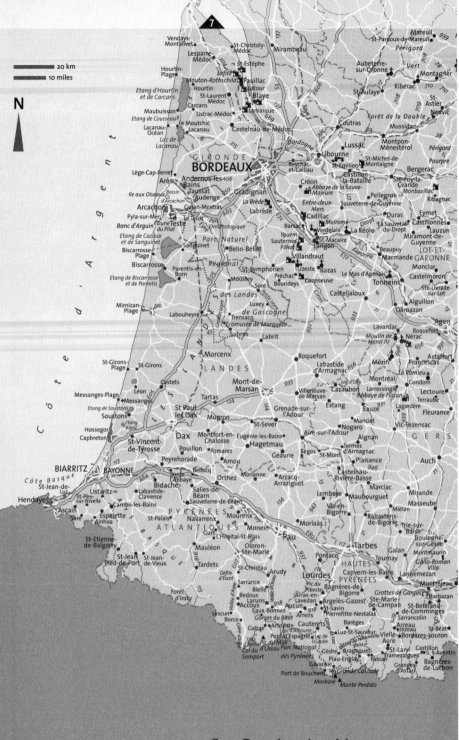

Puyguilhem · Grottes de Villars · Thiviers · Lascaux · Suc-au-May ▲ Chaumeil · St-Angel · 922 · Super-Besse · Besse · Lac Pavin · St-Germain-Lembron · -sur-
Champagnac-de-Belair · Ségur-le-Château · Uzerche · Château du Val · Lac Chauvet · Lac Bourdouze · Lac Montcineyre · Collanges · Mines
Brantôme · Excideuil · Sorges · Chervix-Cubas · Arnac-Pompadour · CORRÈZE · Lac Lôndie · Massiac · Lempdes · Brioude
Bourdeilles · Savignac · Tourtoirac · Bort-les-Orgues · Condat · Riom-ès-Montagnes · Laroute-Chilhac
Périgord Blanc · Auvezère · Hautefort · Donzenac · Tulle · La Roche-Canillac · Mauriac · La Font Sainte · Cheylade · Rocher de Bonneviе · Allanche · Lavoûte-Chilhac
E70 · PÉRIGUEUX · 89 · Montignac · Terrasson-la-Villedieu · E70 · Brive-la-Gaillarde · Pleaux · Le Theil · CANTAL · Salers · Puy Mary · Super-Lioran · Murat · Albepierre-Bredons · Pinols
DORDOGNE · Rouffignac · Grotte de Lascaux · St-Amand-de-Coly · Collonges-la-Rouge · Argentat · Maronne · Tournemire · Plomb du Cantal · St-Flour · 590 · Viaduc de Garabit
Grotte de Rouffignac · La Roque St-Christophe · St-Léon-sur-Vézère · Turenne · Meyssac · Beaulieu-sur-Dordogne · Tours de Merle · Vic-sur-Cère · Monts du Cantal · Alleuze · Barrage de Grandval · 990
Les Eyzies-de-Tayac · Commarque · Font-de-Gaume · Carlux · Martel · Souillac · Carennac · Bretenoux · St-Céré · Aurillac · Cère · Pierrefort · Chaudes-Aigues · St-Alban
Le Bugue · La Mouthe · Sarlat · Lacave · Grottes de Lacave · Montal · Barrage de Sarrans · A75
Trémolat · Cadouin · St-Cyprien · Siorac-en-Périgord · Domme · Grottes de Cougnac · Ste-Lucie
Belvès · Beaumont-du-Périgord · Gourdon · Lacapelle-Marival · Laguiole · Marvejols
Monpazier · Biron · Labastide-Murat · 653 · Assier · Figeac · Capdenac-le-Haut · Entraygues-sur-Truyère · Monts d'Aubrac · Ste-Lucie
Villeréal · Lacapelle-Biron · Les Arques · LOT · Montfaucon · 122 · Espagnac · Ste-Eulalie · Capdenac-Gare · Conques · Espalion · St-Côme-d'Olt · Ste-Eulalie-d'Olt
Monflanquin · Bonaguil · Martignac · La Masse · Marcilhac-sur-Célé · Lot · Estaing · Marvejols
Monsempron · Fumel · Duravel · Puy L'Évêque · Luzech · Bouziès · Cajarc · Cause de Lanhac · Cause du Comtal · Causse de Sauveterre · Ste-Enimie
Villeneuve-sur-Lot · Tournon-d'Agenais · Cahors · Arcambal · St-Cirq-Lapopie · Villefranche-de-Rouergue · Belcastel · Château de la Caze · La Malène
Pujols · Montaigu-de-Quercy · Montcuq · Cause de Limogne · Beauregard · AVEYRON · Rodez · Vézins-de-L · Séverac-le-Château · Les Vignes
Laroque-Timbaut · Beauville · Castelnau-Montratier · Lalbenque · Rieupeyroux · Aven Armand · Le Rozier · Meyrueis
Puymirol · Lauzerte · Montpezat-de-Quercy · Caylus · Najac · Salles-Curan · Montpellier-le-Vieux
Auvillar · Moissac · Abbaye de St-Pierre · St-Antonin-Noble-Val · Cassagnes-Bégonhès · Millau · Trèves
Castelsarrasin · TARN-ET-GARONNE · Lafrançaise · Négrepelisse · Aveyron · Carmaux · La Couvertoirade
Miradoux · St-Clar · Montech · Bruniquel · Penne · Cordes-sur-Ciel · Valence-d'Albigeois · Roquefort-sur-Soulzon · Causse du Larzac
Beaumont-de-Lomagne · Verdun-sur-Garonne · Montauban · Gaillac · Tarn · Albi · Alban · St-Sernin-sur-R · St-Affrique · Sylvanès
Mauvezin · Fronton · TARN · Camarès
Gimont · L'Isle-Jourdain · 124 · Blagnac · Réalmont · Montredon-Labessonnié · Lacaune · Rocher des Vierges · Bédarieux
Saramon · Le Mirail · Lavaur · Graulhet · Brassac · Monts de Lacaune · Lamalou-les-Bains · Mourèze · Clermont-l'Hérault
Samatan · St-Lys · TOULOUSE · Puylaurens · La Salvetat-sur-Agout · Sommet de l'Espinouse · Monts de l'Espinouse · HÉRAULT
Lombez · Muret · Castres · Angles · Parc Naturel Régional du Haut Languedoc · Olargues · St-Pons-de-Thomières · Pézenas
Rieumes · HAUTE-GARONNE · Mazamet · Pic de Nore · Orb
Saissac · Montagne Noire · Roquefère · Minerve · Capestang · Béziers
St-Martory · Montsaunès · Ste-Croix · Artigat · Castelnaudary · Grotte de Limousis · Cesse · Olonzac · Poilhes · Nissan-lez-Enserune · Valras-Plage
St-Gaudens · Salies-du-Salat · St-Girons · Pamiers · Vals · Teilhet · Montolieu · Carcassonne · Trèbes · Le Somail · NARBONNE · Notre-Dame des Auzils
COMMINGES · Le Mas · Montégut-Plantaurel · Micropoix · Capendu · N113 · Lézignan-Corbières · Gruissan
Castillon-en-Couserans · St-Gizier · La Bastide-de-Sérou · St-Jean-de-Verges · Limoux · AUDE · Termes · Abbaye de Fontfroide · Étang de l'Ayrolle
Bethmale · Soueix · Oust · Foix · Lavelanet · Alet-les-Bains · Plateau de Lacamp · Corbières · Port-la-Nouvelle
Mont Valier · Seix · Grotte de Lombrives · Tarascon-sur-Ariège · ARIÈGE · Couiza · Rennes-le-Château · Quillan · Tuchan · Château d'Aguilar · Leucate-Plage
Aulus-les-Bains · Grotte de Niaux · Les Cabannes · Montaillou · Château de Peyrepertuse · Cucugnan · Opoul-Périllos · Fort de Salses · Port-Barcarès
Vicdessos · Ax-les-Thermes · St-Paul-de-Fenouillet · Château de Quéribus · Maury · Tautavel · Salses · Rivesaltes
Cascade d'Arse · Étang de Bays · Sournia · Agly · PERPIGNAN · Canet-en-Roussillon
L'Hospitalet · Villefranche-de-Conflent · Montalba-le-Château · Ille-sur-Têt · Thuir · St-Cyprien-Plage
ANDORRA · Pic Carlit · Prades · St-Michel-de-Cuxa · Têt · Elne · Argelès-sur-Mer
Pyrénées 2000 · Mont Louis · Vernet-les-Bains · PYRÉNÉES · ROUSSILLON · Argelès-Plage · Port Miradoux
Puigcerda · Font-Romeu · Super Bolquère · St-Martin-du-Canigou · Pic du Canigou · Céret · Le Boulou · Port Vendres
Llo · Err · Prats-de-Molo · Arles · Haut Vallespir · Banyuls-sur-Mer · Cerbère · Côte Vermeille

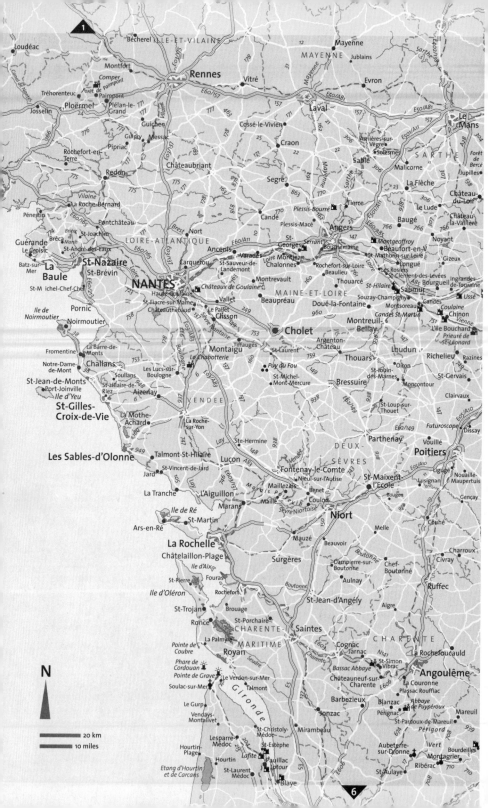

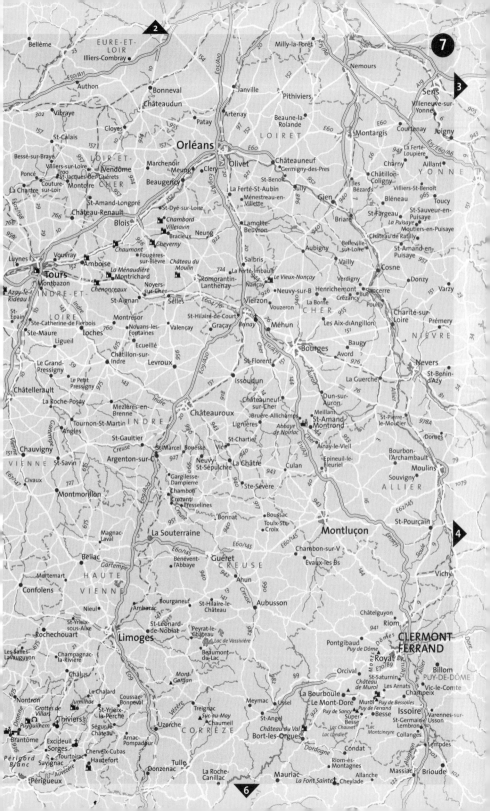

Photo essay
by Monica Larner

2

3

6

7

5 Village fête
6 Vineyard
7 Foods of Nantes

FORUM

France Today

France is not easy to pin down. Most of us are instinctively attracted to France thanks to its high quality of life; but few of us look beyond the immediate gratification it awards. Those who do will know this is a country ripe with contradictions. It is among the most significant European nations in terms of size, political and economic influence. Consequently, it is one of the most complex and troubled. It is among the staunchest supporters of time-honoured traditions and yet it straddles the cutting edge of technological innovation. France was first to give the world bullet trains and a rudimentary form of the Internet. But, only a few kilometres away from the high-tech corridors of France's own version of Silicon Valley, glass-blowers carefully craft vases and wine goblets using the same techniques and craftsmanship their ancestors once perfected.

A long list of adjectives have been used to describe – and often lampoon – the French: arrogant, *bon vivant*, cheerful, curious, friendly, hardworking, impatient, innovative, intolerant, introspective, proud, sophisticated, quarrelsome, moody, superior. One thing is certain: their contribution to civilization has been enormous. One 19th-century writer described France as 'the most brilliant and dangerous nation in Europe'.

Those of us who live here learn that, although 'France' may be a concrete geographical expression, it is not a definition of national identity. Instead of the 'French', this is a country made up of dozens of different people identified by the characteristics of their homeland. Comparing a Frenchman from Normandy with one from Provence makes as much sense as comparing a Briton to a Frenchman. Despite the homogenous appearance, the corners of the Hexagon enclose radically different languages, races, cultures and traditions. By moving to France you yourself will add one more new colour, or one more texture, to the varied cultural patchwork of this fascinating nation.

Government and Major Political Parties

Established by the constitution of 1958, France's Fifth Republic is characterized by strong executive powers held by the president of the Republic and the government (which includes the prime minister). The constitution put an end to the political instability of previous regimes by creating a system whereby a president and a government of contrasting political colours could 'cohabit' (*see* **Getting to Know France**, 'Historical Overview', pp.20–21).

Under the constitution, the president of the Republic is elected to office for a five-year term and may be re-elected unlimited times. He or she appoints the prime minister and approves the government, commands the armed forces and has the last word on foreign policy, presides over the Council of Ministers and the High Council of the Judiciary (which appoints judges), can call referendums

Symbols of a Nation

The French flag was born from the emotions unleashed by the French Revolution. The roots of the 'tricolour' span back to when white symbolized the king and blue and red were the colours of Paris. In the early stages of the French Revolution, rosettes worn on military hats were red and blue. On 17 July 1789, shortly after the storming of the Bastille, Louis XVI came to pay tribute to the new National Guard in Paris and in their honour he attached the same blue and red cockade to his hat. Commander Lafayette approached him and added a touch of white to establish a symbolic trinity. By 1794, the tricolour was recognized as the national flag and laws stipulated that the blue segment be positioned closest to the flagpole. The French rallied around their flag during the First World War and the 1946 constitution established the 'blue, white and red' as the emblem of a nation.

Another proud symbol of France is the Gallic rooster. The Coq Gaulois was first seen on French flags during the Revolution and represents a play on words: the Latin word for France (*Gallus*) is the same as for 'cockerel'.

Roosters, with their head pointed to the sky and their tail feathers standing alert, were shaped from iron and put on the top of roofs as a symbol of vigilance in the Middle Ages. The crow of the cock in the early dawn hours sets the tone for the rest of the day and its image worked its way into folk art, ceramics and embroidery. Its popularity as a symbol grew and the cock became a symbol of the Revolution, at one point replacing the *fleur-de-lys*. Since 1848 the Gallic rooster has appeared on the official seal of the Republic, and it was used as a motif on older coins. Today, it appears on stamps and is a mascot of sporting teams at international competitions.

at will, and has acres of patronage at his disposal. After consultation with the government and the presidents of the assemblies, the president has the power to dissolve the National Assembly.

The prime minister is appointed by the president and directs the operations of the government. He or she is responsible for national defence and has the power to make decrees and ministerial orders. Like all parliamentary democracies, the prime minister must answer to parliament and he or she must be acceptable to the parliamentary majority.

As head of the government, the prime minister's authority is greater than that of the other ministers, who form the Secrétariat Général du Gouvernement. The ministers, in turn, participate in meetings of government bodies and oversee government acts that fall within their areas of control – such as agriculture, defence, justice and education.

The parliament is composed of the National Assembly (previously known as the Chamber of Deputies), which makes its headquarters at the Palais Bourbon in Paris, and the Senate, which meets in the Palais du Luxembourg.

The National Assembly

The National Assembly is composed of 577 deputies, with one deputy representing some 100,000 inhabitants. Each parliament is elected for five years, a term which may be shortened if the president opts to dissolve the Assembly. The National Assembly has a single session that starts on the first day of October and lasts until the last working day of June.

The Senate

The Senate's 321 members are elected for a nine-year term by an electoral college. One-third of senators are elected every three years. In addition to passing legislation and keeping check on government, the Senate is called upon by the 1958 constitution to represent France's local authorities, the *communes*, departments, regions and overseas territories. French citizens living abroad are also represented in the Senate.

The Constitutional Council

The Constitutional Council is a court formed by nine members chosen for a nine-year term, and its task is to safeguard the constitution.

The Council of State

The Conseil d'Etat is the highest administrative court, and acts as an advisory body to the government.

Political Parties

France has dozens of political parties representing a wide spectrum of interests and ideologies. The following is a breakdown of the most important parties in France today.

Parti Socialiste (PS) – Socialist Party

The left-leaning Parti Socialiste has existed since the beginning of the 20th century and was the successor of the SFIO (French section of the Workers International). The PS was reformed and reborn in 1971 under François Mitterrand, although it has fallen in popularity since the 1980s.

Parti Communiste Français (PCF) – French Communist Party

This left-leaning party has often been an instrumental element of ruling coalition governments and was a major force lasting until the late 1970s. It formed an alliance with the Parti Socialiste after François Mitterrand was elected president of the Republic, enabling it to play a part in the 1981–4 left-wing government. The PCF still wins a good number of seats in both the Senate and the National Assembly each election although its general popularity has fallen since the Berlin Wall came down. It was founded at the Tours Congress of 1920 as the French Section of the Communist International, and later became the PCF.

Rassemblement pour la République (RPR) – Rally for the Republic

The RPR has its roots in the Gaullist party established in 1947 and united around Charles de Gaulle as the Rassemblement du Peuple Français (RPF). Its current incarnation was founded in 1976 by Jacques Chirac. As a moderate-to-conservative body, it stands opposed to the trappings of big government.

Union pour la Démocratie Française (UDF) – Union for French Democracy

Founded in 1978 by Valéry Giscard d'Estaing, the Union pour la Démocratie Française was a confederation of parties until 1998, when it became a unified party. Its components are: Force Démocrate, the Parti Populaire pour la Démocratie Française, the Parti Radical, and the Pôle Républicain, Indépendant et Liberal. Its members advocate a move to the centre.

Les Verts – The Greens

Les Verts is a political fusion of the Parti Ecologiste (founded in 1982) and the Confédération Ecologiste (founded in 1983), and promotes environment-friendly causes. The left-leaning party has managed to secure seats in the National Assembly and has gained support thanks to a platform of 'solidarity, global responsibility and citizenship'.

Rassemblement pour la France (RPF) – Rally for France

Founded in 1999, the right-wing RPF is headed by Charles Pasqua and stands against globalization and European federalism. It also promotes French national sovereignty.

Front National (FN)

Founded in 1972 by the controversial Jean-Marie Le Pen, FN calls itself 'a nationalist party of the popular right'. Others consider his party an offence to French values and civil liberties. FN gained little initial electoral support, but since the 1980s its base of supporters has increased culminating in 2002 when its sudden popularity shocked the nation (*see* **Getting to Know France**, pp.20–21). In 1999 a breakaway faction called the Front National–Mouvement National was formed. Le Pen's rhetoric contains a heavy note of racism (*see* 'Immigration and Racism', pp.84–7).

Religion

France's religious kaleidoscope is one of the most fascinating components of its modern identity. About 85 per cent of the French are Roman Catholic and the second largest religious group is comprised of Muslims, who are fast reaching 10 per cent of the population. The rest is divided between small Protestant, Jewish and Buddhist communities and groups not affiliated with any religion.

Although the Roman Catholic majority observes religious holidays and saints' days, the French Republic is wholeheartedly secular. A clear line is drawn separating Church and state, putting France at odds with some of its European neighbours – especially since the EU has set the groundwork for enlargement from 15 to 25 member countries. A new constitution was drawn up to accommodate the newest member states, and one of the most controversial disputes focused on whether the words 'God' and 'Christianity' should be inserted into the draft.

Ireland, Spain, Italy and Poland, urged on by the Vatican, stood on one side of the fence and demanded emphatic recognition of Europe's religious roots in the constitution. They were joined by many of the EU's newest members: Slovakia, the Czech Republic, Malta and Lithuania – which all support a Judaeo-Christian reference in the preamble. The opposing conviction, held most tenaciously by France and Belgium, is that religion does not belong in the governing document of the EU.

Church and state are also divided in domestic politics. In late 2003, President Jacques Chirac called for a law banning the wearing of headscarves for Muslim girls, large crosses for Christians and skullcaps for Jewish boys in public schools. 'Secularism is one of the great successes of the Republic,' he said in an address to the nation. 'It is a crucial element of social peace and national cohesion. We cannot let it weaken.'

Avignon may have been the seat of the papacy from 1307 to 1377, but in recent years active Catholicism in France has been on the decline. For example, newborn baby christenings have dropped from 95 per cent to 55 per cent in the past 15 years. One in two weddings is performed in a church. Only 60 per cent of the French say God exists, and recruitment for new priests and nuns has fallen to an all-time low. All this in a country that houses major religious shrines and pilgrimage destinations such as Lourdes, Lisieux and Chartres.

As one religion loses followers, another – spurred by new waves of immigration – is quickly rising in influence and importance. The Muslim community in France is estimated at between four and five million people, making Islam the second most important religion. This number comprises Muslims from as many as 123 nations worldwide (North Africans from the Maghreb, Africans, Turks and Asians) and is impossible to consider one homogenous group. It is in fact a mixed bag of Islamic groups and cultures. France is home to a growing number of great mosques such as the ones located in Paris, Lyon and Marseille. There are more than 1,000 places of worship for Muslims in France and more than 500 imams operating throughout the French territory. More than 80 per cent of the Muslim population observes Ramadan.

Other religions present include Protestants, who account for two per cent of the population; although their numbers are small, they play a prominent role in French society. Fifteen per cent of Protestants are senior executives or belong to a liberal profession. Prime Minister Lionel Jospin is a case in point.

France's Jewish community is 800,000 strong and is made of Ashkenazi Jews from Central and Eastern Europe and Sephardi Jews from North Africa, notably Algeria. When the second group arrived following Algerian independence in 1962, the Jewish population in France doubled and enjoyed a period of revival refelcted in a growing number of synagogues.

Buddhists number 600,000, making Buddhism the fourth largest religious group in France. The religion has gained influence particularly among youth, intellectuals and artists. France is home to several hundred Zen or Tibetan meditation centres – including the largest centre in the western world located in the Touraine area. Auvergne is home to the biggest Buddhist monastery in the western world.

The Family and Role of Women

All modern nations have witnessed the painful fragmentation of the family nucleus, and France is no exception. The country has seen a decline in marriages and birth rates. The number of divorces and unmarried couples is on the rise. Compare demographic statistics immediately following the Second World War and today and the differences are astonishing. Back then, 420,000 people tied the knot each year and on average the unions produced 2.5 children per couple. Only 10 per cent of marriages ended in divorce. Fast-forward to today and the demographics paint a different picture. One in eight couples don't bother to get married and there are two million unmarried couples (in 1962 there were a mere 300,000). Eighty per cent of married couples start by living together and walk down the aisle at a later date.

The number of babies has fallen dangerously low. The average age in which a women gives birth to her first child increased from 26.8 in 1980 to 28.7 two decades later. In 1994, the birth rate dropped to a record of 1.6 children per couple and has risen only slightly since then. Obviously any country needs to reach a birth rate of 2 per couple to replace the existing population, so this negative birth rate actually puts French population figures at risk.

As recently as 1972, 416,000 marriages were registered, but today that number is half. Church weddings are also down by 50 per cent. In 1972, the average marrying age was 24.5 for men and 22.4 for women. Today it is closer to 30 for men and 28 for women. Nearly 40 per cent of French weddings end in divorce, and in Paris that number tops 50 per cent. Single-parent families are common, and new legislation has created special pacts for homosexual couples who live together which grants them privileges: for example, gay and unmarried couples can apply for a certificate of *concubinage* that establishes limited financial and legal security.

France had its own flourishing and vocal Women's Lib movement in the 1970s, the Mouvement des Libération des Femmes (MLF), and Simone de Beauvoir's classic feminist text *Le Deuxième Sexe*, first published in 1949, was 'rediscovered' by the '68ers. Great strides were made, although many of these reforms took place a number of years after other European countries. Women did not get the vote in France until 1945. Under the 1965 Matrimonial Act, wives gained the right to open a bank account, hold a passport or own property independently of their husband. Further reforms followed in the 1970s and '80s – contraception (1967), legal abortion (1971), more liberal divorce laws (1973) and the legal right to equal pay (1972) – but inequalities still exist in practice, especially in the area of paid work.

In the early 21st century, however, feminism on either side of the Channel and the Atlantic appears to have reached a similar point: '*le droit à la différence*' is the post-feminist mantra. French women still prize femininity over feminism. As one successful woman journalist has remarked, women may have full equality of rights and opportunities, but they have to be *soignée* too – and few seem to wish it otherwise. While women now do better than men overall in education, they are still under-represented at the élite ENA and in the Grandes Ecoles. Marguerite Yourcenar was the first woman to be admitted to the literary pinnacles of the Académie Française, in 1980, but the academy (devoted to the purity of *la langue française*) continues to resist feminization of the language ('*madame la présidente*' has been vetoed, and this may be the nation of *liberté*, *égalité* and *fraternité*, but a feminine equivalent of *fraternité* does not exist in the French language).

Few women have made it to the top echelons of business in France, in large part due to the *phallocratie* that still dominates French public life (*see* 'Internal Issues', pp.82–4). Although 40 per cent of executives today are women, only five per cent of these are heads of companies. In politics, women constitute 11 per cent of deputies and five per cent of ministers, junior ministers, prefects (chiefs of police) and ambassadors. The workforce tends to be divided along gender stereotypical lines, with levels of pay reflecting the divide – women account for 52 per cent of the population, yet their salaries are 25 per cent lower than men's – and finding a balance between work and family is as tough in France as anywhere. The unemployment rate for women is one-third higher than that for men, and significantly fewer women are able to climb professional ranks before hitting the so-called glass ceiling, or *plafond de verre*. Women stay unemployed longer and receive fewer unemployment benefits.

Women have also been slow to enter politics, whether due to male bias or their own reluctance to put themselves forwards: 30 women were elected to the 1945 National Assembly, but only 10 in 1977; following efforts by the Socialists to promote women through the ranks, this number rose to 26 in 1981 and, after the introduction of quotas, to 63 in 1997 (at the same time that New Labour swept to power in Britain with 120 women deputies). Simone Veil became a much-respected health minister in the 1970s, and Edith Cresson a less respected prime minister in 1991; Chirac appointed no fewer than nine women ministers to his cabinet in 1996. But top-level women politicians are still apt to be greeted with 'You're too pretty to be in politics, my dear' (Cresson).

Finally, one very frustrating aspect to being a woman in France has to do with inheritance rights. Even today, unless special provisions are made, a widow can be cut out of property titles and wealth. When a husband dies, these are almost always granted to and divided among the children.

Major Media

Foreigners often have a hard time wrapping their eyes and ears around French media laws. Article 11 of the 1789 *Declaration of the Rights of Man and the Citizen* guarantees that 'every citizen may speak, write and print with freedom'. But when you listen to French radio, for example, you can't avoid noticing that government wields a firm hand when determining what stations can and can't play and in which order. Herein lies the French media paradox.

In 1994, a law passed requiring that 40 per cent of the songs broadcast on popular music programmes be sung in French – with half that number to be performed by new talent. Radio is under the jurisdiction of the Conseil Supérieur de l'Audiovisuel (CSA), or the high council of radio and television broadcasting, which has the power to levy fines and suspend transmissions.

In perfect sequence, every second song is in French. The intent is twofold: to promote French artists and limit the spread of 'cultural contamination' presumably sparked by foreign music. The problem: there simply are not enough good French songwriters and singers to fill the endless hours of open airspace these radio laws have created. You'll spend an inverse proportional amount of time dial-dodging French pop music before finding a song that gets you humming. Although France may not be a hotbed of pop music talent, it is home to some very clever artists. They take first prize in redressing classic rock from England and America and translating lyrics into French in order to slide past media laws. Some are so ingenious (Johnny Hallyday, an aged rocker, has turning English hits into French ones down to an art), they make the CSA's crusade against cultural contamination look like a farce.

Newspapers and Magazines

Generally, the media sector is healthy and France's print media is among the best in the world. There are some 3,000 titles that speak to an immense, and increasingly diversified, readership. France counts 100 national and regional dailies and 49 per cent of the French read a newspaper each morning, according to a recent poll.

The leading newspapers are *Le Monde*, *Le Figaro* and *Libération*, which inform and help create public opinion. Of these, the ultra-serious *Le Monde* has a reputation as one of the world's greatest papers. It is politically independent, left-leaning but more truly oppositionist, and has long stuck by its austere format: small print, lack of photos, long articles and complex language. A revamp in 1995, however, introduced more articles on popular culture, science, social issues – and sport (it published a daily soccer World Cup supplement, to the consternation of the old guard). The conservative, right-wing *Le Figaro* is still going strong too, with the help of innovations such as a Saturday supplement of in-depth features. The radical, left-wing daily *Libération* hit hard times in the 1990s as it failed to find a niche in a post-ideological world. Founded in 1973, with Jean-Paul Sartre as its editor, it gained a reputation for hard-hitting irreverence, but in the last decade its sales fell and, since a sell-off, its old sparkle has dulled. A newer daily is *Parisien-Aujourd'hui*, which has employed smart marketing moves to increase readership.

To ensure democratic debate and prevent concentration of ownership, a single financial interest may control no more than 30 per cent of the total circulation of France's daily newspapers. Before the Second World War, most dailies in France were linked to a political party or group. This is no longer the case, as many publications have broadened their political outlook to reach a wider readership and are no longer defined by a particular ideology. A few party presses remain such as *L'Humanité*, the voice of the communists, or *Présent*, which is a platform for the far right. There is a Catholic daily called *La Croix*.

The regional press (with 400 titles nationwide) is dominated by a few large interests. The Hersant group controls about 30 per cent of the market (*Le Dauphiné Libéré*, *Paris-Normandie*, *Le Progrès de Lyon*, *Les Dernières Nouvelles d'Alsace*, *Nord-Matin*, *Nord-Eclair*, *Le Havre-Libre* and *Midi-Libre*). Hachette-Filipacchi Presse is also a significant force (*Le Provençal*, *Le Méridional* and *La République*). There are smaller groups with publications such as *Ouest-France*, *Sud-Ouest*, *La Dépêche du Midi* and *La Voix du Nord*.

To an Anglo-Saxon reader, the French press may seem Gallicly concerned with ideas over facts, at the same time as being oddly deferential to the establishment, and it is only recently that the press has taken up American-style investigative reporting (in tandem with graft investigations by magistrates). The satirical weekly *Le Canard enchaîné* has long been France's investigative bastion while new, more probing weekly news magazines have begun to eclipse the daily press. Modelled on *Time* or *Der Spiegel*, these offer a weekly news digest and features in a glossy format (with lots of ads). The biggest seller is broad-based *L'Express*. *Le Nouvel Observateur* is slightly more wordy and earnest, while *Le Point* prides itself on its analysis and flippant style. A relative newcomer is the leftish investigative *Marianne*. The veteran *Paris-Match* has also moved away from its glossy photo-story origins to a more newsy style, and the TV listings magazine *Télérama* throws some cultural news into its pop-culture mix.

France has no daily tabloid press like that across the Channel, but the weekly *France-Dimanche* and *Ici-Paris* have been bringing the country celebrity gossip and showbiz scandals since 1946. More recently, German-owned *Voici* and *Gala* have taken sensationalism up a notch: *Voici* openly fabricates its stories, even setting aside a budget for damages payments, which is more than covered by the sales of its fictions.

France has the highest level of magazine readership in the world. A slew of specialist publications – ranging from cars to astrology to women's issues – keep readers flocking to the news kiosks. A good example is *Elle* magazine, which was founded in 1945 and has helped define female beauty ever since; today it has 29 foreign editions. Fifteen magazines cover the automotive industry, six are dedicated to motorcycles, nine on photography and cinema, 20 on food and gastronomy, and seven cover science issues.

The nation's main news agency is Agence France-Presse (AFP), which is one of the three largest in the world with the Associated Press and Reuters. Leading photographic agencies are Gamma and Sipa.

Major media all have internet sites but foreigners will be pleased to find a few sites that keep their needs in mind. Among these are the excellent **www.french-times.com**, **www.livingfrance.com** and **www.francemag.com**.

You can also expect newspaper kiosks to sell international press such as the *Guardian*, the *Independent*, the *Financial Times*, the *International Herald Tribune* and standard news weeklies in English.

Television and Radio

Of course, like elsewhere, the written press has lost power and advertising revenue to broadcast media. Radio and television was a state monopoly but in 1982 media privatization occurred and hundreds of commercial radio stations were finally allowed to broadcast (under the supervision of the CSA). Television channels jumped from three to over 30.

Most television sets without an antenna will receive five terrestrial channels: TF1, France 2, France 3, Arte/France 5 and M6.

TF1 is a private channel that reaches the largest share of audience thanks to its colourful line-up of games, talk shows, soap operas, made for TV-movies and cinema. State-owned **France 2** has similar programming, with a higher dosage of special events, cultural events and interviews. **France 3** is also state-owned and shares some programming with France 2. Generally, it offers viewers more documentaries and nature, wildlife and environmental shows and has excellent regional and national news. **Arte** is a Franco–German joint venture that empha-sizes cultural programming and broadcasts classic movies in original language (*version originale*). **France 5** (also known until recently as La Cinq), which is part of Arte, is France's first educational channel. Last is **M6** – a growing broadcaster dedicated to popular programming, American reruns and music. The public channels are financed by government subsidies and the so-called television tax most set-owners pay. Private broadcasters are funded by advertising.

For an additional subscription fee you can buy **Canal Plus** service – through a satellite dish and a decoder box – to watch the BBC, CNN, Euronews, MTV and more than 300 European broadcasters. Launched as a pay-TV station in 1984, it now boasts more than 4 million subscribers. It specializes in high-quality films (it has its own production wing, co-producing many major European productions) and top-level sport. Every day the channel shows, unencoded, a five-minute political satire called *Les Guignols*, which has a massive, cultish following. Recent newcomers are **Canal Satellite** and **Télévision Par Satellite**, two new satellite digital TV groups, the former an offshoot of Canal Plus, the latter a conglomeration of all the other networks. Between them they have it covered, from sport to feature films, with foreign-language broadcasters (RAI, BBC World) bunched into their bouquets. **Cable TV** is available in Paris and in major towns. **Digital TV** was launched a decade ago and has seen its audience numbers rise thanks to multichannel packages and themed programming.

So, with this increasingly diverse broadcasting base, what can you actually watch on the box? For news, the options are TF1 and F2, which insist on running their main bulletins head-to-head at 8pm. Patrick Poivre d'Arvor is the veteran star newscaster and editor-in-chief of TF1's newscast, throwing in handfuls of his own opinions with the facts. For a broader look at current affairs, try *La Marche du siècle* (F3), *Europe spécial* (F2) or *7 sur 7* (TF1), a heavyweight interview programme. Issues of the day are more likely to be examined through debate than documentary-style investigation (it's both cheaper and more attuned to the argumentative French style). Although TV production is technologically advanced to the point of gimmickry, high professional standards have never been achieved, and presentation tends to be dull and uninventive; TV remains the weakest link in France's cultural apparatus.

Despite foreigners' aversion, the French are particularly attached to their radios. Public radio is grouped under the umbrella of the national radio company, **Radio France**, and offers dozens of stations throughout the territory. It has news programming, job vacancy listings and public service messages, and broadcasts the music of the Orchestre National de France and the Orchestre Philharmonique. The most popular national stations are **France-Inter**, **France-Culture**, **France-Musique** and **Radio Bleue** – which targets older listeners and is specialized in *la chanson française*. **France-Info** offers round-the-clock news.

On the air since 1931, **Radio-France Internationale** (RFI) broadcasts in France and the five continents, and is the cornerstone of the county's foreign broadcasting efforts. **RFO** (Société Nationale de Radio et de Télévision d'Outre-mer) broadcasts radio and television programmes in France's overseas departments and territories.

The main commercial stations that broadcast nationwide are **RTL**, **Europe 1** and **Radio Monte-Carlo**. Other popular options include **Radio-Nostalgie**, **Fun**

Case Study: Making the Morning Show

The way Rob Harrison tells it, success in France comes thanks to love and a really good collection of LPs. Residents of the sun-drenched wonderland between the Italian border and the Var will recognize Rob Harrison's voice. If you don't know the name, tune into Riviera Radio (**www.rivieraradio.mc** at 106.5 FM) the next time you are in the Côte d'Azur to hear France's most loved English-language broadcaster.

Rob Harrison has lived in France for more than 13 years and first arrived from London hot on the trail of a French girl on whom he had set his amorous sights. His other passion was a collection of LPs – numbering in the many thousands – which he dragged abroad with his heavy heart. In 1986, an employee of an Antibes-based station named Radio Sunshine happened to meet Harrison and his record collection and encouraged him to embark on a radio career. Harrison soon moved to the pirate ship Radio Caroline and became presenter of the popular breakfast show. From there, it was a natural jump over to the Monaco-based Riviera Radio.

Since 1991, he has worked every air shift and has held stints as the music, news and sports editor. But his easy mix of humour and a laid-back approach won him the breakfast show – Riviera Radio's most popular slot, with 90,000 listeners on a weekly reach. Harrison has a dream job and knows it: 'Once, because I had a punctured tyre, I drove 10 miles on the metal rims of my wheels from my house in Nice to Monte-Carlo at 4am to make it to work on time.'

Riviera Radio's musical offerings are graciously French-free, which may explain the station's overwhelming popularity. 'We are in Monaco for the obvious reason that is extremely difficult to obtain a licence to broadcast in English in France and the fact that we are in Monaco does mean we don't have to play the French music quota,' he explains.

Off the air, Harrison is occupied by sports, food, drink, his dog and his house-plants. 'I still consider myself English but I wouldn't live anywhere else. I guess you could say I'm an expat Englishman with a European hat.'

Radio and **Skyrock**. And there are hundreds of regional stations to round off the radiowave offerings.

Economic Background and the EU

France is the world's fourth largest economic power, one of two European nuclear powers, one of five permanent members of the United Nations Security Council and a founding member of the European Union. The width and weight of its economic and political influence cannot be underestimated, and it is correct to say that France is among the most important – and loudest – voices on the world stage.

France developed a strong economy post-war. The years 1945–75 are often referred to as 'les trentes glorieuses' – an era of unparalleled growth and prosperity, aided by a state plan which stimulated the rebuilding of industries such as technology, aerospace and car manufacturing. By the 1960s France had fully embraced consumerism, but these glorious years came to an end with global recession after the 1973–4 oil crisis. And just as austerity measures introduced by the centre-right government of Raymond Barre were beginning to take effect, the Socialists came to power in 1981 on a crypto-Marxist manifesto: banks and 'strategic industries' were privatized, and wealth redistributed through a tax on the rich, elevated minimum wage and high welfare benefits. The fragile economy could not support the levels of public spending (there wasn't enough wealth to redistribute), and went into freefall. Unemployment soared to 3 million, and many lived in severe poverty. The government was forced to make a dramatic U-turn, adopting a monetarist realism which has been the prevailing ideology of both left and right ever since.

At the turn of the millennium the economy was booming, and had seen three consecutive years of growth (at over three per cent of GDP) leading up to the September 11 2001 terrorist attacks in the United States. Since that date, and thanks to the global economic slowdown, the French economy has shown signs of wear and tear, like everywhere else. French exports have declined since the turn of the millennium, business confidence has deteriorated, and there is a lower demand for gross fixed investment. Although corporate investments have slowed over the past years, household consumption remains energized thanks to wage increases and tax cuts. Unemployment numbers have been reduced and inflation remains under control. The outlook for the coming years is rosy, with GDP expected to bounce back upwards at an annual rate of up to 3.5 per cent, and unemployment expected at or below the nine per cent mark. Recent reforms have been set up in order to further reduce that figure.

Despite the global downturn and the ripple effects of September 11, France is an economic powerhouse that tightened its belt on spending and trimmed down the deficit in advance of the deadline for European Monetary Union and the introduction of the euro currency. The steps taken back then have helped France fare better today, in more difficult times.

In the 1990s France embarked on an extremely ambitious campaign to reduce the role of the state in the economy through privatization of many industries, deregulation and the reduction of budget deficits. Reforms have

Old Money

If for any reason you need to express prices in francs (for example, when dealing with the elderly), the easiest thing is to divide by 6.5. The exact exchange rate between the old and the new currency was fixed at 1 euro = 6.55957 francs. Conversely, one franc equals roughly 15 euro cents.

The euro became the common currency of Europe on 1 January 2002.

Public and Private

The state has traditionally played a more assertive role in the French economy than in most Western countries. *Dirigisme* (state control of finance and interference in private firms) was useful post-war, promoting telecommunications, the nuclear programme, tourism, *grands projets* and the TGV. State intervention is much diminished now (the state has ceased to shore up 'lame duck' industries: textiles, shipyards and steel have all been left to drown), but the dilemma France faces is whether it can maintain the 'French model' of public services and adjust to globalization. Banking, insurance (where success stories include AXA and Crédit Agricole) and industry have now almost all been re-privatized, while most of the public services are still state-run and subsidized (public spending is 56 per cent of GDP, and revenue from taxes 44 per cent of GDP, the highest levels in the West, while the state employs a quarter of the workforce, heavily unionized). Slowly these services too are being deregulated, initially in the most competitive areas such as air travel. France Télécom no longer has the telephone monopoly, and Electricité de France may come up for grabs if paranoiacs are assured that nuclear safety will not be threatened, but the post and railways (SNCF) will remain state-owned and run (the SNCF is a huge lossmaker, and striking railway workers frequently cripple the country) unless the EU forces a sell-off.

been introduced to allow for more flexibility in the labour market, and France introduced the 35-hour working week – which continues to spark controversy to this very day. Aggressive steps have been taken to create more jobs, but it should be underlined that obtaining a job in France is not easy. This is especially true for foreigners who come to France to look for work (more details concerning foreigners working in France are provided in **Working in France**, pp.229–58).

Yet the truth is, France has not yet reached its full growth potential. The offerings of its industrial sector are already the envy of the world, and it continues to spend generously on research and development. For example, French companies rank among the top European construction and civil engineering firms (France is one of the biggest spenders when it comes to public works projects).

Agriculture

In terms of agriculture and foodstuffs, agriculture in France has been revolutionized over the past 50 years. At the start of the Second World War, 45 per cent of the population lived in rural *communes*. By the mid-1970s agricultural production had doubled, but prices fell and many workers were made redundant, leading to a rural exodus. By 1990, only five per cent of the population was employed on farms. Patterns of farming have changed from traditional peasant farming to large-scale capitalist enterprises growing cash crops (from wheat to cheese and wine), making the most of modern techniques (tractors and fertilizers). The whole sector has been propped up by European subsidies since the Common Agricultural Policy (CAP) was introduced in 1962. France has been involved in what is now the European Union since the Treaty of Rome established the Common Market in 1957 – in fact it has always seen itself as the *de facto* head of Europe. With true *esprit communautaire*, the French have long identified their interests with those of Europe, and seen the EU as a way to control German adventurism. Economically, French farmers have benefited massively from the CAP, and France has been undented by the free-trading Single Market. France is a leader in meat and dairy production, cereals, confectionary and alcoholic beverages thanks to companies like Danone, Eridania, Nestlé and Pernod-Ricard to name a few. It is Europe's most significant exporter and the second largest producer.

Industry

Modern industry has been France's biggest success story, despite reversals in the last few years. The country set off on a well-judged hi-tech path in the 1950s, with telecommunications and information technology companies (France Télécom and Alcatel are leaders in their sectors). Péchiney, Rhône-Poulenc, St-Gobain and Air Liquide (chemicals) and L'Oréal are just a few of the most successful companies (the head of L'Oréal is the world's richest non-royal woman). In the car industry, Peugeot-Citroën and Renault are both doing well, and there is also material processing such as steel, glass, plastics, rubber and aluminium (Michelin is the world's leading tyre manufacturer). France also has Europe's largest aerospace industry: Aérospatiale, as part of a European consortium, based in Toulouse, has taken 40 per cent of the world market in planes with its Airbus and has emerged as a real competitor to the mighty Boeing. And though for many years French scientists resisted funding by industry (the AIDS vaccine was discovered in France, but commercialized in America), the Centre National de Recherche Scientifique is now collaborating with the Patronat in pharmaceutical production. Last is the fashions and luxury goods sector that includes haute couture, jewellery, leather goods and perfumes. Among the principal players are Yves-Saint-Laurent, Vuitton, Chanel and Cartier.

Infrastructure

In addition, France boasts a model infrastructure network and continues to improve and extend it. Not only is it wide-reaching, it is the most sophisticated and technologically advanced in the world, representing an extraordinary investment by the government. For example, two important public works projects currently under way are high-speed train links between Paris and Strasbourg and Lyon and Turin in Italy. France holds the world speed record for trains with its TGV that has reached 515km per hour and travels normally at

Fat VAT Tax

Your suspicion that you are paying more tax by living in France can be confirmed. The mother of all taxes is the 19.6 per cent TVA, *Taxe sur la valeur ajoutée*, or the value-added-tax (VAT in English), which works like a sales tax but is also added to labour, services and insurance. The idea is that anything that can be sold – from a new pair of shoes to an hour of your plumber's time – has added value over things that cannot be sold and the tax therefore applies.

TVA is an enormously important source of revenue for French coffers. For example, in the year 2000, the state generated 51 billion euros in income tax and 103 billion euros from TVA. The TVA figure represents about half of total net receipts. Nevertheless, consumers have understandably had enough of the VAT tax and a movement is under way to reduce it. In fact, it was reduced from 20.6 per cent in 2000. In 1999, the TVA charged for home improvements and renovations was lowered to 5.5 per cent. Keep that in mind when you ask for a *devis* or estimate from your builder, electrician or plumber.

270km per hour on commercial and freight routes. The road network is already the densest in the world and the longest in Europe. Both the aviation and the merchant fleet sectors have weathered hard times. A new terminal was recently added to Nice airport, and 70 million passengers fly with French carriers each year. Marseille is the largest port in France and on the Mediterranean, and the third largest in Europe, handling 95 million tons of goods.

The Service Sector

Financial services and banking, insurance and tourism are the three brightest stars of the service sector. The market capitalization of shares listed on the Paris stock exchange equal 50 per cent of GDP, ranking Paris as the seventh largest *bourse* in the world. Major banks include Crédit Agricole, Société Générale and Banque Nationale de Paris (BNP). The insurance sector is the world's fourth largest and has been consolidated to include a handful of major firms. But tourism is the major cash cow for the French economy. More tourists come to France than any other country in the world, and the income it derives from tourism is the third largest following that of the United States and Italy.

Foreign Trade

France is a force to be reckoned with in this area as well. The country is the second largest exporter of services and farm products and the fourth biggest exporter of goods. Fellow EU countries account for 65 per cent of its trade and its main customers are the United Kingdom, Germany, Italy, Luxembourg, Spain, Belgium and the United States.

Internal Issues

No one is perfect, not even France. Indeed, this great nation is afflicted with many thorny issues that have left painful wounds over the years. Whether these unresolved problems can or will be ironed out remains to be seen.

Labour and the Welfare State

From an economic point of view, France has two weak spots. First is unemployment – particularly, the difficulty of recent university graduates to find suitable work. The second concern is the high cost of the welfare state and how future generations will pay for it. Both have created major tension with labour unions that leads to relentless industrial action and paralysing strikes.

About 10 per cent of French workers are members of labour unions. Some 2.4 million workers belong to the Confédération Générale du Travail (CGT), the largest labour organization in France; the Confédération Française Démocratique du Travail (CFDT), a Roman Catholic-orientated organization; or the Force Ouvrière. Union membership is compulsory in some industries, minimum wages are established by government decree, and pay scales are determined by collective bargaining.

There is consensus that the cost of labour is too high. The complex system of funds for unemployment benefits, health insurance and retirement pensions takes a heavy toll on both the employer and the worker. Employers may have to add to their wage bills up to 45 per cent or even more on top of what they actually pay an employee in the form of contributions to various funds. The worker is not spared either: a sizeable chunk of the wage packet vanishes in his or her contribution to the same funds.

If contributions were to be cut, the money would have to be found elsewhere and the underlying philosophy of the French welfare state would have to be reviewed. There have only been timid steps in that direction.

Elitism and Corruption

Despite a strong economy and a stable political system, France is suffering from a malaise reflected in disillusionment with its political class and institutions. Over the centuries since the French Revolution (1789), France has repeatedly sought a 'new dawn' in politics, but somehow the nation always ends up with another entrenched ruling class. National politics are seen as the domain of self-interested clans, jostling for power among themselves, especially in periods of *cohabitation*, when prime minister and president end up flexing their muscles to oppose each other in the next presidential contest rather than fixing the country's problems.

Critical to the French morale crisis, the élite is seen as inbred, sharing jobs and favours; while France is proud to be a meritocracy, the ruling caste looks after its vested interests. Most of its members are graduates of the Ecole Nationale d'Administration (ENA), set up by De Gaulle to groom a mandarin sect, or of one of the 184 Grandes Ecoles set up by Napoleon (principally the Ecole Polytechnique). Although in theory entry to these prestigious finishing schools is open, in practice the offspring of the establishment are more likely to get in. There are around 4,000 énarques (of whom 20 per cent are women), mostly employed in the service of the state, which has great power and cachet; once launched on a career in the élite Inspection des Finances or Conseil d'État, or one of the more lowly ministries, the members of this class are unbudgeable, and it is hard to break into public life without the right diploma.

The 1990s were dogged by more serious cases of mismanagement and corruption, too, both in public life and in private enterprise. Corruption and sleaze are not new to French politics, nor to business, but over the last decade a new breed of examining magistrates has been taking on prominent figures. More than 500 political or economic leaders have been convicted, accused or put under investigation. Jacques Médecin, Mafia-style mayor of Nice, was imprisoned for fraud and embezzlement. Lyon mayor Michel Noir, Grenoble mayor Alain Carignon, wheeler-dealing businessman and socialist minister Bernard Tapie, Paris mayor Jean Tiberi and state-owned Elf oil were all probed and found lacking.

The crash of Crédit Lyonnais was a high-profile case which epitomized much of what was wrong with the cosy world of finance, where the political and business world overlap. The state bank raced to become a mega-bank with what the European Commission later called 'a bulimia of investments and acquisitions'. Bad judgement was backed up by pay-offs to a socialist minister and a TV news editor, until losses of 140 billion francs were uncovered in 1995. It all happened under the lead of Jean-Yves Haberer, an énarque and former head of the French treasury. Taxpayers paid off debts of 15 billion euros while favoured friends of President Chirac were bailed out and the bank sold off.

This was one of the bigger of the affaires that have brought politicians and corporate chieftains to book for misuse of company funds, bribes to officials, insider dealing, rigged public works contracts, falsifying of accounts and so on. 'Money flowed, everybody seemed buyable,' wrote Le Monde after kickbacks were revealed for the construction of the 1998 World Cup stadium. In another case, dozens of banking executives were hauled in over allegations of money laundering and tax evasion by ready-to-wear clothing firms in Paris. Politicians, the SNCF and public-works companies were all implicated in shady dealing to do with the building of a high-speed TGV link between Paris and Lille. The project was based on entirely false predictions of profitability, with rigged tenders, price-fixing and huge bribes to SNCF executives.

The biggest scandal of them all has been *l'affaire Elf*, with allegations that 3 billion francs were looted from the state-owned oil company in the early 1990s; the political links and top-level contacts of Elf made the scandal an affair of state. Forty-two French business and political figures were charged over the affair, chief among them Loïk Le Floch-Pringent, head of the company from 1989–93, and an international go-between known as Dédé la Sardine, from whom novelist Françoise Sagan had received 4 million francs to lobby President Mitterrand. Elf had been an arm of government since it was founded in 1965, and functioned as a semi-official ambassador for France in Francophone Africa and other former colonies (providing a convenient cover for spies and political agents). Through a banking subsidiary in Switzerland it routinely paid 'royalties' of up to 150 million francs a year each to African leaders. Meanwhile Elf 'interwove' its activities with the French state, with politicians making such frequent use of its private jets that it became known as Air Elf.

After investigations by examining magistrate Eva Joly (sparked off by a complaint from an American investor), Le Floch was accused of having abused his position as chairman and chief executive to 'seek enrichment of himself, his family and friends' through Elf's Swiss and African subsidiaries, and was held in the Santé prison in Paris. Among all sorts of dubious connections, a secret company payroll was found that included French politicians and journalists. Chairman of Elf Gabon André Tarallo, an *énarque* and personal friend of Chirac, was investigated for misuse of corporate funds. The whole affair acted as a reminder of the corruption that had been conducted at the apex of state and business, deepening the cynicism of the French towards the business-political nexus around their rulers.

Another portrait in the gallery of rogues is that of Bernard Tapie, a crooked entrepreneur who sat in the Cabinet as an anointed favourite of a Socialist president. He bought up a swath of ailing companies and made them profitable, plus a leading football club, Olympique de Marseille, living in luxury, dispensing wisdom on TV and making sub-Julio Iglesias records in his spare time. For a while he was everybody's favourite self-made man. He pitted himself against the Front National as mayor of Marseille, and was appointed cabinet minister for towns by Mitterrand. Tapie's fall came over match-fixing payments made to the Valenciennes football team, after which he was up for personal bankruptcy, handling stolen goods, and misuse of corporate property galore.

Immigration and Racism

France has undoubtedly taken on an awkward role in the post-September 11 2001 world. More recently, it has been branded both as courageous and cowardly, following its fierce opposition to the US-led war in Iraq. But, inexplicably, most of the international debate on whether France's position was right

Case Study: Melting Pot

Emmanuel Isaacs, 32, moved to the south of France from London, where he was born and raised, four years ago because of a job with a telecommunications company. His experiences living in France and dealing with local bureaucracy compare to most others. But Emmanuel can offer a new perspective with it comes to race relations.

'In my area of France a black person is more of a novelty,' says the holder of both Nigerian and a British passport. 'You feel like you stand out more than you would in Paris or London, or any other place that is a true melting pot.'

Emmanuel says there is a difference between an ethnically mixed city like London – which sees people of Indian, Chinese, Pakistani, Arab and African descent – compared with a place like France that has more concentration of whites and Arabs. 'France has a comfortable mix, but it doesn't have the same level of mixing that London has.'

Although Emmanuel says he has never been the victim of discrimination in the south of France, he has seen evidence of it around him. 'I think the Arabs get a particularly bad deal; they suffer a lot.' Street graffiti, ethnic jokes and underhand comments are the basis for this impression. 'They are going to have to fight to get out of this situation.'

or wrong overlooked one obvious consideration: how could France enlist in the so-called war on terrorism given the delicate and often volatile Muslim question back home? It could be argued that France did more than other nations to help the anti-terrorism cause by avoiding the tensions that would have surely mounted within its territory had France insensitively turned its back on its internal problems.

Immigration is France's most complicated and misunderstood social issue. People of North African descent have come under target by the far right, especially Jean-Marie Le Pen's Front National party, as a social woe, a burden on public services and the authors of the country's crime problem. Some groups claim that Muslims refuse to assimilate into French society and few extreme politicians advocate compulsory repatriation. Too often patriotism is a cloak for what is really racism.

Many of the people who are labelled 'immigrants' are not immigrants at all. Many are third or fourth generation North Africans who have never even travelled to the counties of their ethnic roots. Many more are the grandchildren of the people who were employed by the French in Algeria until that country gained its independence in 1962.

There are thought to be about three million people living in France born in North Africa (chiefly Algeria, Tunisia and Morocco) or born in France of parents who came to France from North Africa. Immigration has also brought a large number of Europeans and sizeable communities from sub-Saharan Africa and

Jean-Marie Le Pen and the Front National

The menace of populist, racist Jean-Marie Le Pen just won't go away. His political demise has been forecast time and again since his far-right Front National emerged as a force to be reckoned with in 1984, attracting disgruntled voters with its anti-immigrant, anti-Semitic, anti-Europe law-and-order rant; the FN won 11 per cent of the vote in National Assembly elections that year for *la préférence française*. Its biggest success was in 1986, when it won 35 seats in the National Assembly under a new system of proportional representation, quickly reversed. Since then, it has struggled to get more than one seat under the traditional constituency system, but has continued to attract around 10–15 per cent of the vote. In the 2002 elections, Le Pen made it to the second round of the presidential contest, winning 18 per cent of the vote (*see* pp.20–21), and the FN got the third largest tranche of the vote for the National Assembly (ahead of the Communists, Greens and UDF), although no seats. The Front National's power base is stronger in local government, where it took control of the southern cities of Toulon, Orange, Marignane and Vitrolles in the 1990s on a platform of efficient local services, strong police (in black commando uniforms) – and cultural censorship. In Orange, books by 'foreign' writers were removed from the municipal library, and replaced by fascist literature. Near Toulon, the experimental arts centre of Châteauvallon waged war against the FN's repressive cultural policy; the rap band Nique ta Mère sang '*Je pisse sur la police*' at a protest concert, and was imprisoned for it.

The party's main appeal is in the poorer regions of the south, and among unemployed workers in the declining industrial cities of the north, where it attracts votes that would once have gone to the Communists. Le Pen plays hard on fears of lawlessness in *la banlieue*, where high-rise estates built to house immigrant workers have become ghettoes of hopelessness. About a hundred *grands ensembles* of these *habitations à loyer modéré* (HLMs) were built in the 1960s to replace squalid *bidonvilles* (shanty towns). Now inhabited mainly by Arab and African immigrants, they are hotbeds of unemployment, social and racial tension, brutalist architecture, graffiti and neglect. France's crime rate is lower than Britain's, but in the popular mind there is an inescapable conjunction between violent crime and immigrants. Of the 6 million immigrants who make up 10 per cent of the French population, around 1.5 million are *beurs*, reverse slang for second-generation Arabs. They feel no allegiance to a Republic which has abandoned them, and have no economic prospects – so armed

the Far East, but it is the North African first and second-generation immigrants on whom most public attention is focused.

North African youths are certainly concentrated in the low-income housing projects outside the big cities, disproportionately unemployed and unqualified. Following a handful of attacks in France by Muslim fundamentalists, police robbery is a logical career choice. The film *La Haine* made the sink estate of Chanteloupe-les-Vignes famous; several of the extras have been killed in gang warfare since the film was made. Drugs, theft, looting, casual violence and killing constitute daily life among a generation that has nothing more to lose.

The only hope for this parallel society is, ironically, one which strikes dread in the hearts of its rulers: Islam. There are 4–5 million Muslims in France (around ten per cent practising); and the mosques (more than a thousand), women wearing headscarves and halal butchers are all seen as symbols of separateness. Recently, the religion has started to appeal to young delinquents seeking an identity: better to count yourself a Muslim than one of the unemployed. On the extremes of Islam, France felt itself to be a target of fundamentalists even before 11 September 2001: the country was hit by a series of bomb attacks, one of which killed seven people in a Paris station, and a terrorist tried to blow up the TGV train track. These incidents have been rare, but the French establishment is not open to multiculturalism: integration is expected (the government repeatedly tries to ban headscarves in schools), as assimilation becomes less and less likely. Against this background, Le Pen bangs his drum about the 'exclusion' of native French and preferential treatment given to delinquent immigrants (playing on incidents of ghetto youths on subsidized holidays attacking tourists) and pulls in the votes.

As former Socialist premier Laurent Fabius once said, Le Pen asks the right questions, but no one in their right mind thinks he has the answers. However, the mainstream's disdain for Le Pen as a madcap extremist appears to his supporters as a disdain for them and their concerns. When the hectoring, one-eyed thug does his horrible stand-up act in front of a stadium of thousands, it is clear that he is tapping into real fears of the people – made taboo by an excess of political correctness among both orthodox left and right. Astonishingly, though, a significant minority of French people are prepared to throw in their lot with a man who called the Holocaust a 'detail of history', and has commented of respected cabinet minister and concentration camp survivor Simone Veil, 'When I speak of genocide, I always say that in any case they missed old woman Veil.' In a country with a Jewish population of half a million (the largest in Western Europe), Le Pen also taps into a latent anti-Semitism that stretches back through wartime deportations by '*40 millions de Pétainistes*' to the Dreyfus affair.

began stopping dark-skinned people and demanding identity papers. The Education Minister banned the wearing of headscarves and *chadors* in public schools because it violated the tradition of secular education, but many Muslim groups interpreted the law as an affront to them. Mounting hostility resulted in cries of discrimination and a 'climate of intolerance'.

Culture and Art

Even a brief overview of French culture and art couldn't be jammed into the heaviest of volumes. The French contribution to our evolution of intellect and aesthetics cannot be exaggerated, and there is no simple way to sum it up, but we will try anyway.

The French have always prided themselves as a nation on their intellectual élitism, treating the 'intellectual professions' (teachers, academics, artists, writers and journalists) with reverence. But France has also experienced the development of a mass culture in cinema, TV, books, magazines and music over the past 50 years. As a result the arts in France have been torn between high art and populism – as reflected in the cultural policy of a highly interventionist state. In 1959–69, culture minister André Malraux instituted a paternalistic drive to bring canonical culture to the people through provincial *'maisons de la culture'*. But the *maisons* soon fell victim to the polarities that beset the French cultural debate – the bourgeois establishment versus the left; the classics versus avant-garde experimentalism; large-scale national institutions versus smaller local activities – and simply did not appeal to the working classes for whom they were intended. Students and intellectuals, on the other hand, were more interested in experiment, collective creation, street theatre and politics.

Jack Lang's festival of student theatre at Nancy showed him to be a man who believed art and politics were irretrievably intertwined, and when the charismatic Lang came to power as Mitterrand's culture minister in 1981 he turned cultural policy topsy-turvy. He aimed to create *'un désordre créateur'*, a cultural climate conducive to creativity, funding myriad arts groups from circus performers to graffiti artists and hurdy-gurdy workshops.

French culture has long been defended, in particular, against the (perceived) cultural imperialism of America: in the post-war period France was obliged to screen Hollywood films as a condition for aid; now the nation excludes 'cultural products' from free trade agreements and imposes quotas for foreign films and music. All this, and the efforts of the Académie Française to purge the language of anglicisms, have done little more than to maintain national dignity: more than 50 per cent of films screened in French cinemas are American, and the public flocks to see each new blockbuster.

The cultural scene has always been more politicized in France than in Britain or America, and a certain staleness in some areas of the arts may reflect the current sense of political stalemate in the country. Some would argue that France's reluctance to embrace the cultural marketplace has simply impeded the nation's creativity. That said, there is great variation across the arts: broadly speaking, 'social' culture (theatre, music, dance) is more lively now than the more reflective modes of literature and philosophy, while the visual arts are undergoing a renaissance as part of an international scene. Cinema has yet to regain its *nouvelle vague* zenith, embattled between the *film d'auteur* and the mass market. Meanwhile, French intellectual life is under threat in an age without engagement, and the intellectual has morphed into the *médiatique*, or TV personality.

Architecture

The Greeks and the Romans washed into Gaul, bringing their very advanced notions of mythology, theatre and entertaining. There are ancient theatres and amphitheatres and other Roman ruins scattered about the south of the country in places like Orange (it has the only completely intact ancient stage building in the West), Arles (home to an amphitheatre) and Vaison-la-Romaine. What the Romans gave to Gaul helped lay the foundations for a nation that would influence the art and culture of the world over. The Romanesque style of the early Middle Ages, with its inseparable architecture and sculpture, began as a style influenced by these Roman buildings, but quickly diversified to take in the court architecture of Charlemagne, the early churches of the east, and buildings of the Byzantine and Islamic world. Distinctive regional styles rapidly appeared all over France.

During the Middle Ages, France – specifically Paris, home to Notre-Dame – gave the world an artistic movement that would later be dubbed 'Gothic'. Soaring spires, chilling detail in façade carvings and an overall sombre feel set the tone. The countryside of France has undoubtedly been beautified beyond measure by the addition of dozens of Gothic-style cathedrals. Each city competed for the best, most alluring and tallest church, and the results of their efforts are ours to enjoy. There are the Chartres, Reims and Albi cathedrals and the unforgettable Mont-St-Michel in Normandy.

Next, the Renaissance gave us the great châteaux of the Loire and the Louvre in Paris. Throughout the 1500s, architects added black slate towers to the corners of palaces that look like upturned pencils. The interiors were lofty, airy, and filled with precious art and tapestries. By the 17th century, the French for the first time desired national unity; many of the manuscripts of the time reflect this. Meanwhile, designers and builders were indulging in the Grand Siècle and massive rebuilding efforts were unleashed. Paris was almost completely rebuilt and the resulting cityscape has not changed much since then. Spaces, avenues and public squares were created to dwarf mankind amidst the urban splendour. In the era of Emperor Napoleon, starting in the early 1800s, neoclassical architecture made a furious comeback; the Arc de Triomphe in Paris is a brilliant example.

France has always been open to new architectural ideas, and in the 20th century often held competitions for its controversial new projects, which have included the Louvre Pyramid and the new Opéra Bastille.

Philosophy

Tourists still flock to the Café de Flore and Les Deux Magots in search of the spirit of Left Bank philosophers Jean-Paul Sartre, Albert Camus, Simone de Beauvoir *et compagnie* – but all they find is overpriced coffee and each other. To get a finger on the philosophical pulse, they would do better to head for a *café philosophique* (the Café des Phares on the Place de la Bastille was the first), where anyone can join in a debate on contemporary ethics for the price of a drink at the bar – or to listen to the pronouncements of some *médiatique* (most likely Bernard-Henri Lévy) on a TV chat show.

The intellectual has long been a star figure in France, and after the Liberation the Existentialists gave philosophy sex appeal too. Sartre's *L'Être et le Néant* gave a generation the creed that Man creates himself by his actions, for which he has freedom of choice and responsibility – but each choice is absurd, because there is no objective moral framework. By the late 1950s, however, Sartre was losing support through his advocacy of Communism, and the *engagé* intellectual was giving way to a new generation of thinkers – the structuralists – who saw Man as the product of determined systems.

The structuralist group brought ideas from various disciplines – Roland Barthes, literary critic; Claude Lévi-Strauss, ethnologist; Jacques Lacan, psychoanalyst; Michel Foucault, philosopher and historian – to assert that thoughts and actions were governed by pre-existing structures of signs and symbols (semiology), linguistic patterns and so on. The death of Man seemed imminent, as he was in any case just a construct. By the time this rather formulaic, pseudo-scientific vision of the world was catching on in Britain and America, where it has gained huge popularity, it was already waning in France. By 1970 Jacques Derrida was already deconstructing texts, while philosopher Gilles Deleuze examined structures of power (capitalism and schizophrenia), an area that Foucault also turned his attention to (madness, sexuality and prisoners). While American academics are still endeavouring to humanize structuralism and post-structuralism, these thinkers still come under attack: in 1997 Alan Sokal and Jean Bricmont published a book, *Impostures intellectuelles*, criticizing the abstruse writings of post-structuralists like Julie Kristeva; it reignited the whole debate on what these schools of thought contribute to humanity.

New philosophers of the right André Glucksman and Bernard-Henri Lévy stirred things up in the 1970s with scathing attacks on Marxism as depicted in the Soviet Union of Solzhenitsyn's *Gulag Archipelago*. But nowadays, university academics have retreated into their ivory towers and intellectuals are most likely to be found parading their ideas on TV chat shows, without any of the political *engagement* of their predecessors. These *médiatiques* can be relied on to pronounce on topical issues on programmes such as Bernard Pivot's *Apostrophes*, for years the high-point of the intellectual week (succeeded by his *Bouillon de Culture*). Left Bank radical chic persists, however, in the hermetic circles of writers, journalists and academics who keep each other's company at the Dôme. And for those keen to revisit the *philo* they did for the *bac* years ago, the *café philosophique* trend launched by teacher Maurice Sautet in 1992 provides a down-to-earth forum for 'ordinary' people to examine the ethical issues of the day.

Music

There has been a great revival of serious music in France over the last 40 years, from professional performance to amateur playing, with more than a million students (mostly part-time) studying at the *conservatoires* (music schools). This musical renaissance draws on two recent French tendencies: the *repli sur soi* (a turning inwards in search of personal fulfilment) and *la vie associative* (the importance of community), as well perhaps as the pleasure principle of the affluent society. Music may also have gained in appeal through being less ideological than some other arts – although here too there have been tensions between populist promoters such as the first national music director, Michel Landowski, and the avant-garde élitism of composers such as Pierre Boulez.

The heyday of the Paris Opéra was in the 1970s, when it staged productions with renowned directors and conductors (Giorgio Strehler and Georg Solti's *Figaro*) in the sumptuous Palais Garnier. After a fallow period, it is now popular again, with a conservative classical repertoire; large-scale productions are staged at the new Opéra Bastille. The smaller Théâtre du Châtelet pursues a creative, stimulating policy, while the 10 regional opera companies have varied reputations: Lyon and Strasbourg are the best, while Toulouse boasts a successful opera and also the first-rate Orchestre National du Capitole. Music is generally strong in the regions, and some of the summer music festivals, such as those at Aix-en-Provence and Orange, are excellent – partly due to the international performers they attract from abroad; none of the national orchestras is outstanding, and France has fewer star musicians than Germany or Britain.

Back in Paris, the new Cité de la Musique at La Villette (a Mitterrand/Lang enterprise) pulls in the punters for a range of music from Bach to Boulez, *chansons* to flamenco. In fact the French music scene is by no means exclusively highbrow. Since the 1980s, jazz, folk and *chansons*, electric guitar, Breton bagpipes and avant-garde dance have all flourished, with the help of Lang's universal approach to culture. Of France's 40 modern dance companies, the best known is that of Jean-Claude Gallotta at Grenoble, while folklore troupes keep alive the old regional traditions of music and dance. An annual Fête de la Musique is held on the summer solstice, with street music around the country.

Pop and rock have never been France's greatest genres (partly a result of French resistance to American influence): rock 'n' roller Johnny Hallyday has been the idol of French teenagers since 1959, but the home-grown tradition of the *chanson* – poetry set to music – has been endlessly revived, from Edith Piaf to Georges Brassens and Jacques Brel, and more recently Serge Gainsbourg. The 1990s saw a boom in rap and hip-hop – the only area of the arts in which France's immigrant population has gained a voice, speaking for the disaffected of *la banlieue*. Dakar-born poet MC Solaar is one top star; Invasion Arrivant de Mars (IAM) from Marseille, with its Italian, Spanish, Algerian, Senegalese and pied-noir line-up, is another hit; Nique ta Mère and Ministère Amer have been in trouble with the police for the violence with which they evoke the malaise of racism and youth today.

Cinema

The French film reached its zenith with the *nouvelle vague*, and cinephiles still hark back to that golden era. Perhaps it is a symptom not only of the power of American cultural imperialism but also of the paucity of recent French film production that cinema in France today should be so fiercely protected by quotas and free-trade exemptions. Decent movies do still get made, but nothing quite as fresh or interesting has come out of France since the new wave.

Film has always had a special status in France. The Lumière brothers pioneered the medium in the 1890s, and it was already regarded as an art form by the 1920s, with the work of Jean Cocteau. It was the low-budget features of the 1950s and '60s, however, that established the French *film d'auteur*. These films of the *nouvelle vague* varied widely in both content and style, but all were made with an authorial viewpoint, took everyday themes as their subject, and used hand-held cameras, few actors and simple locations. Roger Vadim's *Et Dieu...créa la femme*, starring Bridget Bardot, paved the way with a (then) new subject, the amorality of modern youth in St Tropez. Alain Resnais's *Hiroshima mon amour* shockingly melded a love story with the horrors of nuclear war.

The crest of the wave was a group of writers from *Les Cahiers du Cinéma*, Godard, Truffaut and Chabrol. François Truffaut's *400 Coups* told the semi-auto-biographical story of a boy driven to delinquency by loneliness, although Truffaut is better known for the light touch of *Jules et Jim*. Claude Chabrol also took a bleak personal story for *Le Beau Serge*, about peasant decadence near his home town of Limoges. Jean-Luc Godard launched himself on the world with the stylized *ciné-vérité* style of *A bout de souffle*. Eric Rohmer's films tell low-key tales of human relationships; perhaps the most famous is *Le Genou de Claire*. And Agnès Varda's *Bonheur* analysed the concept of happiness through the life of a middle-class simpleton.

On the fringes of the new wave, Louis Malle made provocative films exam-ining taboos such as alcoholism (*Le Feu follet*); documentarist Chris Marker looked at modern urban life (*Paris nous appartient*) and the religious persecu-tion of women (*La Religieuse*); Jacques Demy spun off into poetic fantasy (*Les Parapluies de Cherbourg*); and Claude Lelouch popularized the new wave with *Un Homme et une Femme*.

Of the directors who have stood out in the years since, Bertrand Tavernier is the finest, a gentle humanist (*Une Semaine de vacances* and *Dimanche à la campagne*). Maurice Pialat is one of the few directors to have addressed social themes (*Passe ton bac d'abord*, about a group of *lycéens* without prospects in Lille). Claude Sautet has specialized in delicate love stories (*Nelly et Monsieur Arnaud*). Alain Corneau has evoked the past through the lives of 17th-century musicians (*Tous les matins du monde*). Patrice Leconte has made a couple of quirky social satires (*Le Mari de la coiffeuse*), while in the 1980s Luc Besson made a splash with *Subway*, and Jean-Jacques Beneix with *Diva*.

The films that stood out in the 1990s were Mathieu Kassovitz's *La Haine*, a dark take on poverty and racial tensions in *la banlieue*, and Erick Zoncka's *La Vie rêvée des anges*, another story of adolescence into adulthood in Lille. Arnaud Desplechin's *Comment je me suis disputé...(ma vie sexuelle)* harked back to a more playful era with three hours of Parisian chatter about sex. The kitsch love story *Le Fabuleux Destin d'Amélie Poulain* (*Amélie*) by Jean-Pierre Jeunet was a surprise hit, *L'Etre et l'Avoir*, about a teacher at a rural school in the Auvergne, another. And for animation fans, *Les Triplettes de Belleville* (*Belleville Rendez-vous*) got an excellent reception.

Theatre

Theatre has been one of the most innovative areas of French cultural life over the last decades, not so much on the strength of new writing but in the work of its directors. It has also been an ideological battleground, between commercial, bourgeois *théâtres de boulevard* and experimental, state-subsidized theatres. Recently there has been a return to slight chamber pieces such as Yasmina Reza's *Art*, but for many years leftist idealism and the avant-garde have been in the ascendant.

In 1951, Jean Vilar established the Théâtre National Populaire at the Palais de Chaillot, with the aim of bringing the classics and serious modern drama to the working class. Vilar's low-price policy attracted plenty of students and intellectuals, but not many workers. The TNP became the core of the Avignon festival – but was vilified for its reactionary nature in 1968. In the 1970s the Comédie Française abandoned the stylized rhetorical tradition it had followed since the 17th century for interesting interpretations of new works such as Ionesco's *La Soif et la Faim*. The Odéon theatre enjoyed a period of glory in the 1960s, as home of the Barrault-Renaud company (forced to move on for backing the rebels in 1968). It saw a resurgence in the 1970s, '80s and early '90s under Pierre Dux, Jean-Pierre Miquel and then Giorgio Strehler, when it became known as the Théâtre de l'Europe, importing the best of international theatre from the Piccolo Teatro di Milano, the Royal Shakespeare Company and the National Theatre from London, a cosmopolitan policy that it shared with the *maison de la culture* at Bobigny. Georges Lavaudant has been the director of the Odéon since

1996. The great Peter Brook has also based himself in Paris since 1971, with his multiracial company at the Bouffes du Nord.

One notable tendency of the French theatre is for avant-garde directors to settle in obscure outer *quartiers* of cities, such as the Théâtre de la Colline at Ménilmontant in working-class eastern Paris – with a mission to bring theatre to the people. Ironically, it is still the intellectual middle-classes who trek out to see all the exciting new productions. Another tendency is for virtuoso directors to radically rework the classics through gesture, lighting and music, or to create their own texts. Ariane Mnouchkine's Théâtre du Soleil has pioneered both tendencies. The troupe, a product of 1968, has performed in a former cartridge factory at Vincennes for more than 30 years, operates as a workers' cooperative and is militantly leftist. The company often uses history as a springboard for political comment, with director and cast improvising around a theme: the French Revolution was reinterpreted as a comment on the events of 1968 in *1789* and *1793* and, more recently, Molière's *Tartuffe* has been adapted as an attack on fundamentalism.

Star directors such as Roger Planchon, Patrice Chéreau and Antoine Vitez have also reintepreted the classics. In the words of Vitez, 'the text must be given a modern force, a 20th-century resonance'. To some critics the sort of directorial fireworks involved are a desecration of the classics; for others at least it keeps the dramatic works of writers like Racine alive, and stimulates a healthy debate.

Literature

Literature is an area of the arts where France is struggling to find a way between abstract theory and popular fiction. Forget Stendhal and Proust, there's no one even to match Camus or Marguerite Yourcenar. Chief culprits may be Alain Robbe-Grillet, Michel Butor, Nathalie Sarraute and the *nouveau roman* of the 1960s. These writers rejected plot, narrative and character portrayal to attack the bourgeois tradition of fiction; bourgeois themselves, they set out to write novels that the ordinary bourgeois reader would not enjoy or even understand. Robbe-Grillet rejected the 'pathetic fallacy' (emotive description of the physical world) for *'chosisme'*, the pseudo-scientific description of objects – to the detriment of any human impetus (*Le Voyeur*). Butor showed a Futuristic concern with the relativity of time and space in the jet age (*L'Emploi du temps*). Sarraute used a stream-of-consciousness technique to depict a world of psychological flickering (*'tropismes'*) – minutely depicted cinematic freeze-frames. While Marguerite Duras also used elliptical dialogue and narrative, her works are *engagé* psychological novels (*Hiroshima mon amour*), if stylistically sophisticated.

Perhaps the good-humoured Robbe-Grillet was simply having a laugh at the reader's expense, but his tyranny of taste continues to exert an influence on new novelists. Alongside the experimental works of Claude Simon, Claude

Mauriac and Philippe Sollers, however, the bourgeois novel still attracts a wider public. Since 1953, the works of Henri Troyat, Jean Lartéguy and Françoise Sagan have sold well in paperback, while today Annie Ernaus and Sylvie Germain top the bestseller lists with their *'petite musique'* – subtle, slight, personal tales which rarely tackle social reality – and Jean Rouaud's *Les Champs d'honneur* was nothing short of a literary blockbuster.

Several writers have turned to the past and mythology for inspiration (Michel Tournier, *Le Roi des aulnes*; Patrick Modiano, *Rue des boutiques obscures*; Pascal Quignard, *Tous les matins du monde*; Sébastien Japrisot, *Un long dimanche de fiançailles*). Others have taken up the baton of stylistic experimentation from the *nouvelle romanciers*. Most famously, Georges Perec wrote *La Disparition* without using the letter 'e', and *Les Revenentes* using only the vowel 'e'. Both Perec (*Les Choses*) and Jean-Marie Le Clézio (*Le Déluge*) have expressed disgust at consumerism and material civilization through their work. Poetic innovators have included Daniel Pennac, Pierre Michon, Jean Echenoz and Marie Darrieussecq's *Truismes*. Much of the best recent literature in France (as in Britain) is by expatriates and immigrants writing about their place of origin, such as Andreï Makine (*Le Testament français*).

One of the few writers to confront the realities of contemporary France has been Michel Houellebecq. His novels *Extension du domaine de la lutte* (1997) and *Les Particules élémentaires* (1998) critiqued consumerism and computerization, and (more tendentiously) the 'liberation ideology' of the '68 generation – in particular sexual freedom and the corruption of human values. His scathing attack on political correctness sparked a frenzied debate on modern values – a return to the *engagé* novel, albeit from the right.

In an era in which the visual is said to be superseding the written word, a peculiarly French phenomenon is the popularity of *bandes dessinées* for adults, which acquired a cult status with the generation of 1968, sanctioned by the *Cahiers de la bande dessinée*. Thirty million copies of these comic-strip albums were sold in 1990, with medical students notoriously avid consumers.

Visual Arts

As mentioned in the history section of **Getting to Know France**, France is home to some of the earliest signs of civilization and the first real evidence of 'art'. Palaeolithic and Neolithic cave drawings have been uncovered, some painted some 35,000 years ago. Skipping a few thousand years, one of the biggest waves to overtake the French nation was Impressionist painting. The names of its protagonists are familiar to anyone interested in colour and light and how these elusive elements are harnessed by mankind: Edgar Degas, Auguste Renoir, Camille Pissarro and Claude Monet. Monet's painting *Impression: Soleil levant* gave a name to the movement. The south was rumbling about the doings of Vincent van Gogh, Paul Gauguin and Paul Cézanne.

In the 20th century the art scene also saw an explosive beginning to the new century. Bohemian painters like Henri Matisse took the Paris art scene by storm. Greatly influenced by the colours and styles of the Impressionists, a new generation headed by artists such as Pablo Picasso and Marc Chagall moved into Cubism and Expressionism. Dadaism came to Paris after the First World War and was followed by Surrealism and the rowdy gang of Salvador Dalí.

After years struggling to live up to its modernist past, France is once again spearheading the avant-garde. A group of French artists (working in a very international scene) is at the forefront of relational aesthetics – a new *tendance* that is all about exchange between artists and viewers. It's a convivial trend, whose catchphrases are sociability and discursivity: art is a means 'of being together in the everyday'. 'I make art,' says one artist, 'so that I can go to the bar and talk about it.' It's all very ephemeral and interactive: casual communities are created at 'places that gather and then disperse', on artistic 'platforms' and at 'stations'.

To join the arty party, head for the Palais de Tokyo in Paris, '*site de création contemporaine*'. An ultra-now venue, it is 'a laboratory of artistic experience', '*un centre de vie permanente*', a meeting place for artists and the public. Alongside exhibitions of artwork (interdisciplinary interactive installations are *de rigueur*) it has gardens, studios, bookshops and lots of space to just hang out in. Go on to the '*galéries de l'association Louise*' – a dozen or so new galleries in the Rue Louise-Weiss, which share premises and *vernissages* to generate the newly fashionable community spirit: Air de Paris, Art: Concept, Emmanuel Perrotin, Almine Rech, Kréo and Praz-Delavallade are a few of the most high-profile.

Collaboration is big among this generation of artists, blurring concepts of authorship and originality beyond even the post-modern. In one work-in-progress, *No Ghost Just a Shell*, prominent practitioners of this new art Pierre Huyghe and Philippe Parreno bought a minor manga character (Ann Lee) from a Japanese animation company and invited other artists to use her in their work. The resulting films have been described as 'the story of a community that finds itself in an image'. In some of Huyghe's other works, too, socialization is a theme as well as a medium. In the installation *Streamside Day Follies*, a film of a inaugural ceremony devised to forge communal identity explores social ritual through a diverse range of cultural representations (19th-century utopian projects, Disney animation, contemporary fiction and Romantic landscape painting).

Like other artists with whom he is associated, both in France and internationally, Huyghe uses video, film, sound, animation, text and photos, architecture and design. One *tendance* has been dubbed 'post-production' for the use of TV shows and Hollywood films, as a reinterpretation of the images that shape our reality. In *Remake*, Huyghe refilmed Hitchcock's *Rear Window* using unknown actors and locations. In *L'Ellipse* the same artist filmed a 'missing' scene from Wenders' *The American Friend*, using the original actor, many years later.

These (and other) works examine the construction of collective and individual identities in relation to various forms of cultural production. In *Third Memory*, Huyghe tracked down the bank robber who inspired the film *Dog Day Afternoon*, starring Al Pacino, and asked him to recount his memory of the day – blurring the boundaries between fiction and reality, memory and history.

Pierre Joseph, whose work *Little Democracy* assembled a gallery of characters belonging to collective mythologies from *Don Quixote* to *Superman*, is also interested in popular culture, exploring the relations between public taste and the avant-garde; his work borrows from sci-fi, techno music, Hollywood, animation and mass-circulation magazines. Parreno also plays with the boundaries of fiction and reality. In his film *La Nuit des héros*, a writer called Dante retreats to a Le Corbusier apartment to write a history of modern art, and suffers delusions as his heroes take over his mind, while Beatrice tries to save him by taking photos of the everyday. Another artist not to miss is Dominique Foerster-Gonzalez, whose series of 'colour rooms' each evoke an atmosphere with the help of sounds and visual 'clues', from which the viewer can attempt to 'generate a narrative'.

The visual arts in France may have been dormant for a while but they were by no means dead. In the Marais (the historical cradle of contemporary art), several galleries exhibit both the new generation and artists harking back to the 1960s and '70s: Marian Goodman (Huyghe, and Daniel Buren, who has been covering the world in 8.7cm-wide vertical stripes since the '60s); Yvon Lambert (Christian Boltanski, whose photographic installations use photos of anonymous people, often taken from death notices arranged as shrines, altars and monuments, playing on themes of death, memory and identity); Daniel Templon (*nouveau réaliste* Raymond Hains, a contemporary of Arman, famous for his coffee-grinder readymades); Chantal Crousel (the commercial home of Sophie Calle, whose work has been based on stalking and snooping; autobiographical narrative constructions; and rules, games and rituals to improve life). One other artist who has attracted a lot of media interest is Orlan, a performance artist who has reconstructed her own face through plastic surgery.

You won't miss out on all the action in the provinces either. The Centre Pompidou at Beaubourg in Paris (opened in 1977) kick-started a public museums revolution with its 'inside out' architecture, open-access libraries and emphasis on confrontation. In the 1980s, culture minister Jack Lang poured money into renovating museums, many in the regions, which are now lively and up-to-the-minute: the Musée d'Art Moderne at Lille Métropole, Museé d'Art Contemporain in Lyon, Musée d'Art Moderne et d'Art Contemporain in Nice, Le Consortium in Dijon, Collection Lambert in Avignon, Les Abbattoirs in Toulouse, and branches of the Fonds Régional d'Art Contemporain and Musée Niepce de la Photographie are among the best. Back in Paris, the Musée d'Art Moderne de la Ville de Paris runs a vigorous contemporary art programme (ARC).

French Cuisine

Food is among the foremost pleasures of life in France, and anyone who has spent time in the country will be enchanted by the attention and care paid to activities of the kitchen. Much of the irresistible appeal of French gastronomy is derived from its immense regional variety. In other words, the personality of French food – shaped by climate, soil, foreign influences and local traditions – is as diverse as the people of France.

Eating Habits

It has become fashionable to snipe from across the Channel that innovative modern British cooking is now superior to dull, decadent French cuisine, but the gastro-renaissance in Britain is a flash in the pan compared with the long tradition of eating well in France. French eating habits have changed, however. Once upon a time, prince and peasant alike enjoyed good food, and the bourgeoisie used to sit down around the family table twice a day to a painstakingly prepared meal of several courses with sauces. Now everyone's in too much of a rush. Lunch for most people is a sandwich on the run (forget *la grande bouffe*), and dinner is more likely to be a steak thrown under the grill at the end of a day's work than a *plat mijoté*. Restaurant standards have slipped, too, as they face competition from *le fast-food*; despite vocal protests, the French wolf down 'McDos'. For a long time the French spent more on what they ate than anything else; in 1960, one-third of the average French household's budget went on food. Today, that figure has surprisingly been shrivelled down to 18 per cent.

Not only do the French spend less on food, they also eat lighter fare. After the Second World War, the average citizen's diet consisted of 2,500 calories. Today it has been whittled down to a leaner 1,900 calories. The French also spend less time eating (down from two hours per day to 90 minutes). And they spend less time preparing meals (cooking time has decreased from 30 minutes to 10 minutes over the past 20 years).

But while good eating is no longer a matter of course, for a special dinner the bourgeois chef may go to extremes to hunt down fresh truffles, authentic wild boar pâté and a genuine *baguette*. As the French move away from the countryside, they become more ardent about fresh local produce.

A gastronomic counter-revolution has been taking place, too, in the temples of *haute cuisine*: the taste for *nouvelle cuisine* is giving way to an appetite for '*la cuisine de grand-mère*'. For decades now the scanty portions made *de rigueur* by '*la bande à Bocuse*' have tyrannized French dining rooms. But the new approach to cooking adopted by chef Paul Bocuse and his gang in the 1960s, using lightly cooked delicacies in unusual combinations, was in its turn a revolution against the rich dishes of Escoffier, laden with cream, brandy, eggs, flour and sugar. It also bred a new generation of star chefs who owned and ran their own restaurants. Most of them are in the provinces; in France the essentials of eating are rooted in provincial diversity. 'Gastronomy, like an art, cannot stand still, it must renew itself,' said Bocuse. The current trend for *cuisine du terroir* has renewed the old country dishes like *bœuf en daube*, in a lighter style. The influence of *nouvelle cuisine* remains in the insistence on top-quality seasonal ingredients.

Sales of quality *charcuterie*, pâtés, cheeses, bread and pastries have all risen in the last decades and, although the taste and texture of the ordinary *baguette* may have declined, owing to mass production and the use of inferior flour, there is a wider range of *pain de campagne* and *pain de seigle* (rye) on offer. No meal is complete in France without cheese, of which the country produces more than 250 varieties, in 'a multitude of guises, sizes, textures and flavours that is quite staggering given that most cheeses have but one ingredient: milk', in the words of food writer Peter Graham. Small farmers are responding to demand with more varieties of apples, free-range chickens and unusual vegetables. Supermarkets such as Carrefour have picked up on the trend and stock a range of first-rate produce. In the far rural provinces, standards have survived, fashion-free, at thousands of small family-run places where you can still eat cheaply – and local farmers' markets are still a routine feature of village life. Even at a *relais routier* for lorry drivers you may find dishes as exotic as *cassoulet de fruits de mer*, or more everyday fare well prepared. And to complement all this good food you have a range of the world's finest wines to choose from.

Regional Specialities

Normandy

Thanks to fertile pastures blanketed with lush barley and grasses, Normandy is home to a centuries-old dairy tradition and France's creamiest cuisine. Milk from Normandy is transformed into distinguished cheeses – such as Camembert – and buttery sauces. Along with white and black spotted cows, apple trees are a fundamental part of the landscape. Apple groves produce the fruit that is baked into piping hot apple pie and many meals are accompanied by the ubiquitous apple cider, poured from terracotta pitchers. *Crevettes au cidre* are shrimps marinated and cooked in apple cider, and another popular menu item is *escalopes cauchoises*, or veal scallops with a cream and mushroom sauce. Calvados, or a powerful apple brandy, is served as an after-dinner *digestif* or is poured over *tarte aux pommes* and lit with a match to produce spectacular blue dancing flames.

Many other specialities of Normandy come from the sea: St-Vaast oysters and Barfleur lobsters; one of the most celebrated seafood dishes is *sole à la Dieppoise*, with a sauce of mussels, prawns and cream. Local chefs will proudly remind you that *gourmande* rhymes with *normande*.

Brittany

The craggy edges of the Breton peninsula are scarred with rocky inlets, tiny bays and thick patches of ocean foam where the Atlantic waves break. Indeed, fishermen offer most of the fresh ingredients used in Brittany's cuisine. Mackerel is marinated in a wine sauce with bay leaf, thyme and fennel for two days before it is eaten cold. *Pot-au-feu de homard breton* is lobster stewed with four kinds of shellfish: shrimp, scallops, oysters and mussels. The ingredients are simmered in Calvados or white wine and shallots and a touch of *crème fraîche* is added to the flavourful broth. Bretons indulge in a wide assortment of fish stews, called *cotriade*. One famous dish is *coquilles St-Jacques* (scallops). Sweetened *crêpes* can be served for dessert, or as a main course. A *galette* is a buckwheat flour crêpe into which seafood, eggs or meat is folded. Ocean winds and salt spray near the coast add taste to local produce, especially Breton's cabbage, with thick, green leaves, and artichoke crop.

Anjou and Touraine

Travel along the Loire River from Nantes and pass through the gateway to gastronomic nirvana. The foods of Anjou and Touraine are characterized by two things: freshwater fish from the river and its tributaries – such as perch, carp and pike – and fertile fields on the riverbanks. The limestone and tufa soils drain well, making them perfectly suited for agriculture and grape-growing, and the geographical positioning of the Loire Valley makes for a mild microclimate where many vegetables and fruits ripen earlier than regions further south. Among the most delicious offerings of the area is *fromage de chèvre*, or goat's cheese, either served fresh (*frais*) or aged until a pungent brown rind is formed. Main dishes include *matelote d'anguille et de carpe* (eel and carp stew with a dash of Cognac), *cul de veau* (braised veal with chunks of bacon, carrots, celery and tomato), and *noisette de porc aux pruneaux* (pork chops with a prune sauce).

Ile de France

The 'island of France' is the geographical equivalent of a reduction sauce. The very best of France's culinary traditions have been simmered down and crammed into a tiny area. In Paris, a foodie oasis, there are more restaurants and bistros than any region. Consumers can also enjoy countless outdoor markets attended by farmers and produce-growers from the surrounding countryside.

Thanks to the sophisticated palates and chefs who flock here, Paris has a special knack for culinary perfectionism. A baker's family may have employed centuries before producing the perfect croissant. But Paris is not limited to French specialities. The capital is a gastronomic mecca where cooks experiment with tastes and spices from far away. Immigration has help to pad menus with so many options, you could go years without eating the same thing twice.

Sologne

Seventy-five kilometres south of Paris is the small province of Sologne, whose genuine and gentle nature give its very name a romantic tinge. Thick forests, unspoiled countryside and time-honoured traditions make this a hunters' paradise. Home cooking usually involves stews or game meat including rabbit, pheasant or wild boar. *Marinade de civet de marcassin* is marinated boar stewed with shallots, garlic, carrots, celery and white wine. Hare is stuffed with vegetables, herbs, bacon and prunes and served with hearty red wine. Wild mushrooms abound and go into *cèpes forestière*, or *cèpes* in a cream and garlic sauce, and potatoes are often sautéed with garlic, butter and chopped parsley (*pommes de terre sautées*). Your sweet tooth will be satisfied by home-made almond cookies (*croquets*), honey spice bread (*pain d'épices au miel de Sologne*) and upside-down apple tart (*tarte Tatin* or *tarte à l'envers*).

Alsace

Proximity to Germany has added new gastronomic vocabulary to the eastern-most French province, which extends from the slopes of the Vosges mountains to the Rhine River plains. Trade and prosperity thanks to its geographic positioning has helped launch Alsace's foods to the forefront of French cuisine. Yet what you eat here shares little with the rest of the country.

Case Study: Slow Simmer

Like a cat with nine lives, Hazel Young has lived many of the best expatriate existences. Having had one foot in France since a young age, Hazel has made the picturesque Var her home; she raised goats on a five-acre property near St-Tropez and made cheese; she has lived on a canal boat in Burgundy; and she has attended the French National Cooking School of Beaune. 'My friends say I should write a book about my life in France – a book filled with my favourite recipes to tell my story.'

Indeed, of Hazel's many hats (she arranges canal barge tours at **www.canals offrance.com**), the one she likes the most is her chef's hat. 'I learned a lot of discipline at French cooking school. First of all it is very difficult to get accepted. The year I went there were just 11 student apprentices,' she explains. 'Once I got a kick in the legs because I had been peeling carrots for two hours and I failed to stand up straight. It was like boot camp.'

That swift kick seems to have paid off. At least that's what friends say after one of Hazel's meals. What are some of her favourite dishes? Caramelized onion tart topped with figs and goat cheese; *bourride*, or white monkfish stew with mussels, tomato, vegetables and garlic *aïoli*; and crisp duck baked with orange peel, honey and a grape *confiture*. 'I had been on transatlantic crossings as a kid and tasted some of the best foods prepared by the best chefs. Fine French cuisine became part of my upbringing.' Now it's the basis of her life.

The quintessential Alsatian dish is *choucroute*, or *sauerkraut* garnished with juniper, bay leaves, potatoes and thick slices of bacon or sausage. Pheasant with *sauerkraut* (*faisan à la choucroute*) is a lesser-known dish. Munster cheese is a local speciality and no gourmand can resist the apple pie (*tarte alsacienne*). Strasbourg *foie gras* pâté or *quiche lorraine* are famous *hors-d'œuvre*.

Burgundy

The book of French cuisine was written in Bourgogne. Born in 1775 in the town of Belley, Brillat-Savarin penned *The Physiology of Taste*. Today, his book – with cooking tips and history – is the manifesto of the true gourmand. Burgundy is home to a plethora of smelly cheeses, gardens and livestock – and vineyards to boot – so its no wonder the author found inspiration in what he ate.

Burgundy's namesake dish is *bœuf bourguignon*, or beef with vegetables slowly cooked in red wine (a high-quality one, nonetheless, like a pinot noir). Food-adventurers will also recognize *escargots*, or snails cooked with garlic, parsley and wine and served in attractive shells. Poultry reigns with the celebrated *coq au vin*, or cockerel stewed in red wine, and *poulet de Bresse* is chicken cooked in white wine and cream and served with morel mushrooms. The art of *charcuterie*, or cured meats, is taken to new levels in Burgundy.

Lyonnais

For a culinary *coup de grâce*, head to Lyon and the nearby Rhône Valley. Lyon has gained a reputation as a leading gastronomic centre of the world thanks to its access to the freshest food supplies. Two rivers cut through the city, and travellers and merchants used these channels for exchanging ingredients and recipes. One could write a dissertation on cheeses alone. From white cheese and tommes from the Dauphiné, the red cheese of the Mâconnais and the blue cheese from Gex, a rainbow of dairy products will tempt your senses.

Local wine is excellent for washing down *andouillettes*, or tripe sausage with veal; *poulet à la demi-deuil*, or chicken with truffles inserted under its skin before it is cooked; and *saucisson en brioche*, or sausage baked in a crispy pastry.

Dordogne

Périgord is one of the great gastronomic regions of France, with a cuisine based on truffles and goose. A classic dish is *confit d'oie*, goose preserved in its own fat, and *magret de canard*, fillet of duck breast.

Provence and Languedoc

Much of the local cuisine in this sun-drenched corner of the world was born from a poor people's tradition. Locals used what nature afforded them and deftly assembled the ingredients. Something as simple as an olive is marinated and aged with spices. The result is a tiny morsel that makes a big impact. The earth's bounty has always been generous in Provence and chefs have perfected their magic touch on everything from pungent basil to cherry tomatoes.

Soupe au pistou is vegetable minestrone flavoured with a basil and garlic paste reminiscent of pesto from neighbouring Italy. Artichokes and aubergine can be stuffed with breadcrumbs and minced meat, and ball-shaped courgettes are served *au gratin*. Lamb and pork is popular but generally fish dishes outnumber the meat ones. Sea bass, or *loup de mer*, is poached, grilled or fried, and no visitor to Marseille can leave without dipping a spoon into the fish stew known as *bouillabaisse* (served with toasted croutons and spicy mayonnaise sauce). More dishes are *daube*, or meat and vegetable casserole, *anchoïade* (an anchovy paste for flavouring) and the Provençal version of ravioli (consisting of only the stuffing, minus the pasta, smothered in tomato sauce). Nice is famous for its finger foods: *socca* (a thin pancake made with chickpea flour), *pissaladière* (a flat onion tart), *pan bagnat* (sort of *salade niçoise* in a sandwich) and *beignets* (fritters, of vegetables or courgette flowers).

To the west, in the Midi and Languedoc, the best-known dish is *cassoulet*, a stew of beans, sausage, pork, mutton and *confit d'oie*. But the region's top offering is Roquefort, a pungent, creamy, blue, sheeps' milk cheese.

Bordelais

Last but not least is the area around Bordeaux. The Basque country shares culinary notes with Spain and many of the surrounding regions, like Périgord, are influenced by inland culinary traditions. But Bordeaux stands alone thanks to its lucrative wine trade and important Atlantic Ocean ports.

You'll find France's most refined cuisine here: *foie gras*, oysters from Arcachon, duck, frogs' legs and pork sausage studded with black truffle (*crépinettes truffées*). Bordeaux gets the best of surf and turf (where wild mushrooms and white asparagus flourish). Curiosity dishes include *huîtres et saucisses au vin blanc*, oysters and sausage with white wine; *anguilles grillées*, grilled eel; and *baron d'agneau de Pauillac*, roast lamb with potatoes and tasty truffles.

Wine

It has been noted that the beauty of France reaches its maximum form of expression in a glass of wine. If you are familiar with the term *terroir*, you know this to be true. An English translation does not exist, but the definition of *terroir* is the magic combination of climate, soil, sunshine and landscape reflected in the character of a vineyard and the wines it produces. In other words, wine is meaningless without reference to the place in which it is made.

Winemakers the world-over believe in the notion of *terroir*, but none more firmly than in France. And, although the French did not invent wine, they certainly played a leading role in perfecting the art of making wine. The clones, techniques, growing practices and the very language of wine were born in this country and its social fabric has been forever grafted to the vine.

Within the French territory, four regions stand out thanks to a consistently outstanding product: Bordeaux, Burgundy, the Rhône, and Champagne. Wine enthusiasts are also smitten by flinty Sauvignon Blanc from the Loire and exciting experimentations under way in Languedoc. The latter will surely help France keep its competitive edge against New World wines from California, Australia and Chile.

All French wines are classified as part of a pyramid system that regulates quality. There are four major areas starting with *vin de table, vin de pays, vin délimité de qualité supérieure* (VDQS) and *appellation contrôlée* at the high end of the quality spectrum. AOC, or *appellation d'origine contrôlée*, was created in 1936 and guarantees the origin, style and quality of a wine. About 40 per cent of French wines falls into this élite category.

France is also home to the family of so-called Noble Grapes. Among them are: chardonnay, merlot, cabernet franc, cabernet sauvignon, pinot noir and syrah, now planted across the globe. Although many of these varietals are not native to France (syrah, for example, is said to originate in what is today Iran), the French kept them vigorous throughout the centuries.

The truth is: France is simply blessed as a land of Bacchus. The soils of France are perfectly suited for vines. In some areas, alluvial rivers laid down a combination of limestone and argillaceous clay. In others, patches of land are granite, loam, sand and sandstone. South-facing slopes are bathed in sunshine and winds are strong enough to keep clusters aerated. Most importantly, the French pour their heart and soul into the bottle.

Bordeaux

Bordeaux has broken most of wine's most coveted records. It makes more top quality wine than any other region and is home to France's highest proportion of large estates. It also makes the world's most expensive and sought after wines. Look out for bottles from Châteaux Margaux, Lafite or Mouton-Rothschild in Pauillac. The region is the undisputed king of cabernet sauvignon, merlot and cabernet franc and a new crop of native varietals like petit verdot and melbec. Whites include sauvignon blanc, semillon and muscadelle.

One secret of its success is water – and the effect it has on climate. Bordeaux is flanked by the Atlantic Ocean and is bisected by the Gironde and Garonne rivers. These give the region a mild, stable climate that varies from one side of the region to another. St-Emilion and Pomerol, which are further inland, enjoy continental conditions with hotter summers and cooler winters. Bordeaux's soils are also excellent. Parts of the region have gravel that allow for easier drainage and is suited for cabernet sauvignon. In other places, higher clay contents trap water and are good for merlot.

Burgundy

Unlike Bordeaux with its monumental château estates and deep-rooted wealth, Burgundy is associated with grass-roots winemakers spread over a patchwork of smaller vineyards, who have carefully crafted a strong identity with their unique *terroir*. Burgundy, south of Dijon, also has one of France's narrowest ranges of grape varietals: reds and whites are made almost exclusively from pinot noir and chardonnay respectively.

Rigid inheritance laws linked to the Napoleonic Code meant Burgundy's vineyards were subdivided over generations, and today their numbers have reached nearly 2,000. Faced with so many small *domaines*, and looking to make sense of it all, the consumer is often left baffled.

Another quirk is Burgundy's unusual relationship, between the grape-grower and *négociant* – or merchant wineries that buy grapes at auctions or contract them to make their own wines. Despite their polarized interests, the wide selection of fruit makes for higher quality wine.

The region includes the grape-growing areas of Côte de Nuits and Côte de Beaune in the greater Côte d'Or *département*, and the Côte Mâconnais and the Côte Chalonnaise. Beaujolais (with granite soils) and Chablis (limestone) are two distinct viticulture areas to be considered separately.

The Rhône

No French wine region has seen its reputation grow faster over the past two decades than the Rhône. France's oldest grape-growing area is divided into two distinct poles along the Rhône River: the northern Rhône and the southern Rhône. Like the ends of a barbell, they are separated by 30 miles of vine-less land. The sun-drenched vertical vineyards that hang perilously to the walls of the river corridor to the north include the *appellations* Hermitage and Côte Rôtie: rivals of the best of Bordeaux and Burgundy thanks to rich expressions of syrah grapes and the wine's natural ability to age. Viognier, with its unmistakable whiffs of violet, is the defining white grape of Condrieu. The southern Rhône, on the other hand, which once saw its grenache juice hauled off in gasoline tanker trucks, is home to excellent wines such as Châteauneuf-du-Pape, Gigondas and Vacqueyras.

The emphasis has unquestionably shifted to lower yields and higher quality, and consequently the Rhône has blossomed into one of France's best wine regions. One of the faces behind the Rhône renaissance is the exceptionally talented Marcel Guigal, a winemaker based in the town of Ampuis.

Champagne

Champagne stands tall thanks to visionary marketing. Rather than make still wine like everyone else, producers in these chalky, northeastern plains added a touch of caprice – the bubble – and invented a luxury brand.

Champagne sales soon became a barometer of global cheer. With links to the Russian court, sales boomed until that market suddenly disappeared in 1917. They did so again in the prosperous post-war decades, and a handful of companies had the foresight to buy vineyards during the rough patch in between, putting them in a strong position today. More recently this region has faced a series of new pressures. Initially, Champenois were flattered by competitors who imitated their unique winemaking methods. But soon competition from growing giants Italy, California and Australia was anything but reassuring. Champagne is responsible for only one bottle in 12 of world production of sparkling wine. By the early 1990s, sales began to slow and many smaller firms were unable to survive on their own, leading to consolidation of the industry. Today, producers are intent on safeguarding their unique identity.

The Loire Valley

The Loire's portfolio of wines concentrates heavily on whites, and some critics see this as a limitation. But the fertile valley offers something the others don't: breathtakingly beautiful wine country that will make your jaw drop as each successive château comes into view. Most of these architectural masterpieces are framed against expanses of trellised vineyard, which boast a wide variety of grapes. Some of the most popular are cabernet franc, malbec, gamay and sauvignon blanc. A delightful white from this region is Sancerre and others include Pouilly-Fumé, Vouvray and Montlouis. The Loire is among the most travelled wine routes.

Other Regions

Smaller wine regions include Alsace and Lorraine, south of Strasbourg, which offer cool-climate, aromatic white wines such as Tokay and Gewürztraminer. Granite and sandstone slopes are also good for pinot blanc, muscat and riesling. The high-altitude Jura and Savoie areas offer similar wines and are France's most overlooked wine regions. Chardonnay and pinot noir is planted and vineyard managers must keep a careful eye on unpredictable mountain weather. Provence and Corsica offer refreshing whites and rosés that are paired well with fish and summer fare.

Languedoc-Roussillon, in the south, is France's most fascinating wine region because it does not adhere to the strict *appellation contrôlée* system. Anything goes and vineyards are planted to an incredibly vast selection: grenache, cabernet sauvignon, merlot, syrah, mourvedre, chardonnay, ugni blanc and viognier. Winemakers are given freedom to experiment with different varietals and blends that are not permitted in other regions. Consequently, it offers quality wines for lower prices. Many regard Languedoc-Roussillon as the sleeping giant of the wine world and the only region armed to compete with the low prices and full-bodied tastes of the New World.

First Steps

04

There is something comforting in the idea of moving to France. This is by no means an exotic destination or uncharted land. Thanks to its geographic proximity, most of us have visited the country at least once. Thanks to our schooling, we can all utter a few words of the language. Thanks to our sophisticated palates, we have savoured French cuisine at home, and sipped its best wines. And, thanks to popular films and newspaper features, we are familiar with the basic contours of the French culture. We instinctively know France better than most foreign nations. Moving to France is not like moving to the Far East, or Africa, or a tiny village lost in the English countryside for that matter. Moving to France means going to a place you already know you will appreciate.

It also means your expectations will be high. Chances are you are moving to France by choice: you want to retire, buy a holiday home, learn the language, start your own business, find other employment or simply reward yourself with lazy afternoons with the smell of lavender hanging heavy in the air. You may well be transferring a great deal of your financial savings and personal energy to your new life in France. The decision to move to France should not be taken lightly, no matter how well you think you relate to the country. The following chapter will paint a basic picture of the various reasons foreigners move abroad and should help you decide if France is right for you. It also provides basic information on getting to France so you can discover the country at your leisure.

Why Work and Live in France?

There is but one answer: quality of life. This is the nation that has added the terms *joie de vivre* and *savoir-faire* to the lexicon of the modern world. If one nation embodies the concept of the good life, it is France. That's not to say it isn't infested with the same problems as other nations. Realistically, there are plenty of painful social woes, inadequate services and suffocating red tape. Despite the cliché, you will probably come up with a long list of unfortunate encounters with language supremacists if your spoken French isn't *parfait*. Yet, like its Latin neighbours Spain and Italy, France also affords those important little indulgences that make us happier inside: you'll breathe a little deeper and walk a little slower.

Better still: it is so close. You are whisked across the Channel by boat, tunnel or aeroplane in a matter of minutes, with slightly more effort than it takes to make your daily commute to the office. Depending on where you settle in France, you can easily live with one foot in Britain and one in your new home. Then there's that unique bond the French and English share. A recent newspaper article observed: 'If there were not a France, the British might have to invent one, and

It's an Expat's Life

If one person can be credited with the love affair the world has with *la vie française*, he is Peter Mayle. A former advertising executive, Mayle bought a 200-year-old stone farmhouse nestled in the foothills of the Luberon mountains and moved to the south of France with his wife, Jenny, and their two dogs. Already a published children's author, his new life inspired him to pen one of the greatest, and funniest, travelogues ever. *A Year in Provence*, published in 1990, shot to the top of the best-seller list thanks to its witty humour, wise storytelling and savoury culinary passages. Descriptions of game dishes, melting goat cheese, aniseed Pastis *apéritifs* and black truffles build a hearty appetite for the expat life.

After that success, Mayle wrote and published an entire genre of 'life in France' books that include: *Toujours Provence, Hotel Pastis, A Dog's Life, Chasing Cézanne, Encore Provence: New Adventures in the South of France*, and most recently *French Lessons: Adventures with Knife, Fork, and Corkscrew*.

Mayle soon discovered that his years in Provence were to lose their idyllic charm. His country house became a Mecca for pilgrims of the sweet life. 'There was a sense of disbelief to start off with and it took me a long time to realize that the book was becoming well known, and it was only when I looked at the printing numbers that I realized it had really taken off. For at least a year or two after I wrote it, nothing much changed as far as I was concerned. I mean, nobody was dancing up and down asking for my autograph. Life just went on as it had been... And then I started getting letters from people, and then I started getting more letters and then I started getting so many letters I had to get a girl to help me out to answer them,' said Mayle in a published interview.

Book fans waited for him to emerge from his house and hunted him down for autographs and property tips. Journalists called so often, he resorted to speaking through the fax machine. It got so bad, Mayle and his wife left their beloved Provence and moved to New York's Hamptons to get away. This glitzy seaside American resort town was an excellent choice: with neighbours like Steven Spielberg, fans paid less attention to the bespectacled Englishman. After four years in the Hamptons, Mayle and his wife could no longer resist the spell of France. They bought another house in Provence, in an undisclosed location, where Mayle continues to write and shop at the local outdoor market for literary inspiration (and a few cooking ingredients as well).

'I have gradually got used to the idea that I really have been able to give a lot of people a few hours of pleasure,' said Mayle. 'It's the most wonderful feeling.'

in a sense they have. Lacking wines, they put claret on the map; subsisting on heavy meat and little vegetable, they embraced French cuisine; cloaked in cloud, they trickled across the Channel into French sunshine.'

There are thriving British enclaves throughout the country: from Paris to the Riviera to the Dordogne region in western France to the French Alps. In fact, they are growing so fast that many of France's institutions are having a hard time keeping up. Estate agents' signs across the country read 'English spoken'; a British mortgage bank, Abbey National, has a branch in France to help new home-owners; web portals help English-speaking residents network, find jobs or even a plumber if needed; Monaco's *Riviera Radio* bypasses French broadcasting laws to bring listeners all-English language programmes; a slew of publications and magazines are aimed at the expatriate community; and even British groceries have carved their own market niche in the country of *haute cuisine*.

According to Abbey National, property purchases by foreigners in France rose by three per cent in 2002. But British purchases soared by 40 per cent. At the end of 2002, the British accounted for 36 per cent of foreign real estate holdings in France, followed by the Italians with 13.5 per cent and the Dutch with 5.2 per cent. There is no other country in Europe, or the world for that matter, with which British expatriates enjoy a more fruitful relationship.

Ask any foreigners why they come and the answer is invariably quality of life. All other considerations – ranging from beautiful surroundings, geography, better weather, good food and wine, healthy living and (sometimes) cheaper prices – fall under this heading. Investing in France doesn't just mean buying a new home or transferring your profession abroad, it means acquiring a new lifestyle.

France will satisfy all your senses. The borders of the country enclose stunning natural beauty; but eyes, ears and taste buds will also be stimulated by what mankind has added to the natural surroundings. France's artistic heritage is second only to Italy's and ranges from prehistoric cave drawing to the glass pyramid in front of the Louvre. And if you could put a value on France's epicurean contributions to the world – from the odd *brasserie* in New York City to the Bordeaux wines exported to Japan – you'd probably be dealing with a monetary figure higher than many nation's GNP.

Buying Property

Among the main reasons Britons move to France is because they want to invest their savings in bricks and mortar or because they want a second home. France is paradise for holiday-home shoppers. There is no shortage of beautiful properties (which hold their value well) or beautiful locations. All of the country is easily accessible through state-of-the-art transportation hubs and regional airports. Waves of artistic and architectural movements over centuries speak to all tastes, from rustic to refined. Most importantly, locals and foreigners by and large cohabit harmoniously. Although there have been backlashes linked to inflated property prices due to what the French have dubbed 'the British invasion', the truth is that cultural assimilation is virtually painless.

Starting a Business or Self-Employment

Many come to France to open the business they dreamed of running back home. A large section of the French economy is fuelled by family-run businesses. Husbands and wives, sons and fathers, mothers and daughters open shops, restaurants and companies together. As a result, the economy and the employment structure cannot survive without them. France is a decidedly pro-small-business environment. Britons with good business ideas can easily insert themselves and there are no major bureaucratic obstacles to stop them. If they don't want to start a formal business, they can opt to work for themselves. For a range of business ideas to get started in, *see* **Working in France**, pp.229–58.

Educating and Raising Children

One of France's most admired virtues is the importance its society gives to the family nucleus. Because family bonds are sacred, foreigners find France to be, by and large, a fantastic place to raise offspring. Tight and generous communities are formed around local schools and, in general, the society proudly lends a hand to help raise its youngest citizens. If you are coming with the children, you and your little ones will fit in famously.

Retirement

For many foreigners, France is a prize enjoyed at the end of a lifetime of hard work spent elsewhere. A pension in England can easily be paid in France to ensure that your golden years are what they are supposed to be. Its famous healthcare system is accessible to foreign pensioners, as are the other perks of the social security system. Retirees will find many communities throughout the country in which to live and people with whom they share common interests, including leisure and intellectual activities.

Getting to France

Getting to France is not a problem. What you need to consider is how you want to get there, and this depends on how many belongings you are bringing. Needless to say, if you are planning a fact-finding mission on where to live in Paris, and only plan to stay a few days, going by aeroplane or Eurostar makes the most economic sense. Renting a car in France is a good option for those who want to enjoy trips into the countryside. Or you could take your own car over the Channel. If you are officially moving to France with children, the dog and your collection of oakwood chairs, you'd better start taking measurements to see how much will fit into the boot.

By Air

France is well served by airports, with main air hubs located in Paris (either Roissy-Charles de Gaulle or Orly), Bordeaux, Brest, Grenoble, Lille, Lyon, Marseille, Montpellier, Nantes, Nice (with its new high-tech terminal), Rennes, Strasbourg and Toulouse. It takes only 45 minutes to fly from London to Paris, and only twice that to reach Nice in the south of the country.

Airline deregulation is the most revolutionary thing to happen to European travel. Within the past 10 years, a whole new crop of budget airlines has surfaced, providing passengers with no-frills, but cheap, air transport to most points on the continent. The pressure exerted by budget airlines has forced national (sometimes state-owned) carriers to slash prices in order to stay competitive. This is excellent news for the consumer.

The downside is that more people are travelling, and you should book well in advance for the best fares and seats, especially in the summer months and around the Christmas holiday. You should also dedicate extra time to shopping around for the best prices. It's amazing how much fares differ from one company to the next. For the latest bargains, check with your travel agent or scan the adverts published in your Sunday newspaper. Online booking agents such as **www.lastminute.com**, **www.opodo.co.uk**, **www.travelocity.com**, **www.bestfares.com**, **www.expedia.com** and **www.cheapflights.com** (from the USA with a special section for UK users) will also give you an idea of how low you can go. Airlines regularly change schedules and destinations. The information below was valid when this book went to print.

Major Airlines

• **Air France** (**t** 0845 359 1000, **www.airfrance.co.uk**) is the French national carrier and offers regular flights from London Heathrow, London City, Birmingham, Dublin, Edinburgh, Glasgow, Manchester, Newcastle and Southampton to Paris Charles de Gaulle (with various connection options within France). It also flies direct from Heathrow to Lyon and Toulouse and from Gatwick to Brest, Nantes and Strasbourg.

• **British Airways** (**t** 0870 850 9850, **www.britishairways.com**) is the British national airline and has daily flights from Heathrow and Gatwick to Paris, Bordeaux, Lyon, Marseille, Montpellier, Nantes, Nice, Toulon and Toulouse (some routes are operated by a partner airline). You can also fly to Paris from Aberdeen, Belfast, Birmingham, Bristol, Cardiff, Edinburgh, Glasgow, Inverness, Jersey, Manchester, Newcastle, Newquay and Plymouth.

• **British Midland** (**t** 0870 607 0555, **www.flybmi.com**): from Aberdeen, Belfast, Edinburgh, Glasgow, Heathrow, Leeds, Manchester and Teesside to France.

• **Aer Lingus** (**www.aerlingus.com**) is the Irish national carrier with services from Dublin to Paris, Toulouse and Nice. Or you could fly to France through a connecting flight in Heathrow. From Cork, Aer Lingus also has a service to Paris.

Budget Airlines

With most budget airlines, the prices go up the closer you are to your departure date. Therefore you really must book in advance for the best fares. You'll also notice that prices are very attractive in odd hours. For example, if you book your flight at 6am you will pay a fraction of the ticket price of a 6pm flight that same day. It is not unusual to find fares as low as £20 for a one-way London-Paris flight (fares are usually one-way only). For more information on low-cost airlines for travel within France *see* **Living in France**, 'Transport', pp.199–200.

• **Easyjet** (**t** 08717 500 100, **www.easyjet.com**), known for its orange planes, bought Go a few years back and acquired additional routes. It operates from London Stansted, Luton and Gatwick (with connections from Belfast, Bristol, East Midlands, Edinburgh, Glasgow, Liverpool and Newcastle) and flies to Paris Charles de Gaulle, Paris Orly, Lyon, Marseille, Nice and Toulouse. Don't expect comfort, the airline is dubbed 'Squeezy Jet' for a reason.

• **Ryanair** (**t** 0905 566 0000, **www.ryanair.com**) has an extensive list of flights throughout France (it acquired Buzz a few years back and gained more routes as well). You can fly to Bergerac, Biarritz, Brest, Carcassonne, Clermont-Ferrand, Dinard (with a bus to Rennes), La Rochelle, Limoges, Montpellier, Nîmes, Paris-Beauvais, Pau, Perpignan, Poitiers, Reims-Champagne, Rodez, St-Etienne (with a bus to Lyon), Strasbourg, Tours and even Disneyland (about 180km from Paris).

• **BMI Baby** (**t** 0870 264 2229, **www.bmibaby.com**) is British Midland's low-cost airline, with flights to Paris Charles de Gaulle, Nice and Toulouse from East Midlands Airport and connections from Dublin.

You could also try **FlyBe, t** 08708 890 908, **www.flybe.com**, and **Jet2, t** 0870 737 8383, **www.jet2.com**.

Charter Flights

For a wider range of options and flights from smaller airports (not listed above) you could explore charter airlines. Schedules and destinations are changed according to demand from season to season. Find out about availability through your local newspaper or travel agent or contact a company such as Thomson Airtours (**www.cheap-holiday-sun.co.uk**) or Unijet (**www.unijet.com**), which offer charter flights to France from a number of UK airports.

Long Distance Flights

If you are travelling from the USA and Canada your options are limited to the major carriers. Remember to check out connecting flights through major international airports in London, New York and Paris.

• **Air France** (**t** 800 237 2747, **www.airfrance.com**) has services from New York, Philadelphia, Cincinnati, Atlanta, Boston, Chicago, Houston, Miami, San Francisco and Washington.

• **American Airlines** (**t** 800 433 7300, **www.aa.com**) flies to France from Boston, Chicago, Dallas, Los Angeles, Miami and New York.

• **Continental** (**t** 800 231 0856, **www.continental.com**) flies from Houston and Newark.

• **Delta** (**t** 800 221 1212, **www.delta.com**) has flights from Atlanta to Paris and New York to Nice.

• **Northwest Airlines** (**t** 800 225 2525, **www.nwa.com**) flies from Detroit to Paris.

• **Air Canada** (**www.aircanada.ca**) also has direct flights to Paris from several Canadian airports.

By Car

Taking your car probably means reserving a place on the **Eurotunnel** train, which is by far the most convenient way to get to France from Britain. It takes only a fast 35 minutes to cross the Channel from Folkestone to Calais. Depending on the time of day, there are as many as four departures per hour and trains run every day of the year. The ticket price includes a car (less than 6.5m in length) plus the driver and all passengers. Fares range from £29 (with return) at night and in the low season to as much as £200 (with return) in the high season. For the latest prices and a timetable of departures, *see* **t** 08705 35 35 35, **www.eurotunnel.com**.

If you wanted, you could also send your car to France by rail or by boat. See the following sections for more information on those options.

Once you get to France, the 8,000km of motorway are yours to explore. Other than the side of the road you drive on, French driving regulations do not differ much from UK ones, although the French habit of sitting on your tail can be a bit disconcerting to begin with.

Is a UK driver's licence valid in France? Yes. Any European Union member state-issued driver's licence, including one from the UK, is valid in France. In the not too distant past, a UK driver's licence needed to be converted into an International Driver's Licence, but thanks to French reciprocal licence exchange this is no longer the case. Make sure your driver's licence has not expired. The minimum driving age in France is 18, which means a 17-year-old UK licence holder may not drive in France (fines can reach €1,500 and the vehicle may

be impounded if they do). Penalty points are non-transferable, but a driver disqualified from driving in the UK may not drive in France.

If you have do not have an EU driver's licence (for example if your licence is from the USA, Canada, South Africa or Australia), you may drive in France with your licence for up to one year. For more information on driver's licences, importing a car, buying a car in France, car insurance, accidents and French driving regulations *see* **Living in France**, 'Transport', pp.200–206.

By Coach

The coach company **Eurolines** (**t** 08705 80 80 80, **www.eurolines.com**) has a regular bus service from London to some 70 cities in France including Paris, Bordeaux, Chamonix, Grenoble, Perpignan, St-Malo, Strasbourg and Toulouse. The trip to Paris from London takes about 8hrs, compared with 22hrs to Toulouse. In the peak season, tickets are more expensive but discounts are offered to senior citizens and children under 12. There are special discounts to those who buy more than one trip.

By Train

Taking a high-speed train is another very attractive alternative for people making short hops into France, or travelling to smaller cities. The French rail network is exhaustive, making it possible to reach the furthest corners of the country. **Eurostar** (**t** 08705 186 186, **www.eurostar.com**) trains leave London Waterloo or Ashford International (in Kent) with direct connections to Paris's Gare du Nord. These high-speed trains will also bring you directly to Lille, Disneyland, and the French Alps for skiing. Fares are cheaper if you book seven days in advance and include a Saturday night stopover. You must check in at least 20mins before departure.

Once inside France, you can move around easily with the TGV (*trains à grande vitessse*), a symbol of the nation's engineering pride. These 'bullet' trains zap from station to station at an average of 180mph, although secondary tracks are not fitted for high speeds. You can count on speedy connections from Paris to Bordeaux, Lyon, Marseille (with a slower onward connection to Nice), Montpellier and Strasbourg. The trip from Paris Gare de Lyon to Marseille, for example, takes only a little more than 4hrs.

Towns and cities not serviced by TGV (and more and more kilometres of high-speed tracks are being put down each year) will be connected to the SNCF network, the country's national railway system. There are overnight sleeper trains to Paris and other destinations. Although these slow trains are cheaper, there have been a large number of robberies reported on them, so pay attention. The timetable and prices are available at **www.voyages-sncf.fr**.

France's Rail Network

ENGLAND

Amsterdam

London

NETHER-
LANDS

Dover

Dunkerque

Calais

Brussels

GERMANY

Boulogne

Lille

Lens

LUX.

English Channel

Arras

Cambrai

Dieppe

Amiens

St-Quentin

Charleville-
Mézières

Cherbourg

Le Havre

Rouen

Reims

Thionville

Metz

Channel
Is

Granville

Caen

Evreux

Mantes

Epernay

Nancy

Sarrebourg

Strasbourg

Brest

Morlaix

St-Brieuc

Alençon

Chartres

Fontainebleau

PARIS

St-Dizier

Epinal

Colmar

Quimper

Rennes

Château-dun

Sens

Mulhouse

Lorient

Le Mans

Vendôme

Montargis

Vesoul

Belfort

Vannes

Angers

Orléans

Auxerre

Dijon

Besançon

St-
Nazaire

NANTES

Tours

Blois

Bourges

Nevers

SWITZER-
LAND

La Roche-
sur-Yon

Poitiers

Châteauroux

Montceau-
les-Mines

Chalon-sur-
Saône

Niort

Vichy

Mâcon

Bourg-
en-Bresse

Geneva

La Rochelle

Rochefort

Royan

Cognac

Angoulême

Limoges

Roanne

LYON

Chambéry

ITALY

Gironde

Périgueux

CLERMONT-
FERRAND

St-Etienne

Grenoble

BORDEAUX

Brive-la-
Gaillarde

Valence

Arcachon

Villeneuve-
sur-Lot

Rodez

Montélimar

BIARRITZ

Montauban

Alès

Orange

AVIGNON

NICE

MONTE-
CARLO

Pau

Tarbes

TOULOUSE

NIMES

MONTPELLIER

MARSEILLE

Lourdes

NARBONNE

TOULON

SPAIN

PERPIGNAN

N

Madrid

- - - TGV rail network

100 km

50 miles

Balearic Islands

By Boat

If you have packed the car and trailer with personal belongings and are making the final move to France, you should consider booking a trip by ferry. The sea route can save you money depending on the time of year you plan your travel and the volume of goods you are bringing. You pay extra for trailers and motorcycles (bicycles are sometimes free), but children under 14 get a discounted rate and children under four travel free altogether. There are lower rates for people planning to stay in France for five days or people travelling in large groups. The trip from Dover to Calais takes about 35mins in a high-speed Seacat or you could sail to ports of call located further away in a slower ferry.

Here are a few ferry services that regularly zip across the Channel. Shop around for the best rates.

• **Brittany Ferries (t** 08703 665 333, **www.brittany-ferries.com**): Portsmouth to Caen (6hrs) and St-Malo; or Poole to Cherbourg; or Plymouth to Roscoff (6hrs). They also sail from Cork to Roscoff.

• **Condor Ferries (t** (01305) 761551, **www.condorferries.co.uk**): Weymouth and Poole to St-Malo.

• **Hoverspeed Ferries (t** 0870 240 8070, **www.hoverspeed.co.uk**): Dover to Calais (35mins), Folkestone to Boulogne (1hr) and Newhaven to Dieppe (2hrs).

• **Norfolkline (t** (01304) 218400, **www.norfolkline.com**) has a good service on large transport boats for cars only (no foot passengers) from Dover to Dunkerque.

• **P&O Portsmouth (t** 08705 20 20 20, t 0870 242 4999, **www.poportsmouth. com**):night ferries from Portsmouth to Le Havre (6hrs) and Cherbourg.

• **P&O Stena Line (t** 0870 242 4999, **www.posl.com**) has a ferry from Dover to Calais (45mins) as well as a service from Hull or even Dublin.

• **SeaFrance (t** 08705 711 711, **www.seafrance.com**) operates from Dover to Calais with a slower boat (90mins).

If you are travelling to France from another Mediterranean port, contact **Southern Ferries/SNCM (www.seafrance.co.uk** or **www.sncm.fr**). They have boats from Marseille, Nice and Toulon to Corsica, Italy (Sardinia, Livorno and Genoa) and North Africa. **Corsica Ferries (www.corsicaferries.com**) also services Corsica and Sardinia.

Red Tape

05

A Latin proverb promises *verba volant, scripta manent* ('spoken words fly away, written ones remain') and is the key to understanding the maniacal attention southern European nations, once on the grid of the mighty Roman Empire, give to paperwork. France is guilty of an obsessive and visceral attachment to the red tape spewed forth by its colossal governmental institutions. It has not reached the infernal depths of neighbouring countries (Italy), perhaps, but it is bad. You will often be reminded that one in four French citizens is employed by the state and, a very large percentage of them perform functions that have never been revealed to or understood by the remainder of the population. It has even been hypothesized that some of the officials (*fonctionnaires*) themselves do not have a full grasp of what their professional duties are. The French government has made gallant attempts to combat unemployment, but the truth is that many of the jobless have been enlisted in an army of willingly servile bureaucrats whose marching orders are, simply, to pound sheets of paper with rubber stamps.

Don't let that put you off. Moving to a new country means taking its cultural idiosyncrasies in your stride and having a laugh or two along the way (nightmare bureaucracy stories are a good way of livening up staid dinner party conversations). Patience is something you might want to store in advance, as you would stock vegetable preserves before the winter. All guidebooks on living in France include lengthy chapters dedicated to red tape and many leave their stunned and confused readers wondering what hit them. Rest assured that there is rhyme and reason behind the gobbledygook. In this chapter we have done our best to make complicated things (such as visas, permits and taxes) as simple as possible. Or at least, sound simple.

Visas, Permits and Other Paperwork

The good news is that the harmonization of European law has made it much easier today to obtain the necessary paperwork for residing in France. If you are a member of an EU state, of which most – but not all – have signed the Schengen Agreement (Austria, Belgium, Denmark, Finland, France, Germany, Greece, Ireland, Italy, Luxembourg, Netherlands, Portugal, Spain, Sweden, the UK and Switzerland – which is treated like an EU country although it isn't) you do NOT need any special paperwork to live, own property or look for a job in France for up to *three months*. If you stay longer than three months, you are advised to apply for a residence permit (*carte de séjour*). If you are an EU citizen and want to learn more about the residence permit, please skip to the 'Residence Permits (*carte de séjour*)' section below.

Note that British nationals may travel to France until the expiry date of their British passport.

Visas

If you are not an EU citizen you will probably need to apply for a visa before you enter France. This applies to all countries *except* Andorra, Argentina, Australia, Bolivia, Brazil, Canada, Chile, Cyprus, Czech Republic, Hungary, Iceland, Israel, Japan, Liechtenstein, Malta, Mexico, Monaco, New Zealand, Norway, Poland, San Marino, Slovakia, Slovenia, South Korea and the USA.

If you are a national of any of these countries, you are allowed to visit France for up to three months without a visa. If you intend to stay longer than three months, and if you intend to look for a job in France, you will need to apply for a visa. Of course many people who don't have visa and stay longer than three months simply leave France – for example, they go to Switzerland for a few hours – and return fresh with another three months to spend in France. There is nothing wrong with this strategy, but remember always to have your passport stamped upon re-entry to France.

Many Americans, Australians and New Zealanders get caught in the following predicament: they come to France as a 'tourist' for three months, and don't realize that it is impossible to change their status to that of an employee, resident or student while they are in France. To change your status, you must return to your country of citizenship and start the paperwork process there.

At the French embassy or consulate in your country, you can apply for one of two types of visas. The first is a short-stay visa (*visa de court séjour*) which is roughly the equivalent of a transit visa. It is usually valid for 90 days and is good for multiple entries into France. There are variations to this, such as a three-day transit visa and a short-stay visa for businessmen which allows multiple stays up to 90 days for up to three years.

More likely, what you are after is the second kind of visa, the so-called long-stay visa (*visa de long séjour*). These are required by all non-EU nationals (including Americans, Australians and New Zealanders) who want to stay longer than three months and want to work, study or live in France. Again, it must be obtained *before* you leave because once you arrive in France it is impossible to change your status. (A long-stay visa is *not* required for EU nationals.)

Although the documentation required for the application process changes according to the type of visa you request (if you intend to work, study or live in France), here is what you might be asked to bring to the French embassy or consulate in your country:

- **your valid passport**
- **eight passport-sized photos against a white background (to affix to the eight visa applications you will be asked to compile)**
- **a certified birth certificate (plus those of your spouse and children)**
- **proof that you have sufficient funds to cover the cost of your stay (such as a bank statement that proves you have money in the account. Credit cards**

and cash are not accepted as proof of financial means. You may need to supply a notarized *certificat d'hébergement*, which is proof that a family or friend will be supplying you with accommodation)

• proof of health insurance (please note that many national health schemes do not cover their citizens abroad so you may need to purchase additional insurance)

• a contract of employment (this must be approved by the French Labour Ministry or the District Labour Department where you will work. The contract must be issued by the employer, who then sends it to the Office des Migrations Internationales (OMI) which in turn forwards it to the French embassy or consulate you are dealing with)

• proof you are a student, such as a letter of admission to an accredited university (sometimes a round-trip airline ticket is also required)

• proof of a medical examination taken three months prior to your expected move to France

• an agreement with a French family, or *déclaration d'engagement* (if you plan to work as an *au pair* in France)

• a marriage certificate (only if you are married to a French national)

• a statement confirming that you do not have a criminal record

• authorization from a legal guardian if you are under 18.

Once your long-stay visa has been issued (the whole process can take up to three months) you are free to travel to France. Once in France you *must* apply for a *carte de séjour* within one week of your arrival. In other words, the visa gets you to France and the permit keeps you there.

Residence Permits

Most people reading this are either EU citizens who want to stay in France longer than three months, or non-EU citizens with a long-stay visa who want to stay in France longer than three months. In both cases, they need to get a *carte de séjour*.

The *carte de séjour* is a residence permit and has until recently been obligatory for pretty much anyone who intends to stay in France for more than 90 days. **In November 2003 the rules were changed (*see* box), and it is technically no longer necessary, but the French may take some time to get used to this and at the moment the word is that it will still make your life much easier to apply for one.**

There are different kinds of residence permits, including ones for long-stay visitors (*visiteur*), workers (*salarié*), family members (*membre de famille*), students (*étudiant*) and businesspeople (*commerçant*).

There are also two general headings under which the residence permit fall. The first is the *carte de séjour* and the second is the *carte de résident*.

> **The Carte de Séjour According to the British Embassy Website**
> 'A new French law, 2003-1119 of 26 November 2003, lifted the requirement for EU nationals (including British passport holders) wishing to reside in France, to hold a *carte de séjour*.
> 'British passport holders (and other EU nationals) can still apply for a *carte de séjour* if they wish to have some form of French identity document.'

Carte de Séjour

A simple translation for the *carte de séjour* is a 'temporary residence permit'. This is issued for EU and non-EU nationals alike and has a term of validity before it expires. For example, a *carte de séjour* issued to a non-EU national may be valid for one year before it must be renewed. If the non-EU national, for example, only has a work contract that lasts six months, his *carte de séjour* will be valid for six months. In most cases the *carte de séjour* for EU nationals is valid for 10 years and becomes a *carte de résident* (*see* below). But if the EU national does not have a job and cannot prove financial means, he will probably receive a one-year *carte de séjour* to be renewed when it expires. If you are under the age of 18, you will be listed on your parent or legal guardian's *carte de séjour*.

If you are a **non-EU citizen** and you have successfully renewed your *carte de séjour* each year for three years in a row, you can qualify for a *carte de résident*.

Carte de Résident

A simple translation for the *carte de résident* is 'permanent residence permit'. This is usually granted to EU citizens and to non-EU citizens who have successfully renewed their *carte de séjour* for three years in a row. The foreign spouse of a French national gets one immediately. The *carte de résident* is valid for 10 years, after which it can be renewed every 10 years (provided the holder can prove financial means).

To apply for a residence permit you need to go to the town hall (*mairie*) or police station (*commissariat de police*, also called *gendarmerie*) nearest you. In Paris, you should head to the 'foreigners' office' (*centre d'accueil des étrangers*) of the Préfecture de Police in your *arrondissement*. Remember, if you hold a long-stay visa, you must do this within one week of your arrival in France (although certain extensions are granted to students).

Here is a list of the paperwork you will probably have to provide:

- **your valid passport (or a national identity card if you are a EU citizen)**
- **your long-stay visa (only if you are a non-EU citizen)**
- **a certified birth certificate**
- **three passport-sized photographs (sometimes more are required and, inexplicably, sometimes the photos must be black and white)**

- proof of a residence in France (a copy of your lease (*quittance de loyer*) or a copy of the deed of sale on your house (*acte de vente*); or an electricity bill with your name on it, or a *certificat d'hébergement* if you are a guest at a friend or family member's home)
- proof that you have sufficient funds to cover the cost of your stay (such as a bank statement)
- proof of health insurance
- a marriage or divorce certificate (if your maiden name is not listed on your British passport, for example, you will be asked for this)
- a contract from an employer if you are working in France (if you are self-employed, take proof of registration for a trade from the *Chambre de Métiers* or proof of registration for a profession from the *Chambre de Commerce*, or proof of registration as a *Profession Libérale* from URSSAF)
- if you are retired, proof of pension payments
- a statement confirming that you do not have a criminal record
- proof of admission to an accredited school or university
- proof of a medical examination (sometimes required for students)
- an *au pair* agreement with a French family
- two self-addressed, stamped envelopes (not always requested).

Hopefully, you will have your paperwork in order upon your first visit. Since this is unlikely, know that you can request an extension (*prolongation*). Some of your documents must be translated by a notarized translator and these can be found under '*traducteurs*' in the local phone book. Your embassy in France can also provide you with a list of translators. Other documents need to be notarized at a public notary (*notaire*).

Until your residence permit is ready, you will be issued a receipt (*récépissé de demande de carte de séjour*). This is usually valid for three months and can be renewed if your residence permit process is delayed. You should keep the receipt with you in your wallet at all times, as you would your residence permit. This is required by French law.

Renewals of the residence permit should be made two months before it expires. A residence permit entitles you to French state benefits.

If you are a **non-EU citizen** and want to change the status of your residence permit you must request a *régularisation*. For example, let's say you are a retired American living in France. If you decide you want to sell antiques at the local fair, you would need to change the status of your *carte de séjour* to *carte de commerçant* to reflect the fact you are becoming self-employed. For more detail on the various steps you would need to take, see **Working in France**, 'Starting Your Own Business', pp.253–5.

As with all bureaucratic procedures, you will be expected to dish out a sizeable sum in fees, taxes and the tax stamps (*timbre fiscal*) that you affix to your documents.

The most frustrating thing about the process is the fact you will undoubtedly be fed conflicting and sometimes wrong information. One source might require three passport photos, the next eight. Plan on making repeat visits, queueing and resisting the temptation to raise your voice. Be prepared to learn things not listed in this book. An excellent resource (in French) for updates in the law concerning visas and permits is **www.prefecture-police-Paris.interieur.gouv.fr**. The embassies and consulates listed below are also extremely helpful.

Useful Addresses

The five British Consulates General in France are located in Paris, Bordeaux, Lille, Lyon and Marseille. The British Consulate General in Paris provides full consular services including full passport and visa services. Those in Bordeaux, Lille, Lyon and Marseille provide general consular assistance to British nationals as well as legalization and notarial services and voter registration information. All of them also provide a range of commercial services.

For more information and emergency contact numbers, go to **www.amb-grandebretagne.fr** or **www.britishinfrance.com**.

British Consulate-General in Paris

18bis rue d'Anjou, 75008 Paris
t 01 44 51 31 00
f 01 44 51 31 27
consulare-mailpavis.consulare-mailpavis2@fco.gov.uk
Open Mon, Wed, Thurs and Fri 9.30–12.30 and 2.30–5; Tues 9.30–4.30

Covers Aube, Calvados, Cher, Côtes-du-Nord, Eure, Eure-et-Loir, Finistère, Ille-et-Vilaine, Indre, Indre-et-Loire, Loir-et-Cher, Loire, Loire-Atlantique, Loiret, Maine-et-Loire, Manche (St-Lô), Marne, Haute-Marne, Mayenne, Meurthe-et-Moselle, Meuse, Morbihan, Moselle, Nievre, Oise, Orne, Bas-Rhin, Haut-Rhin, Sarthe, Paris (Seine), Seine-Maritime, Seine-et-Marne, Yvelins, Vendée, Vosges, Yonne, Essonne, Hauts-de-Seine, Seine-St-Denis, Val de Marne, Val d'Oise, French Guiana, Guadeloupe, Martinique, New Caledonia and Tahiti.

British Consulate-General in Bordeaux

353 boulevard du président Wilson, 33073 Bordeaux cedex
t 05 57 22 21 10
f 05 56 08 33 12
postmaster.bordeaux@fco.gov.uk
Open Mon–Fri 9am–noon and 2–5

Covers Ariège, Aveyron, Charente, Charente-Maritime, Corrèze, Creuse, Dordogne, Haute-Garonne, Gers, Gironde, Landes, Lot, Lot-et-Garonne, Pyrénées-Atlantiques, Hautes-Pyrénées, Deux-Sèvres, Tarn, Tarn-et-Garonne, Vienne and Haute-Vienne.

British Consulate-General in Lille
11 square Dutilleul, 59800 Lille
t 03 20 12 82 72
f 03 20 54 88 16
consular.lille@fco.gov.uk
Open Mon–Fri 9.30–12.30 and 2–5

Covers Nord, Pas-de-Calais, Somme, Aisne and Ardennes.

British Consulate-General in Lyon
24 rue Childebert, 69002 Lyon
t 04 72 77 81 70
f 04 72 77 81 79
britishconsulate.mail@ordilyon.fr
Open Mon–Fri 9–12.30 and 2–5.30

Covers Auvergne, Bourgogne, Franche-Comté and Rhône-Alpes.

British Consulate-General in Marseille
24 avenue du Prado, 13006 Marseille
t 04 91 15 72 10
f 04 91 37 47 06
marseilleconsular.marseille@fco.gov.uk
Open Mon–Fri 9–noon and 2–5

Covers Pyrénées-Orientales, Aude, Hérault, Lozère, Gard, Vaucluse, Bouches du Rhône, Var, Alpes-Maritimes, Hautes-Alpes, Alpes de Haute Provence, Corsica and Monaco.

French Embassies Abroad

French Embassy in Australia (**www.ambafrance-au.org**)
French Embassy in Canada (**www.ambafrance-ca.org**)
French Embassy in Ireland (**www.ambafrance.ie**)
French Embassy in New Zealand (**www.ambafrance-nz.org**)
French Embassy in South Africa (**www.ambafrance-rsa.org**)

French Embassy in the USA
4101 Reservoir Road, NW, Washington, DC 20007
t (202) 944-6000
f (202) 944-6166

www.info-france-usa.org
www.ambafrance-us.org
www.consulfrance-washington.org

Taxes

Now that you've swallowed that pill, here's another choker: taxes. The following is a run-down of some of the basic tax-related questions that may concern you. Please be warned, this is only intended as a general guide and if you have more complicated or pressing tax issues it would be imprudent not to seek the advice of a professional.

• **Must I pay French taxes?** The answer to this question depends on your status: whether you are a resident of France or not. A resident for tax purposes is a person who spends more than 183 days per year in France. If you spend less than 183 days you could still be a 'resident' if you have a permanent home in France, practise your profession in France or if your main economic interests are in France. Anyone who is not officially a resident of France is considered a 'non-resident'. Non-residents are liable for taxes in France in the following cases: if they make money from a rental property in France or if they receive a salary from a French employer.

• **What is taxed as income?** Your annual disposable income is what will be taxed. It includes any payments made with regards to your professional activity, investments and salary. It also includes capital gains received from the sale of real estate or investments. Taxes are calculated at a progressive rate that reaches a maximum of 54 per cent for incomes over c45,000. Remember that many allowances, deductions and provisions are in place thanks to reciprocal tax treaties between France and other countries such as the UK. They help chisel your annual disposable income down to the 'net taxable income'.

• **What else should I pay?** You will have to pay France's famous social charges (either the CSG or the CRDS; *see* **Living in France**, 'Social Services and Welfare Benefits', p.214 for more information on these). The employer usually deducts them. Residents who make money from a rental property or investments in France pay a flat social charge fee of 10 per cent. There will also be local property taxes to be paid in your region.

• **What deductions can be made?** Certain expenses you incur to help you make money can be deducted or are turned into tax credits. These include: business expenses that were not reimbursed, business rent, finance charges, travel to and from work and the social security contributions of self-employed people.

• **Are there personal allowances?** Under the French system, your taxable income is divided by the number of 'allowances' you are entitled to. Those allowances are linked to how many people are in your family. A single person has one allowance. A married couple with two children has three allowances. On the tax form you submit you will be asked to fill in your income, your expenses and your deductions.

• **When are taxes due?** The fiscal year ends at the end of March, covering the period from 1 January to 31 December of the previous year. When you have submitted your tax form, the French authorities calculate the amount due and send you a bill. In general, residents pay one-third in February and one-third in May with the remainder due some time between September and December. If it is more convenient you can arrange to pay in monthly instalments with the balance due at the year's end. Remember that if this is the first time you are paying taxes in France, the tax on the previous year's income is paid in full between September and December of the following year.

Non-residents, on the other hand, file their returns between May and the end of June. All French income must be declared, although you should find out the details of the tax treaties between France and your country of residence because certain exemptions do apply. If your country has a tax treaty with France (as England does) it is likely you will receive a credit against the tax due in your country for taxes paid in France.

• **What happens if I don't pay?** There is a penalty of 10 per cent for taxes filed late and not paid by the due date and you will probably be asked for interest on the outstanding tax (in the past this has been 0.75 per cent per month).

More detailed tax information can be found at **www.inlandrevenue.gov.uk/international** (in English), **www.impots.gouv.fr** (in French) or **www.finances.gouv.fr** (in French).

Living in France

06

You're finally ready to make the move. The following chapter details step-by-step the things the things you need to do – and not do – to make your experience as comforting and rewarding as possible. Information is included on a wide range of topics from how to install broadband for a faster internet service, to which licence you need for driving in France, to enrolling your children in school.

Of all the things we can recommend for a productive life in France, first and foremost is to learn the language (*see* below). Being able to communicate is the key to successful integration in a foreign society, and you will be happier.

Although you're unlikely to suffer from serious bouts of culture shock, other expatriates have identified various phases of cultural adjustment they experienced when they moved to France. First is excitement and enthusiasm. You'll love studying the dozens of cheeses in the supermarket or tuning your radio to the latest French sounds. The next stage is disbelief, frustration and loss. After a few years, or just months in some cases, you start to question why you came to France in the first place. The cheeses stink, as do those songs on the radio – and it takes particular intestinal fortitude to listen to the French ones. In the third stage, you make a renewed effort to learn French culture from a new and balanced perspective. Now you have started to *live* in France and you can mouth the words to your favourite songs. The fourth and last stage is acclimatization and belonging. Your cultural transition is complete (but count on going through round two of culture shock if you move back home).

Learning French

Besides falling in love with a dreamy French man or woman who will tickle your ears with romantic conversation day and night, the only other effective way to learn the language is to study it at the source. Thousands of foreigners come here each year to do just that, and there are more language schools, both public and private, than you can shake a *dictionnaire* at.

Learning French can be a pleasure or a pain, depending on how you approach the task. We are all aware of the infamous unwillingness of the French to brave what they perceive as butchery of their beautiful language by our clumsy tongues and intolerable accents. As a student of the French language there is nothing more frustrating than having your carefully worded and enunciated queries answered in English (bad English at that). Or worse yet is when you finally get that difficult French sentence out, only to receive a sneer of disapproval followed by the blood-curdling: '*Quoi?*' The French can be downright demoralizing to language students and are unparalleled in this respect. Mark Twain said it best: 'In Paris they just opened their eyes and stared when we

Rules of Pronunciation

Vowels

a/à/â between *a* in 'bat' and 'part'
é/er/ez at end of word as *a* in 'plate' but a bit shorter
e/è/ê as *e* in 'bet'
e at end of word not pronounced
e at end of syllable or in one-syllable word pronounced weakly, like *er* in 'mother'
i as *ee* in 'bee'
o as *o* in 'pot'
ô as *o* in 'go'
u/û between *oo* in 'boot' and *ee* in 'bee'

Vowel Combinations

ai as *a* in 'plate'
aî as *e* in 'bet'
ail as *i* in 'kite'
au/eau as *o* in 'go'
ei as *e* in 'bet'
eu/œu as *er* in 'mother'
oi between *wa in* 'swam' and *wu* in 'swum'
oy as 'why'
ui as *wee* in 'twee'

Nasal Vowels

Vowels followed by an **n** or **m** have a nasal sound.
an/en as *o* in 'pot' + nasal sound
ain/ein/in as *a* in 'bat' + nasal sound
on as *aw* in 'paw' + nasal sound
un as *u* in 'nut' + nasal sound

Consonants

Many French consonants are pronounced as in English, but there are some exceptions:
c followed by *e, i* or *y,* and *ç* as *s* in 'sit'
c followed by *a, o, u* as *c* in 'cat'
g followed by *e, i* or *y* as *s* in 'pleasure'
g followed by *a, o, u* as *g* in 'good'
gn as *ni* in 'opinion'
j as *s* in 'pleasure'
ll as *y* in 'yes'
qu as *k* in 'kite'
s between vowels as *z* in 'zebra'
s otherwise as *s* in 'sit'
w except in English words as *v* in 'vest'
x at end of word as *s* in 'sit'
x otherwise as *x* in 'six'

Stress

The stress usually falls on the last syllable except when the word ends with an unaccented **e**.

spoke to them in French. We never did succeed in making those idiots understand their own language.'

The only effective strategy is to overwhelm: rattle off in your French for as long as you can like an automatic weapon, be exceedingly chipper and cheery, but don't stop talking and you will eventually succeed in subduing even the most fervent linguistic fascist into timid submission. *Bonne chance*!

Thankfully, once you get past the beginning stages you will find that French is one of the most rewarding and stimulating languages to learn. It's also a fun language to speak, with an attractive range of vocabulary words and idiomatic expressions, to whet your appetite for French culture, friendships and – yes – politics. You will not integrate successfully until you speak French (for more on the history and evolution of the French language, *see* **Getting to Know France**, 'The French Language', pp.22–4).

Talented and enthusiastic foreigners learn French by chatting with shopkeepers, going to French cinemas and staying active in their community. If learning a foreign language doesn't come naturally to you, you could sign on for private one-on-one lessons (the going rate is about €30 per hour of instruction) or become involved in a language exchange, swapping an hour of English with an hour of French conversation. Or, you could arrange for a wine-tasting or cooking session at home with other Francophiles. Watching French television helps more than you think.

But the fastest and most effective way to learn French is by taking a **language course**. There are intensive courses that last a few months with classes five days a week, or more relaxed courses in which you might study one day a week over many months. The telephone directory and the internet are full of advertisements (check **www.pagesjaunes.fr**).

One important consideration to take into account when choosing a course is whether you need a diploma of French fluency upon completion. Some jobs or applications to a French university may require a fluency certificate. You can even study for diplomas in business French, medical French or French for official translators and interpreters. Most of the private language schools listed in the *Yellow Pages* offer their own 'certificates of completion', but, depending on the reputation of the school, that diploma might not hold much weight. If you are studying for yourself, getting a diploma is probably not your objective. But if you require an officially recognized fluency certificate there are many options available to you.

The **DELF** (*Diplôme d'Etudes de Langue Française*) and **DALF** (*Diplôme Approfondi de Langue Française*), the most recognized exams to test fluency skills, are sponsored by the French Ministry of Education. The DELF has six levels of competency and after you pass the first four you receive a degree. Following successful completion of the last two, you receive an advanced diploma. The DALF exam is often required if you intend to enrol in a French university. The results are scored in terms of *très bien, bien, assez bien* and *sans mention*.

Another alternative is to study for one of the prestigious diplomas offered by the **Alliance Française (www.alliancefr.org)**. These are designed for students of all levels whose native language is not French. The diplomas are recognized internationally (in the 130 countries where the Alliance Française operates) and are based on European Council recommendations as outlined by the ALTE (Association of Language Testers in Europe). Testing centres are in Paris and throughout the country. Alliance Française is also a testing centre for DELF and DALF certificates. Alliance Française exams have different levels including CEFP 1 (*Certificat d'Etudes Françaises*), CEFP 2, the DL (*Diplôme de Langue Française*), DS (*Diplôme Supérieur d'Etudes Françaises*) and the DHEF (*Diplôme de Hautes Etudes Françaises*). The DL and the DS are the most common and the DHEF is recommended for teachers of French. These are 'pass or fail' exams.

Other language certificates are organized by the **Chamber of Commerce and Industry** in Paris and test a candidate's ability to use the language of a specific professional realm. Candidates must participate in a three-month preparatory course to qualify for the exam.

Finding a Home

Whether you intend to rent or buy, making a home in France is by far the most important component of life abroad. In many respects, it *is* your life abroad. Thankfully, there are more resources available now than ever to help turn your dreams of life in France into bricks and mortar. It is relatively easy to set up a home in France thanks to the internet, cheaper air fares, increased financing options, banks that operate internationally, good property prices that keep their value over the long term, a wide range of properties on the market, bilingual estate agents, more reference sources (such as Cadogan's more comprehensive *Buying a Property: France*) and, most importantly, a growing and vibrant ex-patriate community. Thousands of Britons have successfully made a home in France and have paved the way for your own transition abroad.

The most pressing consideration is where you will make your home. Choosing the location that is right for you is paramount; for some help on this, *see* **Profiles of the Regions**, pp.25–48. If you are moving here for a job, choosing a location is probably not an option open to you. But if you are looking for a summer residence, a second home, a retirement spot or a place from which to freelance, France is your oyster.

Buying a Property

Deciding where to make your home is not just a matter of deciding which French region you like best. It entails deep thought and on-the-ground research of other significant factors such as proximity to shops, schools for your children,

Case Study: Barge Life

Carolyn and Roland Muri are certified world travellers – restless and energized. Following years of keeping pace with revved-up Romans, Londoners and New Yorkers, they were suddenly awash in bucolic dreams. But moving to the remote country seemed too extreme.

Barge life was a perfect solution. 'Ten years ago we were invited to help crew a cabin cruiser on the Nivernais canal. This was a totally new experience but after a week we fell in love with the rolling hills of the Morvan dotted with creamy Charolais cattle, the peace and quiet. Each morning we would hop on our bicycles and pedal through the countryside. Mooring under a 14th-century chateau had its appeal too. The week was over too quickly and we vowed we would one day return to the canals.'

A few years ago, they spotted a 20-metre Luxemotor converted Dutch barge with three bedrooms and a lovely living room for sale at St-Jean de Losne, about 30km south of Dijon in Burgundy. This is the barge capital of France – a country with 5,500km of canals from the north Pas de Calais area, through Champagne, Burgundy, to the Camargue and the Canal du Midi as far as Bordeaux.

It was not all plain sailing. 'We probably underestimated the learning curve as far as the actual machinery is concerned: the engine, water pumps, battery maintenance and electrics. We have faced quite a few challenges. Work in dry dock recommended by the survey had to be postponed due to river flooding. The wooden inside of the barge had to be dismantled due to fire risk before welding on the hull could proceed.' Then, came the dreadful summer of 2003: 'Forty degrees centigrade inside a steel hull with no shade is not a barrel of laughs.' They had guests that took too many showers, thus depleting the batteries. Another time the water pump mysteriously filled and the toilet would not flush. They consulted their boat owner's bible, tackled the pump and extracted a small fish.

But they love this lifestyle. 'We have visits on the deck from a pair of swans, we have been woken by mallards demanding breakfast. It's an opportunity to travel without the hassle of roads and hotels and it's a great chance to meet people from all over the world. Flexibility and a sense of adventure are the prime requisites.'

In a nod to their experiences, the Muris named their boat *Otium*. 'It's a Latin word meaning "learned leisure", and was an essential part of a Roman senator's life after he had fulfilled his obligations to society, as in *negotium*. We decided to spend our retirement like the Romans of old, in the country with books, studying and congenial company.'

businesses, doctors, transport and community. You might stumble across your dream home on a remote hilltop in Provence drenched in golden sunlight and surrounded by lavender fields. But when you realize the nearest foreign newspaper shop is some 50km away, that idyllic country life loses its lustre. So many city-dwellers make the mistake of buying homes based purely on aesthetic impact. Once the sun sets, what they thought was 'quaint isolation' becomes *Friday the Thirteenth* terror. They lie in bed with eyes wide open listening to the deafening sounds of nature: screeching owls, human-like wails of felines on heat and the pitter-patter of rats scurrying on tile roofs. After just one night, they're ready to move back to the city.

There are other practical issues to consider. The first is shopping. Country homes are usually only serviced by a small collection of food shops that sell the basics like bread, sugar, cold meats, tinned goods and cleaning detergents, with a produce market open mornings only. Bigger towns are flanked by supermarkets on the outskirts. If you cannot live without the plentiful resources of a full-blown shopping centre, you're better off at least near to a city or town. If you intend to brave country life, make sure you have a large vehicle. Your shopping expeditions will be as momentous as when Noah filled his ark.

Besides food shopping, you'll have to think about various supplies and building equipment such as plywood, bricks, plumbing parts and gardening material. And you'll need to keep an eye on services available nearby. For example, if your water boiler has a nasty habit of breaking down frequently, getting a service representative to travel kilometres over dirt roads might be more trying than braving ice-cold showers.

Choosing a location also means identifying the nearest hospital and accessibility to doctors. This is especially important for the elderly. Transport is another concern. If you often travel for work , you'll need to be close to an airport, major motorways or a train station. You'll need to know if there are schools in your area for your children. If your preference is an English-language education, this will further limit your choices. Thought should be given to whether you want to live near a gym, swimming pool or golf club. Again, most of these things are easier to find closer to urban centres, and if this makes it sound as if some country areas in France are completely desolate, they are.

Foreign homeowners are faced with an additional concern that does not apply to the French. This is finding a location either near to or away from other expatriates. There are two kinds of foreigner in France. The first group is intent on successful full-immersion. These are Britons who would prefer to live as far away as possible from other Britons. They speak French fluently, read French newspapers and have mostly French friends. The second group is the so-called 'cultural colonialists'. They are much larger in number and their primary concern is to make France feel more like home. They watch BBC by satellite, go out of their way to buy British foods, and surround themselves with people who can understand their affection for two countries (almost always other expatriates). Within this group are extremes: those who never make the effort to assimilate, and those who find a happy medium between their British and French halves.

Research

House-hunting usually starts in front of the computer with a meticulous search of properties listed on the internet. Plug in a few key words like 'property', 'buying', 'house' and 'France', and your search engine is likely to throw thousands of web links back at you. There are simply too many to list in this book, and a careful search will produce mouthwatering photographs of properties that go on and off the market each week.

Otherwise you can start your search with traditional media. In the UK, *World of Property* and *International Homes* are two publications with ample listings in France. More specific are *French Property News*, *Focus on France* and *Living in France* magazine – all available in the UK.

France is exceedingly well represented at property shows in the UK and often an entire trade show will be focused on the country. At property exhibitions, you can meet estate agents, lawyers for consultation and financial advisers who can explain the intricacies of mortgages. Seminars are organized, and the exhibition gives you a chance to rummage through thousands of photographs and pamphlets of dream homes. There are two main exhibition series: Homes Overseas and World of Property. For information on when and here the next trade show will take place, see **www.tsnn.co.uk** or **www.internationalproperty show.com**.

Estate Agents

The vast majority of foreigners who buy property in France do so with the help of an estate agent, and opinions on them are polarized. Some estate agents are the subject of frequent complaints and have been tagged with every insult imaginable, from greedy to dishonest. Others are praised for their keen ability to supply the buyer with a wealth of information and knowledge about a particular property. As a result, it is very important that you choose well and establish a strong rapport with your agent. But keep one thought firmly in the back of your mind: the estate agent represents the seller's interests, and these do not usually coincide with yours.

In a sense, the internet is your fiercest ally because it represents a system of checks and balances. You can preview properties from home. You can form impressions – whether positive or negative – with just a few clicks of the mouse. Ironically, the internet makes the estate agent's job both easier and more difficult: easier because the internet connects sellers to agents, and agents to buyers; more difficult because the estate agent can no longer rely on haughty adjectives printed in a black and white advert to attract customers. A picture is worth a thousand words – especially when it can be compressed and downloaded within seconds to buyers. The internet means that estate agents can't afford to misrepresent the truth.

There are two main groups of estate agents, French and foreign, and there are pros and cons to both. Some buyers swear by French estate agents, especially ones based very close to the property in question, because they have a deeper understanding of the practical issues – planning regulations, possible problems and the neighbourhood. Many estate agents are also close friends or relatives of the people surrounding your target property (or even of its owner), which guarantees an 'insider's' approach. Having a French agent to represent you might remove some of the seller's temptation to overcharge. On the other hand, a foreign estate agent – and many are British – can speak your language and therefore better understand your needs; for example, a foreign estate agent has probably dealt more extensively with buyers who want to restore a property or with people transferring large sums of money from abroad. Choosing between the two groups might ultimately be decided by your fluency in French. The importance of good communication between agent and buyer cannot be exaggerated.

A French agent (*agent immobilier*) must be professionally qualified and must hold a *carte professionnelle* to practise. Most have indemnity insurance and a fidelity bond (*pièce de garantie*). The agent's licence is usually framed on display in his office. Most also join the French equivalent of the British National Association of Estate Agents, known as FNAIM (*Fédération Nationale des Agents Immobiliers et Mandataires*) or a competing professional body known as SNPI (*Syndicat National des Professionnels de l'Immobilier*).

In order to sell property, an estate agent must be licensed and must have written permission from the owner (*mandat*). However, many agents operate illegally without the licence or the mandate. Some are Britons selling to Britons or Germans selling to Germans. You will be told to avoid their services, but the truth is many are excellent at what they do.

There are also a growing number of estate agents based in the UK, who are technically not licensed to sell in France but who sell here anyway. They often work in association with French agents, generally covering a wider area than a single French agent would. Most charge a fee or a commission of the sale. They are a convenient alternative for those buying from the UK and you can find them through the internet or at a property exhibition.

Other buyers, particularly those with a good command of French, opt to buy property directly from the seller (*de particulier à particulier*). There is nothing wrong with this; in fact, many buyers prefer it. Un-agented property is common in France, although foreigners usually have a hard time finding it because they instinctively gravitate towards the agencies.

Some 20 per cent of property in France is sold by a notary public (*notaire*) acting as an estate agent. It may seem strange that the person charged with the transfer of ownership on behalf of both the buyer and seller would be representing the property (imagine a solicitor selling a property) – but it is normal here.

Some agents will tell you that you do not need to use a lawyer – that the services of the local notary public will suffice. Ignore that advice. It is quite true that the average French person would not use the services of an independent lawyer when buying a house unless there was something complex about the transaction or about their own circumstances. For a foreigner, however, this is generally not good enough. There are many issues on which you will need guidance that it is no part of the notary's duty to provide. Furthermore, your French notary will almost certainly know nothing about British law and so will be unable to give you any help as far as such vital issues as who should own the property in order to make the most of UK *and* French tax and inheritance rules.

When you make an appointment to visit a property, bring a notepad, a digital camera and a map. If you see more than four homes in one day, the details concerning the first house will be indistinguishable from those of the last. Take notes and pictures of rooms you might like to restore, bathroom fixtures you might like to move and gardening you'd like to plan. These will come in handy when you come back for a second visit. Most experts recommend not seeing more than four properties per day. If you are making appointments with agents from abroad via the internet, take note of the reference or tracking number, and check the property's availability: turnover rates are high and you wouldn't want to travel to France to find that the property you wanted is already sold. After you've seen a batch of possibilities, find a good restaurant, relax with a glass of wine and discuss.

Basic Questions

- **What are you looking for?** Options range from country farmhouse to city apartment; condominium to houseboat/barge on a canal.
- **Where are you looking?** Understand which region best reflects your character and needs.
- **Why are you buying?** Are you looking for a second home where you can spend summers? An investment property? A place to raise your children or a base from which to work? Are you looking for a retirement place?
- **Is your financial picture in focus?** Make sure you understand what the euro can buy.
- **Have you worked out a budget?** As a rule of thumb, most home-buyers purchase properties that cost 1.5 to 2.5 times their annual income.
- **Do you need to secure a loan?**
- **Do you plan to remodel?** Factor this into your budget.
- **How much should you offer for a house?** If you feel it is overpriced, offer 20 or 30 per cent below the asking price to start with. If the property is priced at what you think it is worth, make an offer slightly below the asking price. If it is underpriced, grab it fast.

- Can you talk down the asking price? Usually yes. Factors like a sitting tenant, a leaking roof, warped or un-level floors, termites or damp in walls should be used as 'negotiating chips' in your favour.

- Should you spend money on a home inspection? Yes. Make an appointment with a contractor to check plumbing, roofs, floors and humidity as soon as possible.

- Are there outstanding mortgages or loans on the property?

- Are there outstanding property taxes on the property?

- Are there outstanding utilities connected to the property?

- Does the property have the relevant building licences? If a window has been enlarged, or an extra room added, make sure it has been recorded on the property deed.

- What is the water situation? Some country properties have shared wells. Check that all relevant neighbours have given their consent for water use.

- Have you checked the planning regulations? If you plan to turn a barn into a residence, make sure planning permission is available.

- Is there a sitting tenant in the property? If there is you will have an impossible time kicking them out – even if they simply decide to stop paying rent.

Auctions (*Ventes aux Enchères*)

Property in France can be bought at auction, just as in England. Some auctions are voluntary, others run by court order. The voluntary auctions are run by notaries (*Marché Immobilier des Notaires*). Only notaries are permitted to run voluntary auctions. There are relatively few such auctions. There you will find a combination of properties that the sellers have decided to sell in this way: properties that have 'stuck' in the market, properties that the sellers think will sell best at auction, and properties that have been inherited which the heirs wish to dispose of quickly. One attraction of such auctions for the seller is that his share of the auctioneers' fees (usually one per cent of the price) is lower that the normal level of estate agents' fees (say, five per cent).

Other auctions are judicial auctions (*ventes judiciares*). In theory there are several circumstances where the law requires a sale by auction but increasingly, in practice and by consent, these sales take place as ordinary sales by private agreement in order to save the considerable cost of an auction. In a judicial auction you will find properties sold, for example, as a result of mortgage repossession, unpaid debts, disputes between joint owners, in connection with the administration of the estate of someone who has died or by virtue of some other court order.

Prices can be very attractive. A few years ago, during the last recession, there were incredible bargains at, perhaps, 30 per cent of 'value'. Now auctions usually offer less spectacular bargains. The bargains are because, particularly in many judicial auctions, the process is intended first and foremost to recover someone's debt. Once that and the considerable costs have been covered there is little reason to press for a higher price, even though the owner will ultimately receive the excess.

Buying a property at auction is not simple for someone who does not live in the area and it is vitally important that you have taken all the normal preparatory steps – including seeing a lawyer – before you embark on the process. The procedure leading up to the auction is basically the same whether the auction is a judicial auction or a notarial auction. First, you must know that the auction is taking place. They are usually advertised six to eight weeks in advance. Auctions ordered by the court will be advertised by order of the court in the local press. Notices will also be posted in the area.

Secondly, you must find out what is in the auction. Brief details of the property to be sold should be available, including the *commune*'s land/rating registry (*cadastre*) reference, the arrangements for viewing, the notary dealing with the sale, the reserve price and the deposit that must be lodged in order that you can be allowed to bid. These details of the property will mean nothing to you. The place could be derelict or next door to a nuclear power station. You will need to inspect the property personally and decide whether it is of interest. This is a time-consuming and potentially costly process. Remember that you could have to inspect 20 properties to find three you might like and then you might be outbid on all three. An alternative to personal inspection is to get someone to do it for you. This is not as satisfactory but a local estate agent will, for a fee of about £200, go to look at the property and give you a description of it. Some people buy blind. This is for real poker-players.

Thirdly, you will need to check out the legal situation of the property before the date of the auction. Most of the steps needed in an ordinary purchase will be required.

Fourthly, many properties on sale by auction are not in the best condition. You will therefore need to get estimates as to the likely cost of repairs or improvements so as to make sure that the price you bid is not so high as to make the project non-viable.

Fifthly, you will have to appoint a notary or local lawyer (*avocat*) to act on your behalf at the auction. At a judicial auction individuals cannot turn up and bid as they can in England. Only notaries and *avocats* are entitled to bid. Even at an ordinary notarial auction you would be brave or foolish not to be represented. The lawyer will explain precisely what will need to be done for this particular auction. You will have to tell him the maximum price you want to offer and pay him the bidding deposit – a refundable deposit levied by the auctioneer in order to allow you to enter a bid. You will also have to give your personal details (marital status, occupation, nationality, passport number, etc.) and a deposit of

10 per cent of the price you are offering, less the bidding deposit. The full deposit is paid across at the time your bid is accepted.

You do not need to attend the auction – the lawyer will be able to do so for you. He will probably require a power of attorney for that purpose. He will, of course, charge you for this work. The fee can be substantial, so get an estimate. Even though you do not need to be present, an auction (especially a judicial auction) is a most interesting event, so you might want to go along. The traditional auction, gradually disappearing, is the 'candle' auction (*vente à la chandelle*). The sale is *à la bougie* or *aux trois feux*. This picturesque, if confusing and often noisy, affair sells the property on the extinction of a candle flame. Once the last bid has been received, a 20-second taper is lit. Once it burns out, a second is lit. If no further bids are received, a third – the knock-down candle (*feu d'adjudication*) is lit. Once that splutters out the sale is made!

If you are successful, your deposit will be taken. You will then have to wait 10 days to know whether you have actually got the property, as the results of the auction can be attacked during that period by anyone who is prepared to bid 10 per cent more than the sale price (*surenchère*). This might, for example, be the dispossessed owner of the property that has been sold for a pittance by the bank that repossessed it. If the auction is challenged it will be repeated. It can only be challenged once and it is a rare event.

Although the prices at auction can be very attractive, you must bear in mind that you will face additional costs over and above those on a normal purchase. These are likely to raise the overall costs of buying from the normal 8–9 per cent of the price to perhaps 17–20 per cent of the price paid. The extra costs include the fees paid to your lawyers for dealing with the auction, extra land registry fees for publishing the result, and the fees and charges related to the auction itself.

On the other hand, many people will be entitled to automatic mortgage finance of 60 per cent of the price paid if they buy at a notarial auction. Check with your lawyer if this will apply to you.

What Preparation Should You Make?

Understand the System

The system of buying and selling property in France is, not surprisingly, different from the system of buying property in England or Scotland – on balance, neither better nor worse – just different. It has many superficial similarities, which can lull you into a false sense of familiarity and over-confidence. The most important thing to remember is that buying a home in France is just as safe as buying a home in Cardiff – providing that you take the right professional advice and precautions when doing so. If you do not take such advice there are many expensive traps for the unwary. It will help you to avoid the problems and to ask the necessary questions of those advising you if you have a broad general understanding of the processes involved.

See a Lawyer

It will save you a lot of time and trouble if you see your lawyer before you find a property. There are a number of preliminary issues that can best be discussed in the relative calm before you find the house of your dreams rather than once you are under pressure to sign some document to commit yourself to the purchase. These issues will include:

- **who should own the property, bearing in mind the French inheritance. rules and the French and British tax consequences of ownership**
- **whether to consider mortgage finance and if so in which country**
- **what to do about converting the purchase price into euros**
- **if you are going to be living in France, sorting out the tax and investment issues that will need to be dealt with before your move if you are to get the best out of both systems.**

Only UK lawyers who specialize in dealing with France will be able to help you fully. Your normal English solicitor will know little or nothing of the issues of French law and a French lawyer is likely to know little or nothing about the British tax system or the issues of English or Scots law that will affect the way the transaction should be arranged. The lawyer may also be able to recommend estate agents, architects, surveyors and other contacts in the area you are looking in.

A physical meeting is still the best way to start an important relationship. It has a number of advantages. It allows you to show and be shown documents, and wander off more easily into related topics. Most importantly, it is usually easier to make certain that you have each understood the other in a face-to-face meeting. But, these days, 'seeing' your lawyer does not need to involve an actual meeting. If it is more convenient to you it could be done by telephone conference call or videoconference over the internet.

Decide on Ownership

Who should be the owner of your new home? This is the most important decision you will have to make when buying a property. Because of the combination of the French inheritance rules – which do not allow you to leave your property as you please – and the French and British tax systems, getting the ownership wrong can be a very expensive mistake indeed. It can lead to the wrong people being entitled to inherit the property from you (a particular problem for people with children from more than one relationship) and it can lead to totally unnecessary tax during your lifetime and on your death. Even on a modest property this unnecessary tax can amount to tens of thousands of pounds. See further 'Who Should Own the Property?', pp.154–6.

Get an Offer of Mortgage/Finance

These days, with very low interest rates, more and more people borrow at least part of the money needed to buy their home in France. Even if they don't need to do so, for many it makes good business or investment sense. If you want to borrow money to part-finance your purchase it makes sense to get clearance before you start looking at property. Whether you want to borrow on your UK property or on the overseas property, your lawyers should be able to put you in touch with suitable lenders. They will process your application and give you a preliminary clearance to borrow up to a certain amount. This, of course, is subject to the property and its title later proving satisfactory. Doing this removes the need for an embarrassing call to the agent a week after you have bought the property to tell him that you can't raise the finance. Getting a preliminary clearance in this way does not restrict your freedom to take up a better offer if one comes to light whilst you are looking at properties.

Think about How You Will Pay a Deposit

If you are going shopping for property you will need to have access to some money to pay for it and you will normally need to put down a preliminary deposit of five or 10 per cent of the price of the property. How should you make this payment?

Some estate agencies, particularly those operating from Britain, will ask you to take a banker's draft for the likely amount of any deposit. Fortunately there are few of these. This is not a good idea. It is ideal for the estate agent and the seller, but puts the buyer under subtle but unnecessary pressure to spend the money on something. Happily, the usual way of paying the deposit is still via a British cheque for the sterling equivalent of the euros needed. This is a simple and effective method of payment. There is, however, a further option that people are increasingly using. This is to leave the amount likely to be needed as a deposit with their specialist lawyer in the UK. Then, when you have found the right property and the estate agent is asking you to sign some form of contract, you can tell him that it is your lawyer who has the money. You will sign the contract as soon as he has approved it and that he will then transfer the funds into the estate agent's bank account by electronic transfer. The lawyer should be able to check a contract faxed to him whilst you wait and be able to tell you that its terms appear reasonable, and that any necessary special clauses have been included. He will also be able to tell you the nature of the contract you are signing (formal offer, reservation, option or full contract) and explain, briefly, its legal effects.

This has a number of advantages. It can take a lot of pressure off you. It makes it very hard for the agent to persuade you to sign a document which has – in every case – far-reaching consequences without getting it checked. From the agent's point of view it means that he will receive the cleared funds within a couple of days rather than the two or three weeks it can take for your British cheque to pass through the banking system and be cleared into his account. This preliminary check by the lawyer, though useful, is limited. He will not have seen proof of title or planning consents. He will not have inspected the detailed documentation relating to the construction of a new building. He will not have been able to carry out any checks on the property. But it is a great deal better than nothing.

This really only works well if you have made contact with your lawyer before you go to look at properties, as he will need to understand something about your circumstances before being able to give sensible advice about, for example, the special clauses needed in the contract.

Building from Scratch or Renovation

Prepare a huge reserve of 'elbow grease' if you plan to build or restore your property. If you are not keen on do-it-yourself or if your bank account is close to imploding, think twice before embarking down this path. But if you are a creative and enthusiastic home restorer there is no shortage of derelict property available in all stages of decay poised to become your next pet project.

Building a new home costs about €800 per square metre for finished work (unfinished work, which is just walls and plumbing but not decorative details like carpeting or tiling, is about half that). Restoring an old home also costs €800 per square metre for finished work. That means it costs the same amount to build from scratch as it does to renovate. In most cases, renovation costs more in the long term because demolition costs must also be factored in.

The only way to bring down renovation costs is to do most of the work yourself. You will face steep prices if you have to install electricity cables, water, septic tanks, air-conditioning, broadband wiring for internet service, wells, swimming pools or hook up to utilities if they are far away. Remember that an old country house rarely has these amenities. Although do-it-yourself materials are readily available in France, they can be very expensive (the VAT tax doesn't help keep costs down, either). You will find stores that sell fireplaces, above-ground swimming pools, porcelain for bathrooms, lighting fixtures and everything else. You can also find junkyards or salvage dealers who sell antique bathtubs, masonry and ironwork. Many foreigners drive over with loads of supplies, such as paint, that may cost less in the UK.

French labour is highly specialized and extremely good. Many builders consider themselves artisans and take great pride in being perfectionists and carrying out the trade that was passed on to them by their fathers. The VAT tax should always be included in estimates (*devis*) and should reflect the tax paid on building labour and material. (You should keep the receipts so that the costs can be set against the perceived gain on the resale of the property for French capital gains tax.) If you approve the estimate, you will usually be asked to pay a deposit of 10–25 per cent before work starts and follow up with monthly

Safer Swimming Pools

In December 2002, the French parliament passed the Raffarin Law to make private swimming pools safer for both children and pets. Under the new legislation, pool owners are obliged to install a standardized security system (*dispositif de sécurité normalisé*), which must be in place before 1 January 2006, or face a €45,000 penalty. The law does not apply to indoor pools or above-ground pools. The *dispositif de sécurité normalisé* consists of compulsory fencing around the pool (1.10m high with a child-proof entrance), reinforced pool covers (that cover the surface of the water and the edges of the pool and that must support the weight of an adult), drowning alarms (that detect objects which have fallen in with infra-red technology) and pool shelters. Permission to build new pools will only be granted to those who have applied the new security system to their pool designs.

payments or some other payment scheme depending on what you negotiate. Never give too much money up-front, and check the price of materials to make sure you are not being overcharged. It is always a good idea to establish a completion date with your builder. Like anywhere else, there are stories of builders taking deposit money and then disappearing, or builders who get halfway through the project, become discouraged and then disappear, leaving you roofless or waterless. Some foreigners bring foreign workers with them, but this is usually more costly, and not a smart move since the electricity systems are different and the foreign builder probably won't be familiar with French building and safety regulations.

Property Inspection

Whatever property you are thinking of buying, you should think about having it inspected before you commit yourself to the purchase. In fact – foolishly – very few buyers of property in France do this. There is no tradition of doing so. It costs just as much and causes just as much disruption to repair property in France as in the UK, so you don't want any surprises.

A new property will be covered by a two-year guarantee (*responsabilité garantie biennale*), running from the date of handover (*reception des travaux*), covering defects to equipment in the new property. The property will also benefit from a guarantee in respect of major structural defects that will last for 10 years (*garantie décennale*). As a subsequent purchaser you assume the benefit of these guarantees. After 10 years you are on your own! For property more than 10 years old (and, arguably, for younger property too) you should consider a survey.

Most surveys can be done in seven to 10 days and a number of options are available to you. Whichever report you opt for, its quality will depend in part on your input. Agree clearly and in writing the things you expect to be covered in the report. If you do not speak French (and the surveyor doesn't speak good English) you may have to ask someone to write on your behalf. Your UK lawyer would probably be the best bet. Some of the matters you may wish to think about are set out below. Some of these will involve you in additional cost. Ask what will be covered as part of the standard fee and get an estimate for the extras.

Types of Survey

Estate Agent's Valuation and 'Survey'

It may be possible to arrange for another local estate agent to give the property a quick 'once over' to comment on the price asked and any obvious problem areas. This is far short of a survey. It is likely to cost about £200.

Mortgage Lender's Survey

This is no substitute for a proper survey. Many lenders do not ask for one and, where they do, it is normally fairly peremptory, limited to a check on whether it is imminently about to fall over and whether it is worth the money the bank is lending you.

French Builder

If you are going to do a virtual demolition and rebuild then it might make more sense to get a builder to do a report on the property. A reputable and experienced qualified builder (*maître d'œuvres*) will also be able to comment on whether the price is reasonable for the property in its existing state. Make sure you ask for a binding written quotation (*devis*) for any building work proposed. These are excellent documents that set out clearly the work required and the charge for doing it. As in any country, it is as well to get several quotes, though in rural areas this can be tricky.

French Surveyor

There are a number of options here. There is no single profession of 'surveyor' in France as we have it in England. Instead, different professionals carry out surveys that are different from each other and appropriate in different circumstances. Seek advice about which to use in your case. The local notary or estate agent can put you in touch with the right people. In most rural areas there will be limited choice but, for obvious reasons, it is perhaps better not to seek a recommendation from the estate agent selling the property. Alternatively, if you are using UK lawyers, they will probably have a recommendation. If you prefer you can select 'blind' from a list of local members supplied by the surveyors' professional body.

Architect (Architecte)

An architect's survey will, as you might expect, tend to focus on issues of design and construction although it should cover all of the basic subjects needed in a survey. The people to contact for a list of local architects are the College of Architects. This is not a training establishment but the architects' professional body, as in the Royal College of Surgeons. Costs vary depending on the size and complexity of the house and the distance from the architect's base. Allow £500–1,500 for an average house.

Valuer/Surveyor (Expert Immobilier)

The survey from an expert will focus on measurement and valuation, but will also cover the essential issues relating to the structure of the property. For a list of experts contact the Chambre des Experts Immobiliers. Experts produce two types of report. The more common is the expertise, a report of limited scope – really the initial observations of a trained eye. Such a report will contain little in the way of testing. The less common is the fuller structural report (*bilan de santé*). Not all surveyors produce the latter reports.

As with architects, costs vary depending on the size and complexity of the house and the distance from the surveyor's base. They will also vary to reflect the depth of report required. Allow £200–500 for a basic report on an average house and £500–1,500 for a more complex report.

Whichever type of report and whether it is from an architect or a surveyor, you will find that it is different from the sort of report you would get from an English surveyor. Many people find it a little 'thin', with too much focus on issues that are not their primary concern. It will, hardly surprisingly, be in French. You will need to have it translated unless you speak very good French and have access to a technical dictionary. Translation costs amount to about £60–100 per 1,000 words, depending on where you are located and the complexity of the document. Always use an English person to translate documents from French into English. An alternative to translation of the full report would be to ask your lawyer to summarize the report in a letter to you and translate any areas of particular concern.

A few French surveyors and architects, mainly in the popular areas, have geared themselves to the non-French market and will produce a report rather more like a British or German survey. They will probably also prepare it in bilingual form or at least supply a translation of the original French document.

UK-qualified Surveyor Based in France

A number of UK surveyors – usually those with a love of France – have seen a gap in the market and have set themselves up in France to provide British-style structural surveys. They usually offer the brief 'Homebuyers' Report' or the fuller 'Full Structural Survey'. This is not as simple as it would first appear. To do the job well they must learn about French building techniques and regulations, which are different from those in Britain. Without this knowledge the report will be of limited value. Prices are generally slightly more expensive than a French report, but it will be in English and so avoid the need for translation costs. Your UK lawyer should be able to recommend a surveyor able to do a survey in your area. Alternatively, look for advertisers in the main French property magazines.

Check they have indemnity insurance covering the provision of reports in France. Check also on the person's qualifications and experience in providing reports on French property and get an estimate. The estimate will only be an estimate because they will not know for sure the scope of the task until they visit the property and because travelling time means that visits to give estimates are not usually feasible.

Contracts 'Subject to Survey'

This is most unusual in France. Legally there is nothing to stop a French preliminary contract (*compromis de vente*) containing a get-out clause (*clause suspensive*) stating that the sale is conditional upon a satisfactory survey being obtained. It is unlikely to meet with the approval of the seller, his agent or notary unless the transaction is unusual – for example, the purchase of a castle where the cost of a survey could be huge. In an ordinary case the seller is likely to tell you to do your survey and then sign a contract. This does expose you to some risk. The seller could sell to someone else before you get the results of the survey. You may be able to enter into a reservation contract to take the property off the market for a couple of weeks and so avoid this risk. Alternatively, you may make a (probably) unenforceable 'Gentleman's Agreement' that the seller will not sell to anyone else for the next two weeks and so allow you to have your survey done. It helps if you have established a good relationship with the seller or his agent and have shown you are a serious player, perhaps by having already placed the deposit money with your lawyer.

Checklist – Things You May Ask Your Surveyor to Do

You might ask your surveyor to carry out:

- **an electrical condition and continuity check**
- **a drains check including assessment of drains to the point where they join mains sewers or septic tank**
- **a septic tank check**
- **a rot check**
- **a check on cement in property constructed out of cement**
- **a check of underfloor areas, where access cannot easily be obtained**
- **a check on heating and air-conditioning**
- **a check on pools and all pool-related equipment and heating**
- **a wood-boring insect check (roughly half of France is infested with termites, so this is important)**

Raising Finance to Buy a Property in France

If you decide to take out a mortgage you can, in most cases, either mortgage your existing UK property or you can take out a mortgage on your new French property. There are advantages and disadvantages both ways. Many people buying property in France will look closely at fixed-rate mortgages so they know their commitment over, say, the next five, 10 or 15 years. Again there are advantages and disadvantages.

Mortgaging your UK Property

At the moment there is fierce competition to lend money and there are some excellent deals to be done, whether you choose to borrow at a variable rate, at a fixed rate or in one of the hybrid schemes now on offer. Read the Sunday papers or the specialist mortgage press to see what is on offer, or consult a mortgage broker. Perhaps most useful are mortgage brokers who can discuss the possibilities in both the UK and France. All in all, a UK mortgage is generally the better option for people who need to borrow relatively small sums and who will be repaying it out of UK income.

A number of people have found that, in today's climate of falling interest rates, re-mortgaging their property in the UK has reduced the cost of their existing borrowing so significantly that their new mortgage – including a loan to buy a modest French property – has cost no more, in monthly payments, than their old loan.

French Mortgages

A French mortgage is one taken out over your French property. This will either be from a French bank (or other lending institution) or from a British bank that is registered and does business in France. You cannot take a mortgage on your new French property from your local UK branch of a building society or high street bank.

The basic concept of a mortgage is the same in France as it is in England or Scotland. It is (usually) a loan secured against land or buildings. Just as in England, if you don't keep up the payments the bank will repossess your property. In France, if they do this they will sell it by judicial auction and you are likely to see it sold for a pittance and recover little if anything for the equity you built up in the property. Mortgages in France are, however, different in many respects from their English counterparts. It is important to understand the differences, which are explained below.

French mortgages are governed by, amongst other rules, the *Loi Scrivener* (so called because Mme Scrivener was the minister responsible for the law). This creates a complex, and typically French, administrative regime for the granting of mortgages and gives some significant elements of consumer protection. Key elements of the *Loi Scrivener* (which applies only to commercial mortgages of residential property) are described below.

• Every purchase contract must contain either a statement that the sale is subject to a mortgage and give details of the loan, or a statement in the buyer's own handwriting that the buyer has been informed of the law and that the purchase does not depend upon a mortgage.

• If the purchase is subject to a mortgage the contract is automatically subject to a get-out condition (*clause suspensive*) for at least one month to the effect that if the loan is refused the contract is null and void and your deposit will be returned. The buyer must make every effort to obtain a mortgage and, if he does not do so, will lose the protection of the law. This clause needs to be drafted most carefully to ensure your protection. If you are offered a contract containing such a clause, always get it checked by your lawyer before you sign it.

• Every offer of a mortgage must be in writing and contain full details of the loan including its total cost, interest charges, mechanisms for varying the interest rate and what ancillary steps the borrower must take to get the loan (such as taking out a life policy). It must also state any penalties for early repayment of the loan and that it is valid for acceptance for 30 days.

• The loan offer cannot be accepted for a period of 10 days from receipt and no money can be paid to the lender until that time. This is a 'cooling off period' that can cause some difficulty if the mortgage offer takes some time to appear and the buyer is anxious to proceed.

• The loan must be subject to a condition that the contract is completed within four months of acceptance of the loan.

• There are restrictions on the ability to impose penalties for early payment of the loan.

The Main Differences Between an English and a French Mortgage

• French mortgages are almost always created on a repayment basis. That is to say, the loan and the interest on it are both gradually repaid by equal instalments over the period of the mortgage. Endowment, PEP, pension and interest-only mortgages are not known in France.

• The formalities involved in making the application, signing the contract subject to a mortgage and completing the transaction are more complex and stricter than in the UK.

• Most French mortgages are granted for 15 years, not 25 as in England. In fact the period can be anything from two to (in a few cases) 25 years. Normally the mortgage must have been repaid by your 70th (sometimes 65th) birthday.

• The maximum loan is generally 80 per cent of the value of the property and 75 or 66 per cent is more common. Valuations by banks tend to be conservative – they are thinking about what they might get for the property on a forced sale if they had to repossess it. As a planning guide, you should think of borrowing no more than two-thirds of the price you are paying. The rate of interest you pay is likely to be less if you borrow a lower percentage of value and for a shorter period.

• Fixed-rate loans – with the rate fixed for the whole duration of the loan – are more common than in the UK. They are very competitively priced.

• The way of calculating the amount the bank will lend you is different from in the UK. As you would expect, there are detailed differences from bank to bank but the bank is not allowed to lend you more than an amount the monthly payments on which amount to 30 per cent of your net disposable income.

• There will usually be a minimum loan (say £20,000) and some banks will not lend at all on property less than a certain value.

• The way of dealing with stage payments on new property and property where money is needed for restoration is different from in England.

• The paperwork on completion of the mortgage is different. There is (usually) no separate mortgage deed. Instead the existence of the mortgage is mentioned in your purchase deed (*Acte de Vente*).

Applications for a French Mortgage

The information needed will vary from bank to bank. It will also depend on whether you are employed or self-employed. Applications can receive preliminary approval (subject to survey of the property, confirmation of good title and confirmation of the information supplied by you) within a few days. A formal letter of offer will take a couple of weeks from the time the bank has received all the necessary information from you. The documents you are likely to need are:

Documents Needed to Apply for a French Mortgage

Employed	Self-employed
Copy passports of all applicants	
Application fee	
Completed application form	
Proof of outgoings such as rent or mortgage	
Copy of last three months' bank statements	
Cash flow forecast for any anticipated rental income	
Proof of income (usually three months' pay slips or a letter from your employer on official paper)	Audited accounts for last three years Last year's tax return and proof of payment of tax

The Mortgage Offer

Allow four weeks altogether from the date of your application to receiving a written mortgage offer as getting the information sometimes takes a while. It can take longer. Once you receive the offer you will generally have 30 days from receipt of the offer in which to accept the offer, after which time it will lapse. You cannot accept it for 10 days from the date of receipt, so as to give you a period of reflection This is very frustrating if the offer has taken ages to arrive and you are in a hurry! Have the mortgage explained in detail by your lawyer.

Payments for New Property

In France when buying a new property one normally takes title to the land at an early stage and then makes payments as the development progresses. You will need to tell your bank that you want to draw down the mortgage to make the stage payments. Usually you will pay off the amount you are providing yourself and then take the further money from the bank as and when it is due. During this period (the *période d'anticipation*) before the completion of the house you will only be borrowing part of the agreed loan and so you will usually pay only interest on the amount paid by the bank thus far. Once the property has been delivered to you (and thus the full loan has been taken) the normal monthly payments will begin.

Property Needing Restoration

Not all banks will finance such property. If you have enough money to buy a property but need a mortgage to renovate it, you *must* apply for the mortgage before buying the property as it can otherwise be difficult to find a lender.

The Cost of Taking Out a Mortgage

This will normally involve an arrangement fee of one per cent of the amount borrowed, a 'valuation' fee of about £150–200 and notaries'/land registry fees of 2.5 per cent of the amount borrowed. Occasionally there will be extra charges. Therefore taking out a French mortgage is not cheap. These charges are in addition to the normal expenses incurred when buying a property, which normally amount to about eight to nine per cent of the price of the property.

You will probably be required to take out life insurance for the amount of the loan, though you may be allowed to use a suitable existing policy. You may be required to have a medical. You will be required to insure the property and produce proof of insurance – but you would probably have done this anyway.

The offer may be subject to early payment penalties. These must be explained in the offer and cannot exceed the penalties laid down by law. The details of these rules vary from time to time. Early payment penalties are of particular concern in the case of a fixed-rate mortgage.

The Exchange Rate Risk

If the funds to repay the mortgage are coming from your sterling earnings then the amount you have to pay will be affected by fluctuations in exchange rates between sterling and the euro. Do not underestimate these variations. Over the last 15 years – a typical period for a mortgage – the French franc has been as high as FF6.5 = £1 and as low as FF11 = £1. The same will almost certainly happen with the euro. Indeed, in the period since its launch it has varied from €1

= €0.57 and €1 = £0.70. This can make a tremendous difference to your monthly mortgage repayments. A monthly mortgage repayment of FF5,000 (about £500 at today's value) would on some occasions during the last 15 years have meant paying £454 and on other occasions £769.

Equally, if sterling falls in value then your debt as a percentage of the value of the property increases in sterling terms. Your property will be worth more in sterling terms but your mortgage will also have increased in value. This is probably not of too much concern to most people. Of course, if sterling rises in value against the euro then the situation is reversed.

Foreign Currency Mortgages

It is possible to mortgage your home in France but to borrow not in euros but in sterling – or US dollars or Swiss francs or Japanese yen. There may be some attractions in borrowing in sterling if you are repaying out of sterling income. The rates of interest will be sterling rates, not euro rates. This will currently mean paying more. Usually the rates are not as competitive as you could obtain if you were remortgaging your property in the UK as the market is less cut-throat. You will have all the same administrative and legal costs as you would if you borrowed in euros – i.e. about four per cent of the amount borrowed. This option is mainly of interest to people who either do not have sufficient equity in their UK home or who, for whatever reason, do not wish to mortgage the property in which they live.

Other Loans

When moving to France permanently, you may not need to incur the expense of mortgaging your property in France. If you have already paid off your UK mortgage and your UK home is on sale, yours may be the following scenario. You have found the perfect place in France and have, say, £180,000 of the £200,000 available from savings and pension lump sums. The balance will be paid from the sale of your UK home, but you are not sure whether that will take place before you are committed to the purchase of the house in France in a few weeks' time.

It is probably unnecessarily complicated to mortgage the UK home for such a short period, and indeed, it could be difficult to do so if the bank knows you are selling. In this case it is often simplest to approach your bank for a short-term loan or overdraft. This might be for the £20,000 shortfall or it could be that you don't really want to sell some of your investments at this stage and so you might ask for a facility of, say, £50,000.

Some people choose to take out formal two- or three-year UK loans for, say, £15,000 each whilst still resident in the UK prior to leaving for France to cover a gap such as waiting to receive a pension lump sum. Despite the high interest rates on such loans the overall cost can be a lot less than taking a short-term mortgage on the French property and paying all the fees.

Who Should Own the Property?

There are many ways of structuring the purchase of a home in France. Each has significant advantages and disadvantages. The choice of the right structure will save you thousands of pounds of tax and expenses during your lifetime and on your death. Because, in France, you do not have the total freedom that we have in the UK to deal with your assets as you please on your death, the wrong choice of owner can also result in the wrong people being entitled to inherit from you when you die. This is a particular problem for people in second marriages and unmarried couples.

Sole Ownership

In some cases it could be sensible to put the property in the name of one person only. If your husband runs a high-risk business, or if he is 90 and you are 22, this could make sense. If you intend to let the property and want all the income to be yours for tax purposes it might be worth considering. It is seldom a good idea from the point of view of tax or inheritance planning.

Joint Ownership

If two people are buying together they will normally buy in both their names. There are two ways of doing this: separate ownership (*en indivision*) or in a loose equivalent to an English 'joint tenancy' called *en tontine*. The choice you make is of great importance.

If you buy *en indivision* then your half is yours and your fellow owner's is theirs. On your death, and subject to the owners' matrimonial regime (*see* 'Your Civil State (*Etat Civil*)' p.161), your half will be disposed of in accordance with the fixed rules laid down by French law. You may not be able to give it to the people you want to. If you buy *en tontine* then your half will pass to your fellow owner automatically on your death. The fixed French succession rules are bypassed. There are other differences. A person who owns *en indivision* (even if they own by virtue of inheritance) can usually insist on the sale of the property. So if your stepchildren inherit from your husband (as is likely under French law) they could insist on the sale of your home. A person who owns *en tontine* cannot usually insist on the sale of the property during the lifetime of the other joint owners. Creditors of other joint owners cannot claim the asset. But ownership *en tontine* can lead to more being paid overall by way of inheritance tax.

If you decide to buy *en indivision* then, in certain cases, it can make sense to split the ownership other than 50/50. If, for example, you have three children and your wife has two then to secure each of those children an equal share on your death you might think about buying 60 per cent in your name and 40 per cent in your wife's name. You might also think of giving the property to your children (or other preferred beneficiaries on your death) but reserving for you and your co-owner a life interest over the property (*usufruit*). This is the right to use the property for their lifetime. So, on your death, your rights would be extinguished but your second wife or partner, who still has a life interest, would still be able to use the property. Only on their death would the property pass in full to the people to whom you gave it years earlier. This device can not only protect your right to use the property but also save large amounts of inheritance tax, particularly if you are young, the property is valuable and you survive for many years. As ever, there are also drawbacks, not least being the fact that after the gift you no longer own the property. If you wish to sell, you need the agreement of the 'owners', who will be entitled to the proceeds of the sale and who would have to agree to buy you a new house.

It is very important to seek clear advice from your lawyer about the form of ownership that will suit you best, both with regard to the consequences in France and the consequences in the UK.

Adding Your Children to the Title

If you give your children the money to buy part of the property and so put them on the title at the outset you may save quite a lot of inheritance tax. On your death you will only own (say) one-fifth of the property rather than one half. Only that part will be taxable. It may be such a small value as to result in a tax-free inheritance. This only works if your children are over 18. Of course, there are drawbacks. For example, if they fall out with you they can insist on the sale of the property and receiving their share.

Putting the Property in the Name of Your Children Only

If you put the property only in the name of your children (possibly reserving for yourself a life interest as explained above) then the property is theirs. On your death there will be little or no inheritance tax and there will be no need to incur the legal expenses involved in dealing with an inheritance. This sounds attractive. Remember, however, that you have lost control. It is no longer your property. If your children divorce, their husband/wife will be able to claim a share. If they die before you without children of their own, you will end up inheriting the property back from them and having to pay inheritance tax for the privilege of doing so.

Limited Company

For some people owning a property via a limited company can be a very attractive option. You own the shares in a company, not a house in France. If you sell the house you can do so by selling the shares in the company rather than transferring the ownership of the property itself. This can save the roughly nine per cent acquisition costs that the new owner would otherwise have to pay and so, arguably, allow you to charge a bit more for the property. When you die you do not own 'immovables' (*immeubles*) – land and buildings – in France and so you will not run into the difficulties that can arise as a result of the French inheritance laws, which (as far as foreigners are concerned) usually only apply to land and buildings. There are drawbacks as well as advantages.

UK Company

It is rare for a purchase through a UK company to make sense for a holiday home or single investment property. This is despite the fact that the ability to pay for the property with the company's money without drawing it out of the company and so paying UK tax on the dividend is attractive. There are still times when it can be the right answer. Once again you need expert advice from someone familiar with the law of both countries.

Offshore (Tax Haven) Company

This has most of the same advantages and disadvantages as ownership by other types of company, with the added disincentive that you will have to pay a special tax of three per cent of the value of the property *every year*. This is to compensate the French for all the inheritance and transfer taxes that they will not receive when the owners of these companies sell them or die. For a person who is (or intends to be) resident in France for tax purposes there are additional disadvantages. If he owns more than 10 per cent of an offshore company he will have to pay tax in France on his share of its income and assets. This tax treatment has more or less killed off ownership via such companies, yet they still have a limited role to play. A 93-year-old buying a £10 million property, or someone who wishes to be discreet about the ownership of the property, might think three per cent per year is a small price to pay for the avoidance of inheritance tax or the securing of privacy respectively. Needless to say, anyone thinking of buying through an offshore company should take detailed advice from a lawyer familiar with the law of both countries.

Which Is Right For You?

The choice is of fundamental importance. If you get it wrong you will pay massively more tax than you need to, both during your lifetime and on your death. For each buyer of a home in France one of the options set out above will suit him perfectly. Another might just about make sense. The rest would be an expensive waste of money. The trouble is, it is not obvious which is the right choice! You need in every case to take advice. If your case is simple so will be the advice. If it is complex the time and money spent will be repaid many times over.

The Process of Buying a Property in France

Buying a property in France is as safe as buying a property in the UK. On reading the following pages – which must explain the potential pitfalls if they are to serve any useful purpose – it can seem a frightening or dangerous experience. If you go about the purchase in the right way it is not dangerous and should not be frightening. The same or similar dangers arise when buying a house in the UK. If you are in any doubt, look briefly at a textbook on English conveyancing and all of the horrible things that have happened to people and which have led to our current system of enquiries and paperwork. You do not worry about those dangers because you are familiar with them and, more importantly, because you are shielded against contact with most of them by your solicitor. The same should be true when buying in France. Read this section to understand the background and why some of the problems exist. But ask your lawyer to advise you about any issues that worry you and leave him to avoid the landmines!

If you and the owner agree on a price you make an offer (*promesse de vente*) and sign a document or preliminary sales agreement (*compromis de vente*). It is accompanied by a down payment (*indemnité d'immobilisation*) of usually 10 per cent of the negotiated price. A 2001 law establishes a mandatory seven-day cooling-off period at this stage (*période de rétractation de sept jours*) during which either party call pull out. Otherwise, the *compromis de vente* determines the final date by which the transfer of ownership will take place (usually three months). A *notaire* will prepare this document as well as the next one (*acte authentique de vente*). The *acte authentique de vente* is the final deed and marks the official change in ownership, which is cemented by the signing (*acte final*).

General Procedure

The general procedure when buying a property in France seems, at first glance, similar to the purchase of a property in England: sign a contract; do some checks; sign a Deed of Title. This is deceptive. The procedure is very different and even the use of the familiar English vocabulary to describe the very different steps in France can produce an undesirable sense of familiarity with the procedure. This can lead to assumptions that things that have not been discussed will be the same as they would be in England. Work on the basis that the system is totally different.

Choosing a Lawyer

The Notary Public (Notaire)

The notary is a special type of lawyer. He is in part a public official but he is also in business, making his living from the fees he charges for his services. There are about 8,000 notaries in France. Notaries also exist in England but they are seldom used in day-to-day transactions.

Under French law only deeds of sale (*actes de vente*) approved and witnessed by a notary can be registered at the land registry (*bureau des hypothèques*). Although it is possible to transfer legal ownership of property such as a house or apartment by a private agreement not witnessed by the notary, and although that agreement will be fully binding on the people who made it, it will not be binding on third parties. Third parties – including people who want to make a claim against the property and banks wanting to lend money on the strength of the property – are entitled to rely upon the details of ownership recorded at the land registry. So if you are not registered as the owner of the property you are at risk. Thus, practically speaking, all sales of real estate in France must be witnessed by a notary. The notary also carries out certain checks on property sold and has some duties as tax collector and validator of documents to be presented for registration. His fee is fixed by law, normally 1–1.5 per cent of the price, though there can sometimes be 'extras'.

The notary is appointed by the seller but, if the buyer wishes, he can insist on appointing his own notary, in which case, such is the generosity of the fees that the law allows him to charge, the two notaries share the same fee! In simple transactions this is seldom a necessary step as it can cause unnecessary delay and complication, but it can be useful in certain cases. It is particularly worth thinking about if the notary is also acting for the seller as estate agent, in which case you may be more comfortable with independent scrutiny.

The notary is strictly neutral. He is more a referee than someone fighting on your behalf. He is, in the usual case, someone who checks the papers to make sure that they comply with the strict rules as to content and so will be accepted by the land registry for registration.

Many French notaries, particularly in rural areas, do not speak English – or, at least, do not speak it well enough to give advice on complex issues. Very few will know anything about English law and so will be unable to tell you about the tax and other consequences in the UK of your plans to buy a house in France. In any case, the buyer will seldom meet the notary before the signing ceremony and so there is little scope for seeking detailed advice. It is very unusual for notaries to offer any comprehensive explanations, least of all in writing, to the buyer.

For the English buyer the notary is therefore no substitute for also using the services of a specialist UK lawyer familiar with French law and international property transactions. This is the clear advice of every guidebook, the French and British governments and the Federation of Overseas Property Developers, Agents and Consultants (FOPDAC). It is therefore baffling why so many people buying a property in France do not take this necessary step.

The Price

This can be freely agreed between the parties. Depending on the economic climate there may be ample or very little room for negotiating a reduction in the asking price. There is still some scope if buying in undiscovered France, especially if the property needs repair. There is also scope in the case of more expensive properties.

In every area there are properties that have stuck on the market, usually because they are overpriced and/or in a poor location. Find out when the property was placed on the market. Ask to see the agent's sale authority (*mandat*). Of course, negotiating a reduction is always worth a try, but if your advances are rejected do bear in mind the probability that it is not mere posturing but a genuine confidence that the price asked is achievable. Also remember that once a formal offer is accepted it is binding upon both of you, so the price cannot be reduced. Better, if unsure, to start a little low and test the water. You can always increase the offer if the first is rejected.

If you are unsure of the value of the property, it is often possible to obtain a valuation. This is unusual in France, but useful in the case of properties, especially in rural areas, where there may be few obvious similar properties on the market to use for price comparisons. The estate agent may also be able to give you some guidance, but he is being paid by the seller to sell the property, and receiving a commission based on the amount he receives, so treat his input with caution.

Above all, don't get carried away. There will always be another property. Fix a maximum budget before you set off on your visit – and stick to it. Make ample allowance for the likely costs of repair/refurbishment. They are always 25 per cent higher than you think! If necessary get estimates before committing yourself.

Which Currency?

The price of the property will be recorded in the deed of sale (*acte de vente*) in euros. Usually the euro will also be used in the reservation agreement and contract (*compromis*).

In France you have the right to enter into a contract on whatever terms you please and so some people may choose to agree a price in sterling, US dollars or whatever. This would involve the buyer paying and the seller receiving the currency of their choice, which might be useful if, for example, both were British and living in the UK as it would remove the risk of exchange rate fluctuations for both parties. It would also avoid the expense of the buyer converting sterling to euros and the seller then incurring the similar expense of converting them back again.

It will be necessary for an agreed figure in euros, representing the approximate value of the foreign currency, to be inserted in the *acte de vente* and land register and for the taxes due to be paid on the basis of this figure. This can prove a problem with the notary, who will almost certainly not have access to a sterling or US dollar bank account and so will not be able to perform his normal task of receiving and paying over the funds. Because he does not do this, the protection afforded to the buyer is less than would otherwise be the case. If you are paying direct to the seller, try to use a 'stakeholder', typically your solicitor, who will receive the money and keep it safe until the deed of sale is signed and then release it to the seller. Generally, unless you are very worried about movements in exchange rates, it is better to do the deal in euros.

How Much Should Be Declared in the Deed of Sale?

For many years there was a tradition in France (and other Latin countries) of under-declaring the price actually paid for a property when signing the deed of sale (*acte de vente*). This was because the taxes and notaries' fees due were calculated on the basis of the price declared. Lower price, less taxes for the buyer and, for a holiday home (*résidence secondaire*), less capital gains tax for the seller. Magic! Those days have now largely gone. In rural areas you can still sometimes come under pressure to under-declare, but it is now rare. Under-declaration is foolish. There are severe penalties. In the worst case the state can forcibly buy the property for the price declared plus 10 per cent. In the best case there are fines and penalties for late payment. Don't do it!

Nevertheless, there is scope for quite legitimately reducing the price declared and so reducing tax. For example, if your purchase includes some furniture (or, in the case of a holiday home, even a boat or a car) there is no need to declare the value of those items and pay stamp duty on the price paid. You can enter into a separate contract for the 'extras' and save some money.

Where Must the Money Be Paid?

The price, together with the taxes and fees payable, is usually paid by the buyer into the notary's bank account and then passed on by him to the seller, the tax man, etc. as applicable. This is the best and safest way. Any money paid to the notary is bonded, and so safe. Try to avoid arrangements, usually as part of an under-declaration, where part of the money is handed over in cash in brown-paper parcels. Apart from being illegal it is dangerous at a practical level. Buyers have lost the bundle, or been robbed on the way to the notary's office. Sometimes there is even a suspicion that the seller, who knew where you were going to be and when, could be involved.

General Enquiries and Special Enquiries

Certain enquiries are made routinely in the course of the purchase of a property. These include a check on the planning situation of the property. This *note de renseignement d'urbanisme* will reveal the position of the property itself but it will not, at least directly, tell you about its neighbours and it will not reveal general plans for the area. If you want to know whether the authorities are going to put a prison in the village or run a new TGV line through your back garden (both, presumably, bad things) or build a motorway access point or TGV station 3km away (both, presumably, good things) you will need to ask. There are various organizations you can approach but, just as in England, there is no single point of contact for such enquiries. If you are concerned about what might happen in the area then you will need to discuss the position with your lawyers at an early stage. There may be a considerable amount of work (and therefore cost) involved in making full enquiries, the results of which can never be guaranteed.

Normal enquiries also include a check that the seller is the registered owner of the property and that it is sold (if this has been agreed) free of mortgages or other charges. In order to advise you what other enquiries might be appropriate your lawyer will need to be told your proposals for the property. Do you intend to rent it out? If so, is it on a commercial basis? Do you intend to use it for business purposes? Do you want to extend or modify the exterior of the property? Do you intend to make interior structural alterations? Agree in advance the additional enquiries you would like to make and get an estimate of the cost of those enquiries.

Your Civil State (*Etat Civil*) and Other Personal Details

This is something you will not have thought about. For most of the time it is a matter of unimportance in England. It is something the French get very worked up about. When preparing documents in France you will be asked to specify your civil state (*état civil*). This comprises a full set of information about you. They will not only ask for your full name and address but also, potentially, for your occupation, nationality, passport number, maiden name and sometimes the names of your parents, date and place of birth, date and place of marriage and, most importantly, your matrimonial regime (*régime matrimonial*).

What is a *régime matrimonial*? It is something we do not have in the UK. In France when you marry you will specify the *régime matrimonial* that will apply to your relationship. There are two main options for a French person: a regime of common ownership of assets (*communauté de biens*) or a regime of separate ownership of assets (*séparation de biens*). Under the first, all assets acquired after the marriage, even if put into just one party's name, belong to both. Under the second, each spouse is entitled to own assets in his or her own name, upon which the other spouse has no automatic claim. The effect of marriage under English law is closer to the second than the first. If possible the notary, when specifying your matrimonial regime, should state that you are married under English law and, in the absence of a marriage contract, do not have a regime but your situation is similar to a regime of *séparation de biens* – '*mariés sous le régime anglais équivalent au régime français de la séparation de biens à defaut de contrat de marriage préalable à leur union célébrée le* [DATE] *à* [PLACE]'.

This is no idle point. The declaration in your *acte de vente* is a public declaration. It is treated in France with great reverence and as being of great importance. It will be hard in later years to go against what you have declared. If you say that you are married in *communauté de biens*, even if the money came from only one of you, the asset will be treated as belonging to both. This, in turn, can have highly undesirable tax and inheritance consequences.

If appropriate you will declare that you are single, separated, divorced, widowed, etc. at this point. The authorities are entitled to ask for proof of all of these points by birth certificates, marriage certificates, etc. If the documents are needed, the official translations into French may be needed. Often the notary will take a slightly more relaxed view and ask you for only the key elements of your *état civil*. It is worth checking in advance as to what is required, as it is embarrassing to turn up to sign the *acte* only to find the ceremony cannot go ahead because you do not have one of the documents required. In the worst case that could put you in breach of contract and you could lose your deposit!

The Community of Owners (*Copropriété*)

This is a device familiar in continental Europe but most unusual in the UK. The basic idea is than when a number of people own land or buildings in such a way that they have exclusive use of part of the property but shared use of the rest then a *copropriété* is created. Houses on their own plots with no shared facilities will not be a member of a *copropriété*. Most other property will be.

In a *copropriété* the buyer of a house which shares a pool with its neighbours, or of an apartment, owns his own house or apartment outright – as the English would say, 'freehold' – and shares the use of the remaining areas as part of a community of owners (*en copropriété*). It is not only the shared pool that is jointly owned but (in an apartment) the lift shafts, corridors, roof, foundations, entrance areas, parking zones, etc.

The members of the *copropriété* are each responsible for their own home. They, collectively, agree the works needed on the common areas and a budget for those works. They then become responsible for paying their share of those common expenses, as stipulated in their title.

The *règlements de copropriété* set out how the *copropriété* should be run and also set out how your share of the expenses is to be calculated. (This is usually by reference to the size of each apartment, with (probably) a larger fraction going to any commercial area included in the *copropriété*.)

The supreme ruling body of any *copropriété* is the general meeting of members (*syndicat des copropriétaires*). The general meeting must meet at least once per year to approve the budget and deal with other business. You must be given at least two weeks' notice of the meeting and the opportunity of putting items on the agenda. Voting is, for most issues, by simple majority vote. If you can't attend you can appoint a proxy to vote on your behalf. Your *règlements* may make additional rules but not take away your basic rights. Day-to-day management is usually delegated to an administrator (*syndic*). The *copropriété* should provide not only for routine work but, through its fees, set aside money for periodic major repairs. If they do not – or if the amount set aside is inadequate – the general meeting can authorize a supplemental levy to raise the sums needed.

The rules set by the *copropriété* are intended to improve the quality of life of residents. They could, for example, deal with concerns over noise (no radios by the pool), prohibit the use of the pool after 10pm, ban the hanging of washing on balconies, etc. More importantly they could ban pets or any commercial activity in the building or short-term holiday letting. Check them.

The *règlements de copropriété* are an important document. Every buyer of a property in a *copropriété* receives a copy of the rules. If you do not speak French you should have them translated or, at least, summarized in English. Check the rules, the level of fees and the pending items of expenditure before you buy.

Initial Contracts

In France most sales start with a preliminary contract. The type of contract will depend upon whether you are buying a finished or an unfinished property. Signing any of these documents has far-reaching legal consequences, which are sometimes different from the consequences of signing a similar document in the UK. Whichever type of contract you are asked to sign, always seek legal advice before signing.

All contracts to buy property are now subject, by law, to the right to cancel the agreement within seven days of receiving the copy signed by the seller. Do this by recorded delivery (AR) post. Strict compliance with the rules and timetable for cancellation is essential. Any money paid should be refunded.

Generally the preliminary contract is prepared, in simple cases, by the estate agent – who is professionally qualified in France – or by the notary. Estate agent's contracts are often based on a pre-printed document in a standard format. It is very important that these contracts are not just accepted as final. In every case they will need to be modified. In some cases they will need to be modified extensively. Some contracts coming from estate agents who are not familiar with dealing with foreign buyers can contain extra clauses into the contract that are potentially harmful to the foreign buyer. More likely, they will leave out one or more of the 'get-out clauses' (*clauses suspensives*) needed to protect your position by cancelling the contract if all turns out not to be well.

If You are Buying a Finished Property

You will be invited to sign one of three different documents. Each has different features. Each has different legal consequences. Each is appropriate in certain circumstances and inappropriate in others. Seek legal advice as to which will be best in your case.

• **Offer to Buy (*Offre d'Achat*)**: This is, technically, not a contract at all. It is a formal written offer from the potential buyer to the potential seller. It will state that you wish to buy the stated property for a stated price and that you will complete the transaction within a stated period. The offer will normally be accompanied by the payment of a deposit to the estate agent (if he is licensed to hold the seller's money) or to a local notary who will be dealing with the transaction. The deposit is not fixed but will usually range from two to five per cent of the price offered.

This document binds you. It is not a mere enquiry as to whether the seller might be interested in selling. If he says that he accepts the offer then you (and he) become legally bound to proceed with the transaction. Until then, of course, the document has no effect on the seller and it is certainly not a guarantee that the seller will sell you the house.

Its main use is in situations where the property is perhaps offered through a variety of estate agents and the seller wants to wait for a week or two to see what offers come in before making up his mind to whom to sell. Generally we do not like *offres*. We prefer the idea of making a verbal enquiry as to whether the seller would accept a certain price and, once he says yes, for a binding bilateral contract of sale (*compromis de vente*) to be signed.

- **Promise to Sell (*Promesse de Vente*)**: This is a written document in which the seller offers to sell a stated property at a stated price to a stated person at any time within a stated period, up to a maximum of six months. It is the mirror image of the *offre d'achat*. The seller will usually require that any person taking up his offer pays him a deposit (*indemnité d'immobilisation*). The amount of the deposit is not fixed by law, but is usually five or 10 per cent of the price of the property. Once he has received this deposit the seller must reserve the property for you until the end of the period specified in the contract. This is similar to an English option contract. If you want to go ahead and buy the property you can but you are not obliged to do so. If you do not go ahead you lose your deposit.

The *promesse* should contain special 'get-out clauses' (*clauses suspensives*) stipulating the circumstances in which the buyer will be entitled to the refund of his deposit if he decides not to go ahead. These might include not being able to obtain a mortgage, finding the property was infested with termites, finding the property could not be used for a certain purpose, etc. The drafting of these clauses is of vital importance. See your lawyer.

If you do want to go ahead you can exercise the option (*lever l'option*) at any point up to the end of the agreed period. If the seller refuses to go ahead the buyer is entitled to claim compensation.

This agreement requires certain formalities for it to be valid. It does not need to be signed in front of a notary but must be recorded at the local tax registry (*cadastre*). This type of agreement has its place but, in general, the full binding bilateral contract of sale (*compromis de vente*) to be signed wherever possible is preferable. The *promesse de vente* can give rise to substantial problems if either the seller dies before completion of the sale or if he refuses to complete. This structure is, however, still common in several parts of France and, in those areas, it may be difficult to persuade the sellers, estate agents and notaries to use the *compromis*. If this is the case then the *promesse* should be drafted with particular care, especially as far as the consequences of non-completion are concerned.

- **Full Contract (*Compromis de Vente*)**: This is also known as a joint promise of sale (*promesse synallagmatique de vente*) and, in most parts of France, is the most common type of document. It is an agreement that commits both parties. The seller must sell a stated property at a stated price to a stated person on the terms set out in the contract. The buyer must buy.

This is the most far-reaching of the three documents and so it is particularly important that you are satisfied that it contains all of the terms necessary to protect your position. Take legal advice. Remember that under French law by signing this contract you become the owner of the property (though you will need to sign a deed of sale (*acte de vente*) and register your ownership to be safe as far as third parties are concerned).

The contract must therefore contain all of the safety clauses to make sure that, for example, if all is not well with the title to the property you will be released from your obligations and get your money back. These will include clauses about any mortgage you are applying for (the *Loi Scrivener* clauses), clauses requiring proof of various planning matters, clauses as to what should happen if a right of pre-emption is exercised. The contract will contain a variety of 'routine' clauses:

- The names of the seller and buyer should both be stated fully.
- The property should be described fully, both in an everyday sense and by reference to its land registry details.
- A statement is usually made that full details of the title will be included in the final deed of sale (*acte de vente*).
- A date for the signing of the *acte* will be fixed. This is usually 60 days after signing the contract. The delay is because there are various documents that must be obtained from the French authorities (particularly a confirmation that SAFER does not intend to exercise its right of pre-emption and a planning certificate (*certificat d'urbanisme*) and these typically take eight weeks to obtain. SAFER is the French Rural Development Agency (*Fédération Nationale des Sociétés d'Aménagement Foncier et d'Etablissement Rural*).
- A statement will be made as to when possession will take place – normally, on the date of signing the title.
- The price is fixed.
- A receipt for any deposit is given.
- A statement is made that the property is sold subject to any rights that exist over it (which, incidentally, you will not have checked at that stage) but that the seller has not himself created any.
- The property should be sold with vacant possession.
- It will state the notary who is to prepare the *acte*.
- It will provide for who is to pay the costs of the purchase.
- It will confirm the details of any agent involved and who is to pay his commission.
- It will set out what is to happen if one or both of the parties breaks the contract.
- It will establish the law to cover the contract and the address of the parties for legal purposes.
- Finally it will contain the all-important special clauses.

If the buyer or seller drops out of the contract or otherwise breaks it, various arrangements may be made. A deposit (*les arrhes*) might be payable by the buyer. If he fails to complete he will lose the deposit. If the seller fails to complete he will have to return double the deposit paid. Alternatively the contract may provide for a sum of agreed compensation to be paid (*un dédit*). The *dédit* for the buyer could be the loss of his deposit. The *dédit* for the seller could be fixed in the contract. If either party is in breach of the contract, the other can serve notice requiring him to sign the *acte* and complete or pay the *dédit*.

There can be a penalty clause. This was a large penalty, designed to frighten both parties into complying with the contract. Its popularity has reduced since the courts were granted the power to decrease such penalties if they thought it reasonable to do so.

If the parties fail to comply with their obligations there is the ultimate remedy of seeking a court order. As in any country, this is very much a last resort as it is costly, time-consuming and (as in any country) there is no guarantee of the outcome of a court case. If a court order is made in your favour this order can be registered at the land registry.

If You Are Buying an Unfinished Property

• **Full Contract**: There are two types of contract in this case. The first is a *sale à terme*. You agree to buy a plot of land and building. You agree to pay once it has been built. Simple! You take title and pay the money at the same time. This type of contract is little used. The second is *en l'état futur d'achèvement*, more commonly known as 'on plan'. Here the seller transfers his interest in the land and anything he has so far built on it to the buyer at once. As the building continues it automatically becomes the property of the buyer. In return the buyer pays an initial sum representing the value of the asset as it now exists and further payments, by stages, during the construction process. The contract must give details of a guarantee to secure completion of the construction in the event, for example, that the seller goes bust.

• **Reservation Contract (*Contrat de Réservation*)**: Usually in these cases there is a preliminary contract. This is the reservation contract. There are various very detailed statutory rules governing how such contracts must be drafted and carried through in order to avoid the obvious risks that arise in such circumstances.

• **The contract must be in writing.**

• **A copy must be given to the seller before any money changes hands.**

• **It must contain a full description of the property to be built, its size and number of rooms.**

• **It must set out any central facilities or services to be provided.**

- The price must be specified as must any arrangements to charge for extras or to vary the price such as, for example, its increasing in line with the official cost of construction index.

- The scheme for stage payments must be stipulated.

- The deposit or reservation fee (*réservation*) must be agreed. This cannot exceed five per cent of the price if completion of the work will take place within one year of signing the reservation contract or two per cent if it will take place more than one year but less than two years from the date of signing. If it will be more than two years until completion of the work, no deposit may be taken.

- The contract must state the circumstances in which the reservation fee is to be repaid, if requested. These include where the *acte de vente* is not signed on the date agreed because of the seller's default, the final price (even if calculated in accordance with the variation terms agreed) is more than five per cent above the initial price agreed, any stipulated loan is not obtained or the property is reduced in size or quality or some of the services are not supplied.

- It must provide for the buyer's receiving a draft title deed (*acte de vente*) at least one month before the date for signing.

- It must contain details of the guarantees in place to secure the monies paid by the buyer if the seller cannot complete the building.

The stage payments are made on receipt of architect's certificates confirming that progress has reached a certain point. There is a maximum level of stage payments permitted at any point:

- foundations – 35 per cent of total price
- building watertight – 75 per cent of total price
- completion of building – 95 per cent of total price.

The building is 'complete' when your part of it and all the common parts indispensable to your use of the building are finished. Minor deficiencies or small outstanding jobs are not a failure to complete and therefore not an excuse for delaying the final payment. If there are outstanding jobs or defects they are normally listed at completion and a timetable is agreed for rectifying them. Any noticed by the buyer within one month of taking possession must be fixed by the seller. This is your strongest guarantee. You should seriously consider having the property inspected by a surveyor or architect before you accept it as being built to specification. The remaining five per cent of the price is held back until all of those issues have been cleared. If the defects will cost more than five per cent to rectify, the seller's liability is not limited to that five per cent. Once that has been done the buyer will, of course, remain entitled to the seller's compulsory two-year and 10-year guarantees.

Other Documentation

You will be given a full specification for the property, a copy of the community rules (*règlements de copropriété*) if the property shares common facilities, and a copy of any agreements you have entered into regarding ongoing management or letting of the property. All are important documents. Pay particular attention to the specification. It is not unknown for the show flat to have marble floors and high-quality wooden kitchens but for the specification to show concrete tiles and MDF.

Renegotiating the Terms of the Contract

If you have signed a contract before seeking legal advice and it turns out that it has deficiencies that, though not legally sufficient to cancel the contract, cause you concern it may be possible to renegotiate the contract. The sooner you attempt to do this, the better.

Checklist – Signing a Contract

Property in the Course of Construction	Existing Property
Are you clear about what you are buying?	
Have you taken legal advice about who should be the owner of the property?	
Have you taken legal advice about inheritance issues?	
Are you clear about boundaries?	
Are you clear about access?	
	Are you sure you can change the property as you want?
	Are you sure you can use the property for what you want?
	Is the property connected to water, electricity, gas, etc?
	Have you had a survey done?
Have you made all necessary checks OR arranged for them to be made?	
Have you included 'get-out' clauses for all important checks not yet made?	
Is your mortgage finance arranged OR a 'get-out' clause inserted in the contract?	
Is the seller clearly described?	
If the seller is not signing in person, have you seen a power of attorney/mandate to authorize the sale?	
Are you fully described?	
Is the property fully described? Identification? Land registry details?	
Is the price correct?	
Are any possible circumstances in which it can be increased or extras described fully?	
Are the stage payments fully described?	Does contract say when possession will be given?
Do stage payments meet the legal restrictions?	Receipt for the deposit paid?
Is the date for completion of the work agreed?	In what capacity is the deposit paid?

Is the date for signing the *acte* agreed?
Does the contract provide for the sale to be free of charges and debts?
Does the contract provide for vacant possession?
Which notary is to act?
Is the estate agent's commission dealt with?
What happens if there is a breach of contract?
Are all the necessary special 'get-out' clauses included?

Mortgage?	Mortgage?
Increase in price?	Pre-emption by SAFER?
	Other pre-emption
	Survey?
	Planning certificate?
	Other?

Steps Between Signing the Contract and Signing the Deed of Sale (*Acte de Vente*)

Power of Attorney (Procuration; Pouvoir; Mandat)

Completion dates on French property are notoriously fluid and so you could plan to be present but suffer a last-minute delay to the signing that makes it impossible. If you cannot sign the *acte de vente* in person, the solution to this problem is the power of attorney. This document authorizes the person appointed (the *mandataire*) to do whatever the document authorizes on behalf of the person granting the power (the *mandant*). The most sensible type of power to use will be the French style of power that is appropriate to the situation. (In theory an English-style power should be sufficient, but in practice the cost and delay associated with getting it recognized will be unacceptable.)

The type of French power of attorney that you will need depends on what you want to use it for. Your specialist English lawyer can discuss your requirements with you and prepare the necessary document. Alternatively you can deal directly with the French notary who will ultimately need the power.

Getting the Money to France

There are a number of ways of getting the money to France:

• **Electronic transfer:** The most practical is to have it sent electronically by SWIFT transfer from a UK bank directly to the recipient's bank in France. This costs about £20–35 depending on your bank. It is safer to allow two or three days for the money to arrive in a rural bank, despite everyone's protestations that it will be there the same day.

IBANK numbers (unique account numbers for all bank accounts, incorporating a code for the identity of the bank and branch involved as well as the account number of the individual customer) should be quoted, if possible, on all international currency transfers.

You can send the money from your own bank, via your lawyers or via a specialist currency dealer. For the sums you are likely to be sending you should receive an exchange rate much better than the 'tourist rate' you see in the press. If you do a lot of business with a bank and they know you are on the ball you are likely to be offered a better rate than a one-off customer. For this reason it is often better to send it via your specialist UK lawyers, who will be dealing with large numbers of such transactions.

You or your lawyers might use a specialist currency dealer to make the transfer of funds instead of a main UK bank. Such dealers often give a better exchange rate than an ordinary bank, but do make sure that the dealer you are using is reputable. Your money is paid to them, not to the major bank, and so could be at risk if the dealer is not bonded or otherwise protected.

However you make the payment, ensure that you understand whether it is you or the recipient who is going to pick up the receiving bank's charges. If you need a clear amount in France you will have to make allowances for these, either by sending a bit extra or by asking your UK bank to pay all the charges. Make sure you have got the details of the recipient bank, its customer's name, the account codes and the recipient's reference precisely right. Any error and the payment is likely to come bank to you as undeliverable – and may involve you in bearing the cost of its being converted back into sterling.

• **Banker's drafts**: You can arrange for your UK bank to issue you with a banker's draft (bank-certified cheque) which you can take to France and pay into your bank account. Make sure that the bank knows that the draft is to be used overseas and issues you with an international draft. Generally this is not a good way to transfer the money. It can take a considerable time – sometimes weeks – for the funds deposited to be made available for your use. The recipient bank's charges can be surprisingly high. The exchange rate offered against a sterling draft may be uncompetitive, as you are a captive customer. If the draft is lost it can, at best, take months to obtain a replacement and, at worst, be impossible to do so.

• **Cash**: This is not recommended. You will need to declare the money on departure from the UK and on arrival in France. The exchange rate you will be offered for cash is usually very uncompetitive and the notary may well refuse to accept the money in his account. Don't do it.

• **Exchange control and other restrictions on moving money**: For EU nationals there is no longer any exchange control when taking money to or from France. There are some statistical records kept, showing the flow of funds and the purpose of the transfers. When you sell your property in France you will be able to bring the money back to the UK if you wish to do so.

Final Checks about the Property

All of the points outstanding as *clauses suspensives* must be resolved to your satisfaction, as must any other points of importance to you.

Fixing the Completion Date

The date stated in the contract for signing the *acte* could, most charitably, be described as flexible or aspirational. More often than not it will move, if only by a day or so. Sometimes the *certificat d'urbanisme* may not have arrived. On other occasions the seller's dispensation from paying French capital gains tax may be delayed. Occasionally your money to buy the house will get stuck in the banking system for a few days. For this reason it is not sensible to book your travel to France until you are almost sure that matters will proceed on a certain day. That may mean a week or two before signing.

Checklist – Steps Before Completion

Property in the Course of Construction	**Existing Property**
Prepare power of attorney	
Check what documents must be produced on signing the *acte*	
Confirm all *clauses suspensives* have been complied with	
Confirm all other important enquiries are clear	
Receive draft of proposed *acte de vente* – one month in advance if possible	
Check seller applied for exemption from CGT	
Confirm arrangements (date, time, place) for completion with your lender if you have a mortgage	
Confirm arrangements (date, time, place) for completion with notary	
Send necessary funds to France	
Receive rules of community (*règlements de copropriété*)	
Insurance cover arranged?	
Sign off work or list defects	Proof of payment of community fees
	Proof of payment of other bills

The Deed of Sale (*Acte de Vente*)

This must be signed in front of a French notary either by the parties in person or someone holding power of attorney for them. The document itself is, largely, a repeat of the contents of the preliminary contract with some additional elements. Because it is such an important document it is worth looking at in some detail. A typical *acte* might contain the following sections:

- **Name and Address of Notary** (*Nom et Adresse du Notaire*).

- **Identification of the Parties** (*Identification des Parties*): This will set out the full details of both buyer and seller (their *états civils*) and the same details of any persons apperaring on their behalf under a power of attorney together with details of the power.

- **Designation** (*Désignation*): This sets out a full description of the property, its land registry details and plot numbers together with details of any restrictions affecting the property. If it is an apartment it will also give details of the common parts – i.e. community property – from which you will benefit.

- **Ownership and Possession** (*Propriété – Jouissance*): This justifies the current claim to ownership of the property and states the date on which the buyer will take over possession of the property (normally that day). It will also confirm that the property is free of tenants (or not, as the case may be) and confirm liability on the part of the seller for all bills up to that date.

- **Price** (*Prix*): The price is stated. Methods of payment are stated. A receipt for payment is given.

- **Administrative Declaration** (*Déclaration pour l'Administration*): This stipulates the nature of the sale and thus the nature of the taxes payable in respect of the sale.

- **Capital Gains Tax** (*Plus-value*): This states the vendor's situation regarding any possible capital gains tax liability on the sale.

- **Calculation of Taxes** (*Calcul des Droits*): This section, if present, will calculate all of the duties payable on the sale.

- **Persons Present or Represented** (*Présences ou Représentations*): Details of all people present at the sale are set out.

- **Sale** (*Vente*): The sale is confirmed to have taken place.

- **Planning and Roads** (*Urbanisme – Voirie*): Details of the town planning situation and reference to the *certificat d'urbanisme* are attached.

- **Rights of Pre-emption** (*Droits de Préemption*): Confirmation that the various (named) people and organizations who might have pre-emptive rights have renounced them.

- **History of the Property** (*Origine de la Propriété*): How the present owner came to own the property – e.g. by inheritance from X or by purchase from Y on [DATE]. Details of the penultimate owner might also be given.

- **Ownership and Occupation** (*Propriété – Occupation*): The date on which the buyer becomes owner of the property and confirmation of vacant possession.

- **Charges and General Conditions** (*Charges – Condition Générales*): Any charges or burdens registered against the property together with the seller's warranties and guarantees.

- **Loans** (*Prêt*): Details of any mortgage finance used to buy the property. This will only refer to any French mortgage. It is of no concern to the French if you mortgaged your UK home for this purpose.

- **Statement of Sincerity** (*Affirmation de Sincérité*): A statement that both parties confirm the truth of all statements in the *acte*, that the price has been fully stated and (usually untrue) that the notary has warned the parties of the sanctions that may flow from false declaration. Because it is rare for notaries to perform this important part of their duty it is worth setting out some of these sanctions. Firstly, the right to raise a supplemental demand for tax not paid + interest + penalty. And secondly, if there is a clear and intentional understatement, the right to buy the property at the price stated plus 10 per cent. This right must generally be exercised within six months.

Formalities

Certain procedures are followed at the signing of the *acte*. The parties are identified by their passports or identity cards. This will normally be done, at least initially, by the notary's clerk. The notary should also ask to see the proof of identity. The notary's clerk will also go through the content of the *acte* with the parties. This tends to be very superficial and often the person concerned will have limited English.

The parties will then be ushered into the presence of the notary. In addition to the buyer and seller it would be possible for the group to comprise also the notary's clerk, the other notary if a second has been appointed, your lawyer, a translator, a representative of the *copropriété*, a representative of your mortgage lender, the estate agent and any sub-agent appointed by the estate agent. Most of these people are there to receive money. Needless to say, if they all turn up it can get a little loud and confusing!

After the *Acte* Has Been Signed

The signing of the *acte* is not the end of the matter. Aterwards, the notary will, from the money you have sent him, pay your taxes to the state and settle his fees. From the money due to the seller he will pay off any sums due to the estate agent and the *copropriété* (if it has been agreed he is responsible for these), any debts on the property that are not being taken over by the buyer, and any other agreed sums. Eventually the balance is sent to the seller. The notary is allowed one month to pay the taxes, but should do so much sooner.

Once the taxes are paid, your title and any mortgage should be presented for registration at the land registry. This must, by law, be done within two months, but again should be done more quickly as there is a potential danger of someone registering another transaction (such as a debt or judgement) against the property. He who registers first gets priority.

After several months the land registry will issue a certificate (*expédition*) to the effect that the title has been registered. This is sent to the notary who dealt with the transaction. The notary will then send you the certificate and other paperwork related to the purchase together with his final bill and a statement showing how he has used the money you sent him. Some notaries are very slow at sending out this final paperwork, possibly because they usually ask at the outset for a little bit more than they are actually likely to need and so will have to make you a small refund!

The Cost of Buying a Property in France

These are the fees and taxes payable by a buyer when acquiring a property in France. They are sometimes known as completion expenses or completion or closing costs. They are impossible to predict with total accuracy at the outset of a transaction. This is because there are a number of variable factors that will not become clear until later. We can, however, give a general guide.

These costs are calculated on the basis of the price that you declared as the price paid for the property in the *acte de vente*. The size of these expenses, coupled with the French dislike for paying tax, has led to the habit of accidentally under-declaring the price in the *acte*. These days are now largely over and we can only suggest that the full price of the property is declared.

The notary will ask for payment of these sums (plus his fees and a small margin in case of the unexpected surprise or error) before the signing of the *acte*. It is normal to send them at the same time as the price of the property.

Notary's Fees

These are fixed by law, so are not negotiable. They will depend on the type of property being bought and its price. As a general guide, allow 1.3 per cent for properties less than £50,000 and one per cent for properties over £50,000. If you have asked the notary to do any additional work over and above the transfer of title to the property, or for any advice, there will be additional charges. All of the notary's charges will be subject to VAT (*TVA*) of 19.6 per cent.

New Property: VAT (*TVA*) and Land Registration Fees

In this context, a 'new' property is one that is less than five years old *and* being sold for the first time). The total of the taxes and land registry fees usually amounts to about 20 per cent of the declared price of the property:

- **VAT (*TVA*):** This is 19.6 per cent of the declared purchase price of the property. This is normally included in the price of the property quoted to you. Check to see whether it is in your case.
- **Land Registry Fee:** Usually 0.615 per cent.

Resale Property: Taxes and Land Registration Fees

- **Departmental Tax** (*Taxe Départementale*).
- **Communal Tax** (*Taxe Communale*): Always 1.2 per cent, whichever *commune* you live in.
- **Levy for Expenses** (*Prélèvement pour Frais*): This is based on 2.5 per cent of the *taxe départementale*.
- **Land Registry Fee:** The total of the taxes and land registry fees amounts to 4.89 per cent of the declared price of the property.

Mortgage Costs (if applicable)

If you are taking out a mortgage there will be additional costs. These typically amount to three per cent of the amount borrowed. Most of these charges will be subject to *TVA* at 19.6 per cent.

Estate Agent's Charges (if payable by the buyer)

If an estate agent has sold the property, his fees, usually between three and five per cent depending on the location and value of the property, are usually paid by the seller. This can be varied by agreement. If a notary has sold the property his fee will be paid by the buyer. These will be subject to *TVA* at 19.6 per cent.

Miscellaneous Other Charges

Architect's fees, surveyor's fees, UK legal fees (typically one per cent), first connection to water, electricity, etc. Most of these will be subject to French *TVA* at 19.6 per cent, but your English lawyer's fees will be outside the scope of English VAT.

Home Insurance

Insurance is big business in France – so big that two of the largest groups, Groupement d'Assurances Nationales and Assurances Générales de France, are nationalized. There are over 500 companies regulated by a *Code des Assurances* and overseen by a Commission de Contrôle des Assurances. The main difference between insuring your house in France and Britain is that, in France, you must have third-party coverage by law. How likely it is that your house is going to damage somebody or something is debatable, but this is a legal requirement.

Property Taxes

There are two types of property tax in France: the *taxe foncière* and the *taxe d'habitation*. The first is a land tax levied on the owner of any plot of land registered with the land registry (*cadastre*). The second is an 'occupancy' tax levied on the person living inside the house regardless of whether they are the owner or the tenant. If the property is being renovated or is uninhabitable, you should be able to negotiate an exemption with the Direction des Impôts, Trésor Public. The *taxe d'habitation* usually does not add up to very much. The bill will come in the autumn and can be paid at the local post office like any utility bill.

Renting

Your options for finding rental property include hiring an agent, scanning the internet, and searching local publications or the property section of a local newspaper. The best option is word of mouth.

Leases

If you are not renting for a short period, for example, the duration of a holiday, most leases (*contrat de location* or *bail*) last a fixed time, say, three years, and are renewable. Contracts lasting three months, six months, one year or any length of time can be negotiated with the owner. To lease in your own name (*bail au nom propre*), you will be asked to provide your passport and proof of some kind of financial stability like a work contract or bank statements.

Deposit

You will be required to pay one or two months' rent in advance as a safety deposit (*dépôt de garantie*). If the property is found to be in good condition upon your departure, the deposit is refunded.

Expenses

In addition to the monthly rent, you will be expected to pay utilities and other expenses. These include water, gas for heating, telephone service, electricity, cleaning and maintenance of the building, lift expenses and the porter's fee. Maintenance is usually paid quarterly and is calculated by the administrator of the building based on the size of your apartment and the floor it is on (for the lift fee). The tenant is also responsible for the occupancy tax (*taxe d'habitation*).

Appliances

Make sure you check them well (especially the refrigerator and washing machine) before renting. The high calcium content in French water makes dishwashers and washing machines clog easily and you don't want to have to fix damage done by a previous tenant. Also, make sure the water heater functions well. Check all appliances with the owner before signing the lease.

Repairs

As a rule of thumb, major repairs such as wiring, plumbing and blinds are the owner's responsibility. Minor repairs due to wear and tear are your responsibility.

Inventory

It's a good idea to make a detailed list of all the furniture, cutlery, kitchen and bathroom items before you sign the contract. Itemize everything and make a note of its condition.

Semi-furnished Apartments

These usually include major appliances, like a stove and refrigerator, and little-to-no furniture.

Unfurnished Apartments

These are usually bare, with tubes protruding from the walls for you to connect your own kitchen appliances.

Porter

The *concierge*, or custodian, usually lives on the ground floor of an apartment building and sits in a little booth at the entrance. He does light repairs and cleaning, collects mail, signs for packages that don't fit in the post box (important if you're not often home during the day) and guards the building against strangers during working hours. You should tip him at Christmas and when extra services are provided.

Rent

Paid monthly (sometimes quarterly) by direct bank transfer, by cheque or cash.

Notice

Most leases call for six months' advance notice in writing prior to the termination of the lease (sent via registered-return receipt mail). Three months' notice is required on leases of one year. In general, if you help the landlord find a replacement tenant, you can arrange your departure with the owner without waiting.

Home Utilities

France offers a painfully simple system when it comes to utilities. Because most are state-run monopolies, you don't have to bother shopping around for the cheapest rates. You take what you get and make sure you pay your bills on time.

Computer-generated bills come by post and contain a remittance slip for making payment. The bill (*facture*) will contain your personal data, account number (*numéro de compte* or *numéro de contrat*), the amount owed (*montant à régler*) and the due date for payment. If your utilities are paid by direct debit from your bank (*prélèvement automatique*), there is no remittance slip but you will see the amount deducted (*montant prélevé* or *montant facturé*) and the date of the next withdrawal (*prochain relevé*). Remember that many bills are not itemized. A phone bill, for example, might list 18 local calls (*appels locaux*) and 10 calls to a foreign mobile phone (*vers mobiles internationaux*) but won't tell you the numbers dialled. Other bills are calculated by your 'estimated' consumption, which is then adjusted either up or down when the meter (*compteur*) is read. When installing your electricity, water and gas, make sure you know where the meter is located so you can keep track of billing. If you leave the house empty for long periods, request that the meters be placed on an outside wall (even if the meter is in your basement a wire can be brought to street level) so that the gas and electricity company can make readings when you are not home. The electricity meter must be read once a year.

To set up a new service you should contact each utility and be able to produce documentation such as your *carte de séjour*, lease if you are letting, and bank account details if you intend to pay by direct debit.

Utility Companies

Utility	Name of Company	Website
Electricity	*Electricité de France*	**www.edf.fr**
Gas	*Gaz de France*	**www.gazdefrance.com**
Water	*Générale des Eaux*	**www.generale-des-eaux.com**
Telephone	*France Télécom*	**www.francetelecom.com**

Note that in the majority of cases EDF (*Electricité de France*) and GDF (*Gaz de France*) are billed on the same statement. France's water company, *Générale des Eaux,* is privatized, so you may be billed by any one of its subsidiaries under a different name.

Payment

There are several options for paying, but by far the most convenient is direct debit from your bank account (*prélèvement automatique*) especially for foreigners who travel often. Bills usually come every two months or six months depending on the service. These are the ways of paying:

• **Pay at the utility company**: This is highly inconvenient because it usually means trekking across town at dawn to queue with everybody else.

• **Pay at the post office**: Bring your remittance slip from the utility company and the amount due in cash. Based on the information on your remittance slip, the post office knows where to send your money but keeps your receipt as proof of payment. You can also pay taxes and magazine subscriptions at the post office. Most also accept payment by cash debit card (not a credit card).

- **Pay through your bank**: Give your bank information to the utility (your name or *nom du titulaire du compte*, your bank's name or *nom de la banque*, the account number or *numéro de compte*, the bank code or *code établissement* and the branch number or *code guichet*) and wash your hands of the whole affair. The bank will charge you a small fee for this service. The utility company will send you an invoice every two months so you can keep track of the amounts deducted and you will see them on your bank statement. Make sure you keep of a reserve of ample funds in your bank account otherwise the service might be cut off. A few years back, my water pipe broke underground and water bled away without my knowing it. When the extremely expensive water bill hit my account, it dried it of available funds and when the next round of utilities arrived there were insufficient funds. As luck would have it, all this happened when I was abroad. I wish they had pulled the plug on my water service, because when I returned I was forced to pay for the many cubic meters of water I had contributed to the aquifer.

- **Internet**: You cannot yet pay your bills on the internet, although this will probably change soon. But you can keep track of your expenses and account online.

If you need to dispute a bill, don't expect an easy ride. The best thing to do is never get to this point by regularly and religiously checking your meters and comparing notes with what the utility company billed. If you make a convincing argument, the amount you were overcharged will be subtracted from the next billing cycle.

Electricity (*Electricité de France*)

France generates two-thirds of its power by nuclear reactors with the remaining coming mostly from environment-friendly hydro-electric plants. For this reason, electricity is cheaper than almost anywhere else in Europe and consequently most appliances run on electricity (such as electric hobs and ovens). Home heating is generally electric.

Contracts can be set up for various levels of power – from three kilowatts to 36 kilowatts. Three, six and nine kilowatts are not very much: you won't be able to vacuum your floors and toast bread at the same time without blowing a fuse. If you don't want to be left in the dark looking for the circuit box, make sure you know how to reset your system *before* you overload it! Systems lower than nine kilowatts can't support electric heating, which requires at least 12 kilowatts. There are different tariffs available that carry different pricing schemes according to usage and the time of day. The French have juggling these tariffs

Air-conditioning

Air-conditioning is considered a luxury item in France and is expensive to install and operate (reflected in your electricity bills). Once you have spent a sleepless night at the end of July (you can't open windows to cool down otherwise vicious mosquitoes will turn you into a bloody pulp), you'll run to the nearest appliance store. It is highly recommended that you install air-conditioning, especially if you are a retiree or expect to have elderly visitors. Some 13,000 deaths were blamed on the summer 2003 heatwave and many lives might have been saved if more hospitals and private homes had had air-conditioning.

down to a science. For example, if the cheapest tariffs are at night, they will set heaters and water boilers to run then and reserve enough hot water for the next day. There are two domestic tariffs: blue tariff (*tarif bleu*) divided into *option base* and *option heures creuses*, and *tempo*. In *option base*, night and day rates are priced the same. In *option heures creuses*, you can select your own reduced rate period. With *tempo* you are encouraged to use electricity when demand is lowest.

French wiring is different from English so you should not bring an electrician from home to do work here, nor attempt it yourself. Fiddling with incompatible wiring is downright dangerous. Almost all property is connected at 220/240 volts. Any property still connected at 110/120 volts can be converted. Because of old wiring, power outages and surges are frequent. Get a UPS (uninterruptible power supply) and a surge protector to protect your television sets, video recorders and especially computers. Electric plugs are two-pronged or sometimes have a third 'earth' prong.

Your EDF bill serves as proof that you have an address in France, and you might find a copy useful when you open a bank account or perform other bureaucratic tasks.

Gas (*Gaz de France*)

Although gas is available in towns and cities, gas pipes do not extend to many remote rural areas. Like electricity, the gas company offers different tariffs and bills you every two months. For all practical purposes, EDF and GDF are a combined company and both are billed together. Some hob and oven units rely on a combination of gas and electricity (gas for the hob and electricity for the oven) and many larger houses and apartment complexes will have gas-generated centralized heating. If your area is not connected to gas mains, you can buy refillable gas tanks (more expensive in the long run). Bottled propane or butane is found at the supermarket and petrol station and you arrange to have it delivered to your home.

Water (*Générale des Eaux*)

Water is supplied by a number of private companies, which fall under the *Générale des Eaux* umbrella. Water is priced per cubic meter and the tariffs vary according to reserves, rainfall and how much water is used. For example, if you live in an area with many swimming pools, you will have a higher water tariff. If you share a meter with neighbours, you will be billed in equal parts even if someone else takes 12 showers a day.

When you go on holiday, make sure you turn off your water as much of the plumbing is old and leaks are frequent. Pipes burst especially in August when the mass exodus of vacationers influences water pressure. If you live in a rural area, you should also expect water shortages. The result is restrictions on supply, particularly in summer months, so it's a good idea to think ahead and fill a storage tank to meet your needs, especially if you have a garden.

Here are some other water-related issues to keep in mind:

- **Boilers:** Make sure yours is big enough. A small boiler only holds enough warm water for one quick shower or one dish-washing session.

- **Wells:** Even if you don't intend to draw drinking water from a well, they are a useful and cheap way of watering your garden or filling your swimming pool (you don't pay for water from wells or natural springs). Some wells (*puits*) dry in the summer and others acquire such a high salt content that they can't be used for irrigation.

- **Septic tanks:** Most rural properties depend on a septic tank for drainage and waste removal. A septic tank acts like a filter and treats sewage by breaking it down with bacteria. Modern equipment treats all the waste you produce and discharges it safely. Septic tanks have a natural lifespan and will need to be replaced. If you are installing a new one, make sure you get the right size (a 3,000-litre tank should be fine for a three-bedroom house and a 4,000-litre tank is good for a two-family home). If your tank is too small, you will spend more time and money emptying it.

- **Swimming pools:** If you live in an arid area with frequent water shortages, your town hall might not grant you a permit to build one.

Telephone (*France Télécom*)

Partially privatized France Télécom has dramatically improved its service and quality in recent years. Because the nation's wiring and infrastructure belongs to France Télécom, it has been able to branch off and add more vital services in a country dependent on the internet.

Through the company Wanadoo, France Télécom offers broadband lines for faster connection speeds (*see* 'The Internet', pp.183–5), and second phone lines for your fax machine or for your computer modem. Remember that slower baud rates may make faxing and dialling up the internet pricey. It also offers a range of services you are familiar with such as call waiting, call forwarding, caller identification and automatic answering services. These will add a bit more to your phone bill. Rates are competitive and you can negotiate different pricing schemes according to your needs. For example, the *tarif général* is for private users who call mostly at weekends and the *tarif professionnel* favours daytime calls. Every area has its own phone prefix: for example, Paris is 01, and 02 is for the northwest. Mobile phones start with 06, special rates with 08. All operations concerning your telephone (obtaining a phone line, laying the cables, billing options and payment, special services) can be done through the local France Télécom bureau (Agence Commerciale des Télécommunications), or by dialling 1014. For billing queries call 3000 (a free automated service).

Since 1998, the telephone market has been deregulated and there are two new national operators, CEGETEL and Bouygues, which both compete with France Télécom on long-distance calls only. France Télécom keeps its monopoly on local calls. You can sign a contract with one of these private companies in department stores such as FNAC, Darty, Auchan or in shops specializing in telecom equipment.

There are a few other ways to steer clear of France Télécom. You could use a British phone card for long distance. Or, you could buy one of the pre-paid phone cards (*télécartes*) available at the *tabac*. There are many cards to choose from that come in different denominations (€5–100) and offer attractive rates (as low as 300 minutes of phone time to the UK for €10). The drawbacks are that you must dial a tiresome series of numbers and secret codes (provided when you purchase the card) to access the system. But you dial into a free number so you can use the card from a payphone or from your home phone with no cost.

In recent years, more working professionals and busy travellers opt not to install a fixed-line telephone service in their homes (thus avoiding the monthly base charges and taxes) and instead rely exclusively on their mobile phones (*see* next section).

Mobile Phones

The three main mobile phone companies are SFR, Orange and Bouygues and each offers competitive rates and similar service. To sign up, visit one of the thousands of telecommunication shops throughout the nation (recognized by the large number of mobile phones in their display window) or the local electronics store.

To apply for a subscription, you will need a billing address (and proof of an address such as an EDF bill in your name) and identification, such as your *carte de séjour*. If you opt for a subscription, your mobile phone company will often throw in a mobile for free or almost free and you will be billed at home. Your mobile phone bill is like any other utility and can be paid via direct debit from your bank account.

The alternative is to buy a phone at full price (or use your British phone, remove the SIM card – the memory chip that contains your phone number – and buy a French SIM card, which means you will have a French mobile phone number that starts with o6 and will pay French rates, thus avoiding international calling rates from your British SIM) and recharge it with pay-as-you-go cards (*mobicarte*). No address or identification is required for the prepaid cards. Most foreigners find this method to be the most convenient as there are no bills or contracts involved. You can buy the prepaid 'recharge' cards at any *tabac* or supermarket. Remember that when your money runs out, you can no longer make calls or receive calls when you are outside France. If you are in France with zero credit you can only receive calls.

As far as the handsets are concerned, you can choose from the same models you will recognize from the UK. GSM is the standard technology, and new third generation phones let you surf the internet, take digital photos or short movies and send them to other users. All phones let you send SMS or text messages and have answering machine and address book functions.

The Internet

Almost two decades ago, France invented the Minitel (a small computer that hooked into the phone system to provide information, train timetables and booking services to users). Although the Minitel never reached global scope, it is still used in millions of French households. It is the grandfather of the internet as we know it and a symbol of France's determination to stay on the cutting edge of technology.

Partly due to France's affection for the Minitel, the internet had a slower start here. But what started as an ember has burst into flame and French public institutions, universities and small businesses have launched some of the world's most beautifully designed and informative websites. France may have missed out on the 'dot.com' glory years that sparked the rapid rise and fall of so many companies, but that may be the reason why it is so enthusiastic about the internet today.

The main internet service provider is **www.wanadoo.fr**, which technically offers free ISP service – although you do pay for your time online and this is reflected on your France Télécom bill. Beware: although the fee is only a few euro cents per minute, time does add up very fast. Wanadoo will provide free software to connect to the internet and you will receive an e-mail address with a wanadoo.fr suffix. France Télécom offers special deals to keep connection costs down. You can pay per minute of internet use, or sign on for a monthly fee that gives you a limited number of hours online per billing cycle. To set up

Jargon Justice?

As if *internautes* didn't already have enough English–French translations to do when surfing the 'universal spider web' (*toile d'araignée universelle*), the French government, in conjunction with everybody's favourite language conservationist group, the Académie Française, banished the word 'e-mail' from French usage in 2003. In its place now is the nationalistically correct '*courriel*'.

Courriel is the official French term for those electronic mail messages you receive via a computer modem. The Culture Ministry announced that all government offices, documents, publications and websites should immediately discontinue using the word formerly known as e-mail.

According to the ministry's General Commission on Terminology and Neology, French people never liked 'e-mail' anyway and had long adopted *courrier électronique* as part of the world wide web lexicon. *Courriel* is meant as a fusion of the two words, much in the same way 'e-mail' is a combination of 'electronic' and 'mail'. Coincidence?

The Commission was very proud of its new term. 'Evocative, with a very French sound, the word *courriel* is broadly used in the press and competes advantageously with the borrowed "mail" in English,' it boasted in a public statement. However, the Académie Française has not enjoyed much success in outlawing other interlopers such as '*le week-end*' and '*le shopping*'.

Critics said the new word sounded contrived. But given the global nature of the internet it is doubtful if anyone outside France will know what to do when they receive an incoming *courriel*.

an account, all that you need is a fixed phone line and a contract for France Télécom service.

Far more interesting, however, is Wanadoo's **broadband** service. There are different packages available that offer various speeds – from 128K, 512K and higher (up to 20 times faster than normal internet connections). Selecting which is right for you depends on whether you download and upload heavy graphics and music files. Downloading a two-hour feature film, for example, might take a few hours via broadband and a few days via the normal phone line. Wanadoo's ADSL eXtense packages start at €30 per month, although promotional fees are available throughout the year. In addition to the monthly fee that can be paid by direct bank debit (you sign a contract for a minimum of 12 months), you pay a one time €100 fee to rent the ADSL modem. The fee is returned to you when you terminate your contract and return the modem.

Broadband means your internet is always turned on and you pay a flat fee no matter how long you use it. You can use your phone and fax normally even when your computer is logged on. The French phone company and Wanadoo are betting on broadband business to outpace mobile phone profits in the long term and are engaged in an aggressive campaign to attract new subscribers.

Anyone who spends a lot of time on the internet would be foolish not to sign on for ADSL. Unfortunately, it is not available everywhere; Wanadoo can tell you if your town or area is set up for broadband service.

If you decide to stay with your British ISP, make sure it has an access number in France. Also check that it doesn't charge surplus fees when you dial up from abroad. To connect, you might need to check 'ignore dial tone' if your modem has difficulty communicating with French phones.

The most popular search engines are **www.voila.fr** and **www.google.fr**. The French *Yellow Pages* are online at **www.pagesjaunes.fr** and are an incredible resource for people looking for language schools, cookery classes, builders or anything else in their neighbourhood. Site **www.laposte.net** details the functions of the postal system. In addition, there are a slew of sites to help foreigners in France. These include **www.angloinfo.com**, **www.paris-anglo.com**, **www.rivieraradio.mc** (with a listing of jobs and used goods for sale), **www.rivierareporter.com** (with very good advice cornering bureaucracy), **www.escapeartist.com**, **www.expatica.com**, **www.french-news.com** and **www.discoverfrance.com**.

Television and Satellite Service

Although there has been talk of phasing it out, France has a mandatory television tax (*redevance*) due each year (your bill will come by post and you can pay it at the post office). Anyone who owns a TV is technically obliged to pay it (unless they are over 64 or are poor). Don't bother bringing your UK television to France because it won't work.

What does your money buy? For starters, you'll get five main terrestrial channels that many French avoid whenever they humanly can. They are TF1, France2 and France3, Arte/France 5 (La Cinq) and M6. (For more information on French media, *see* **France Today**, 'Major Media', pp.75–7.)

You can opt for a vast number of pay-TV channels through **Canal Plus** (there is a monthly fee). With one of their decoder boxes and a satellite dish, you will receive film channels and get a plethora of football channels. Some 200 channels broadcast variety shows (complete with scantily clad dancers), shopping clubs and basement shows with a long cast of questionable characters. Otherwise, you can buy a satellite dish and decoder box and *not* sign on for Canal Plus. In that case, you will still get hundreds of channels, but the most interesting ones (especially football programmes) will be scrambled.

If you are a Sky user your UK card does not authorize you to receive pictures in France because Sky is not licensed to operate outside Britain. Look again. Thousands of holidaymakers and British residents in France happily use their British cards anyway. If you go to a specialized satellite serviceman, he will even arrange a card for those who never had one in England. At the time this book went to press, there was talk of abolishing the address requirement in order to receive a Sky card.

Postal Services

Recognized by their blue and yellow colouring, the post office (*la poste*) is much more than a place to buy stamps. In many respects it is a public service station where you can open a sort of bank account, receive welfare payments, pay your utility bills and, of course, send and receive mail. For more information, go to **www.laposte.net**. Many post offices also have free internet stations (complete with free e-mail addresses for clients ending in laposte.net) and Minitel service.

Your use of *la poste* will probably be limited to sending mail. The overnight service is *Chronopost* and is equivalent to UPS or Federal Express. A registered letter is *lettre recommandée simple* and a registered letter that must be signed for upon receipt is *recommandée avec accusé de réception*. You can buy pre-stamped envelopes at the supermarket or the post office for both domestic and international mail.

You can also buy stamps in your nearest *tabac, see* 'Shopping', p.192.

Money and Banking

Anybody can open a bank account if they are over 18, have proof of identity and an address in France (bring a copy of your EDF bill). The type of account you open will ultimately depend on whether you are a resident or non-resident of France. Banking needs vary dramatically from person to person. If you are running a business or have multiple sources of income, you may require fairly sophisti-cated banking services. Otherwise your banking needs are likely to be very simple. For most foreigners, the only real concerns are finding a bank nearby and with English-speaking staff. France's biggest banks – Banque Nationale de Paris (BNP Paribas), Crédit Lyonnais, Société Générale and Crédit Agricole – fit the bill perfectly.

The best advantage of French banking is having your utilities, mobile phone service and broadband internet bills paid by direct debit. All the big banking institutions offer internet banking free of charge that allows clients to keep track of deposits and deductions. You can even arrange to send money online. Or, you can check your account by phone or Minitel; your bank will send you the secret codes for accessing these services to your home address. If you are choosing between various banks, select the one that has the most affordable charging structure for receiving money. French banks charge for absolutely

Quick Banking Tips

- Learn to write the date on your French cheque: 5 November 1970 is 5/11/70, not 11/5/70.

- Remember to cross the '7' so that it is not confused with a '1'.

- In French, a comma replaces a period and vice versa. We write €2,500.00. A French person would write €2.500,00.

- Often foreigners can't work out where to sign their cheques. The blank space at the lower right is for your signature.

- If for any reason you must deal with prices in old francs (like with the elderly), the exact euro–franc exchange is €0.1522449 for one franc and 6.55957 francs for €1.

everything and some charge for receiving funds from abroad. If you choose to use Barclays or another British bank, remember the services will not differ much from a French bank.

French banking hours are generally Mon–Fri 9am–4.30pm, although some banks close for lunch noon–1.30 or 2pm. Others are open on Saturday.

If you are a resident of France and have a *carte de séjour*, you can open a normal French account (*compte courant*), with a cheque book (*carnet de chèques*) and debit card (*carte bleue*, or CB) included. The latter can be a simple debit card or a combination of debit and credit cards (*carte de retrait* and *carte de crédit*). You generally cannot withdraw more than €500 per day, although you can negotiate individual limits with your bank branch.

Among the various accounts are a chequing account (*compte-chèques*) and a savings account (*compte sur livret*), which pays interest. Your *relevé de compte* is your bank statement that is sent monthly. You will have no problem sending or receiving wire transfers (*virement*) as long as you can supply the sender with the following information: your bank name, the bank code (*code établissement*), agency code (*code guichet*), your account number (*numéro de compte*) and the key number (*clé*). International transfers will require a SWIFT number, IBAN code or bank identifier code (BIC).

All this information is listed on your statement. Funds wired in different currencies will be automatically converted into euros based on the day's exchange rate.

The *compte non-résident* is for non-residents and functions much like a regular account. You can open a cheque account, savings account and get a *carte bleue* as a non-resident and you can deposit or withdraw in any currency you like. The only major difference is that a foreign account automatically lists your foreign address. You can ask for your statements to be sent to you in France as a courtesy, but the official address on the account will be in your home country. That means someone back home must retrieve the secret bank codes and replacement debit cards sent to your official address and then forward them to you in France.

Cheques

Do not even think about writing a cheque on your French account if there are insufficient funds (*un découvert*). This is a criminal offence. Bounced cheques lead to substantial bank charges and your bank can force closure of the account. In extreme cases, you will be banned from opening another account for five years.

'Offshore' accounts

Some people think that by having an offshore bank account they do not have to pay tax in France. This is not the case. The only way not to pay tax is by illegally hiding the existence of the bank account from tax authorities.

Shopping

Shopping habits are a good example of how France embraces the forces of the Old World and those of the New World. Not too long ago, France was a staunch promoter of the concept of speciality and boutique shops. In order to make a meal, shoppers were forced to visit almost as many shops as ingredients they required: one for bread, one for meat and one for vegetables. The payoff for the consumer was a guarantee of quality and a higher standard of service. (The local shop is always the best place to plug into juicy neighbourhood gossip as well.) The drawbacks were inflated prices and inconvenience.

The overriding philosophy was that shopping was not meant to be 'convenient'. Selecting the best head of cabbage involves deep thought and consideration; having the baker dig around for a large loaf of bread for you is expected, and having the pharmacist wrap your medicines in paper (to save you the embarrassment of other people knowing what you purchased) is part of the service. The French approach shopping as one of the day's principal activities, like going to work. They get dressed up, put on lipstick and generally take care to look good in the neighbourhood shop (or, God forbid, they risk becoming the focus of back-handed chatter). If you are not on familiar terms with your local shopkeeper, you will be treated with a certain formal distance that is meant to convey respect.

As in so many other countries, this kind of shopping is sadly on its way to extinction. Busy office workers and parents with better things to do than queue up opt to shop at the nearest supermarket where everything is under one roof.

France is the birthplace of a mutant species of supermarket so big it is technically a 'hypermarket'. The Carrefour chain is an excellent example. Employees get around on rollerskates and shoppers can reach for a new motorboat, mountain bike or kitchen unit in the aisle after the milk and butter.

Hypermarkets are so big, and cast such a long shadow, that they have permanently changed France's consumer landscape by wiping out the corner shop. My town, Biot, is a perfect example. Before Carrefour came we had three bakeries and two butchers. Now there is one of each, and because of the virtual monopoly each holds in its sector, both bread and meat quality has declined. In a sense, one is forced to shop at Carrefour and so the vicious circle perpetuates itself.

Shopping Hours

France's employment laws dictate the hours and days a shop can be open for business. But these regulations have been relaxed, giving more autonomy to the individual shop owners. You would expect most stores to be closed Sunday. That's not always the case. In my town, a strange phenomenon has developed: because Carrefour is closed on Sunday, the local shops stay open for business and rake in the biggest profits then.

Shops are generally open 9am–7pm and take a lunch break 1–3pm. This depends on the shop as these hours apply to clothes shops and most food shops. A bakery, for example, will be open just as the ovens are hottest, at about 6am. In big towns and cities like Paris, shops are known to keep their doors open until 10pm.

You can count on smaller shops to take two to four weeks off in the height of the summer, usually in and around the month of August. At the same time, larger shops usually expand their summer opening hours and stay open seven days a week to accommodate the number of holidaymakers. When small shops close in a town or neighbourhood, shop owners usually compare notes. If the butcher across the way from you shuts down in August, the butcher two streets up will stay open.

Payment

As you would expect, cash is golden; cheques are accepted sometimes reluctantly and bank cards are perfectly acceptable. Beware that many international bank debit cards seem to have a hard time communicating with the French system. Problems always seem to happen in dire situations, for example, when you are trying to fill your car with petrol from an automatic dispenser on a deserted road at midnight.

French credit cards use the 'chip and PIN' system, soon to be introduced in the UK, where instead of signing a slip you tap in a 4-digit PIN number into a machine by the till.

Sales

Twice a year, at the end of January and the beginning of July, clothing shops hold sales (*soldes*). The event sparks nationwide euphoria and shoppers bounce out of bed in the small hours to queue up for the best deals. By 4pm, shops look as if they were hit by a runaway hurricane. Prices are slashed up to 50 or 70 per cent and most sales are final.

Returns

Bringing an item back to the shop after it was purchased was almost unheard of several decades ago. Now, in a sudden about-face, it is common practice. Big chain stores have no problem with returns as long as you have a receipt and are making the return within 30 days of the purchase. Smaller shops may need more convincing.

Basic Shops

Alimentation Générale

These are mini-supermarkets that stock everything from eggs to tights. You will find detergents, hygiene products, canned goods, frozen foods, milk and cheese, cold cuts and meats, wine and bottled juices and more. The 'general store' is also known as an *épicerie* ('grocer'). Many also sell fresh produce. Some are open until late, and in bigger cities like Lyon and Marseille you will find many that cater to a North African clientele. They stock exotic items – from couscous spices to imported tinned vegetables.

Boucherie

If you're in the market for chicken, beef, pork, lamb, fowl, rabbit, veal or any other warm-blooded mammal to stick in a pot, this is your source. Butchers also sell eggs and sometimes have take-away meat dishes, such chicken roasted on a spit or vegetables stuffed with minced pork. You can discuss the cut of meat you want with the butcher and order items ahead that are not easy to find, such as blood sausages from the country farmer. A good butcher will even be able to get hold of a whole turkey for Americans celebrating Thanksgiving Day.

Boulangerie (also Pâtisserie)

This is where you'll want to press your nose against the glass. It is impossible to find a single item you won't like at the French bakery/pastry shop. That's not an exaggeration. It carries a wide variety of breads (from the ubiquitous *baguette* to bread with sesame seeds, rye bread, *pain de campagne* and sweet rolls), croissants, *pain au chocolat* and much more. Many bakeries complete

Baking Baguettes

The following recipe makes four loaves of sourdough French bread.

Ingredients
6 cups of unbleached whole grain white flour
½ to 1 cup of coarse wholewheat flour
3 teaspoons of salt
2¾ cups of warm water
1 cup sourdough starter
1 teaspoon of baker's yeast
2 tablespoons of olive oil
½ cup of cornmeal

The night before, combine 3 cups of white flour and the wholewheat flour with 2 teaspoons of salt, 2 cups of water and the sourdough starter. Mix and cover with a towel and let it sit for 10–18 hours. The following morning, prepare the dough by adding the other 3 cups of white flour, ¾ cup of warm water, 1 teaspoon of salt and yeast. Using a food processor with a metal blade, mix at low speed for 2 minutes and than at high speed for 5 minutes. Place onto a floured wooded board and knead the dough by hand until desired consistency, adding flour as necessary. Place the dough in a bowl coated with olive oil and smear some of the oil on to the dough to prevent drying. Let it rise threefold in volume. When this has occurred, punch down the dough slightly and place it on to a floured board again. Cut into long pieces and shape into baguettes with points at the end. Heat the oven to 425°Fahrenheit (220°Centigrade) and slash the top of the loaves with a razor or blade. Place them in the oven and spray every 2 minutes with water for the first 10 minutes. Reduce heat to 350° Fahrenheit (180°Centigrade) and bake for another 15 minutes. Remove the bread and allow it to cool.

three baking cycles per day – to keep consumers supplied with 'oven-hot' bread – and the delicious smell lingers all day long. The *pâtisserie* specializes in desserts like fruit tarts, éclairs, cakes, mousses and sweet cheese pies.

Charcuterie

Unlike the butcher, this shop sells spiced and cured meats, hams, and regional speciality dishes such as ratatouille, roast beef, picked vegetables, dried tomatoes, pâté, dried sausage (*saucisson*), salads and a wide range of appetizers and snacks.

Fromagerie

A reason in itself to move to France. You won't be able to govern your appetite for gluttony, echoing Charles de Gaulle's famous question: 'How can anyone govern a nation with 246 kinds of cheese?' Good question, but France has more like 2,000 kinds of cheeses. Creamy, rich and absurdly decadent *fromage* is something of a French national emblem and citizens have dedicated much effort to thinking up variations of the lactic treat. There is goat's milk cheese, cow's milk cheese, sheep's milk cheese, aged cheese and cream cheese. A *crèmerie* also sells dairy products such as fresh cream, milk, butter and yoghurt.

Poissonnerie

If you live by the sea, you'll see plenty of fishmongers hawking their goods each morning near the port. Top items include shellfish and molluscs (from prawns to mussels and oysters) to fish such as John Dory, sea perch, bream, cod fish, swordfish, anchovies, flounder, monk-fish, salmon, sardines, scorpion fish, sea bass, tuna, trout and red mullet. It's fun to compare what Mediterranean and Atlantic fishermen find in their nets. The shopkeeper will clean and de-bone a fish if you ask for it *'préparé'*.

All big supermarkets have a good fish section.

Primeurs

These are produce markets or greengrocers that sell everything ripened under the French sunshine. If the outdoor market has closed for the day (see below) you can find fruit and vegetables here.

Tabac

You can obviously buy cigarettes at the *tabac* and you can also get prepaid charge cards for your mobile phone, international phonecards, lottery tickets, postage stamps and tax stamps for various paperwork. How you actually get a *tabac* licence involves backroom dealings and genealogical privileges (the licences were originally given to war veterans, jealously guarded and passed down through the generations). Therefore, count on the local *tabac* owner to be a person of certain local influence.

Kiosques

These are the official outlet of printed goods such as magazines, newspapers, comic books and other small books. The larger *kiosques* will always keep a supply of foreign-language press on hand. You will have no problem finding the *Guardian*, the *Financial Times*, the *Independent* or the *International Herald Tribune* as well as a slew of English-language monthlies (from news to gardening and home decorating magazines).

Miscellaneous Shops

In addition to the shops outlined above, you could also need the services of the following: hairdresser (*coiffeur*), shoe repair shop (*cordonnier*), beautician (*esthéticienne*), florist (*fleuriste*), printer or engraver (*graveur*), stationery store (*papeterie*), pharmacy (*pharmacie*), dry cleaner (*pressing*), locksmith (*serrurier*) and cleaner (*teinturier*).

British and American Food Products

Unbelievably, English food is making inroads in the land of *haute cuisine* thanks to the growing expatriate community. From Paris to Antibes, you'll find speciality shops that cater to those with nostalgia for flavours from back home: from Cadbury's to Colmans. Indian, North African, Korean, Chinese and South American groceries are also available depending on the ethnic mix of your area. Even supermarket chains have a standard foreign foods section where you can pick up a carton of cranberry juice or kits for making Mexican tacos.

Shopping for Clothes

France is firmly planted on the fashion map thanks to international brand names – Hermès, Christian Dior, Chanel, Louis Vuitton, Yves Saint-Laurent, etc. In fact, France is the 'nation of fashion' and you can confirm the hyperbole yourself with a walk down any grand avenue. But if you live and work in France – and are not on a holiday shopping spree – you'll need to pinpoint alternative clothing options. In other words: find the cheap stuff.

Large department store chains – such as Printemps or the well-known and well-placed Galeries Lafayette – carry clothing for the whole family. The women's accessories and lingerie departments are mind-blowing. Perhaps less exciting, you'll find linens and kitchen goods too. The British chain Marks & Spencer came and went. There are cheaper shoe stores such as Eram – and the ubiquitous Carrefour has a range of basic clothing for adults and children.

Outdoor Markets

Every small town and city neighbourhood will have an outdoor market a few mornings a week, if not every morning. This is where France is at its most picture-perfect. Vendors haul in fresh produce from the countryside and lavishly decorate their tables with the colours of France: yellow *Cavaillon* melons, round courgettes, courgette blossoms, brown *cèpes* mushrooms, red beets, aubergines, purple-skinned onions, wild *mesclun* salad and rows of neatly trimmed leeks. All produce is rigorously sold in season. Large markets sell kitchen crockery and marked-down clothing and some areas have monthly antiques fairs or flea markets as well.

Supermarkets and Chain Stores

You know the drill. Besides the aggressive Carrefour chain, other supermarket franchises include Casino, Champion, Leclerc and Monoprix. Auchan, FNAC and Darty are good for electronics and home articles and Decathlon has sporting clothing and equipment. FNAC is the place to go for CDs, books and tickets.

DIY

Castorama (affectionately knows as 'Casto' among its faithful followers) is a DIY mecca. You'll find power tools, floor tiling, home insulation, locks, paints and carpentry materials such as wood. Lapeyre is another good name to know for home improvement. This national chain sells prefabricated kitchens, doors, windows and bathroom fixtures.

Life in Cafés, Bistros and Culinary Notes

France seduces all the senses but casts an especially strong spell on olfactory and taste. If I could launch a personal theory, I'd say 50 per cent of what makes France a wonderful place to live has to do with what its inhabitants put on the dining table.

France is even grander because not all its edible delights go on the table immediately. Shopkeepers and inn-owners exhibit their culinary specialities on the street, tempting pedestrians with a siren song to the stomach. Walking past the many *fromagerie*, *charcuteries* and *pâtisseries* in Paris, for example, it becomes impossible to tame those gastric juices.

The *Café*

The rest of the world has the internet as a forum for exchanging ideas but France has the café. It's a social and cultural institution and the quintessential place to linger. Cafés are always located on busy streets and usually have wicker tables and chairs that spill on to the pavement. The defining concept behind the café is you can stay as long as you'd like: read a book, sip your *panaché* (shandy, or beer with lemonade) for an entire afternoon and watch the people drift by. Many, many people do just that for hours on end, making a city like Paris echo with that irresistible *joie de vivre*. To cynics, the café culture is an indicator of an awful social woe: unemployment.

Most cafés have small things for nibbling (snacks and sandwiches, such as the *croque-monsieur*, a toasted cheese and ham sandwich, and the *croque-madame* with a fried egg on top), but their main mission is to quench your thirst. A French **coffee** (*café*) is black, served in a small cup, and is slightly larger than an Italian-style espresso (*express*). For most French people, the day starts off with a *café au lait* in a big cup, which they dip their breakfast bread or croissant in. Decaffeinated coffee is *déca*. On colder days you can warm your palms around a cup of **tea** (*thé*), which is served with lemon or milk (*thé au citron* or *thé au lait*). Herbals teas are *tisanes* and camomile is *camomille*. **Hot chocolate** (*chocolat chaud*) offers more calories to burn on those really chilly days.

Beer is happily a popular café beverage. Draught beer is *pression* and the standard glass size is 25cl, although your waiter will be happy to bring you a bigger one. Popular French beers include Kronenbourg 1664, Fischer/Pêcheur, Kanterbräu and Perlforth. Stella Artois is from Belgium. Normandy is home to apple **cider** (*cidre*) that has lower alcohol and you can always settle for a soda or grenadine. If you're on the wagon or just very thirsty, **water** (*eau minérale*) comes with bubbles or without (*gazeuse* versus *non-gazeuse* or *plate*).

Wine is served by the glass or by the carafe. The better stuff comes in bottles but can be expensive at the café. One delicious *apéritif* is *kir* or white wine or Champagne coloured by a drop of blackcurrent (*cassis*). All common **spirits** are available, such as gin and tonic and whisky. If you are in the south, you must partake in the local drinking ritual and order a glass of *pastis*, an aniseed-flavoured drink that turns white when you add water. Ricard or Pernod are good brands served with a small carafe of water and ice.

Take-away Food

There are plenty of places to order food to take away (*vente à emporter*) and among the most common are pizzerias and Chinese restaurants. Mr Pizza is a popular franchise that will deliver steaming pizzas to your home thanks to a squad of scooter-riding delivery boys – who are also something of a road hazard.

The *Brasserie*

A *brasserie* is like a café only it serves hot meals throughout the day – roughly the French equivalent of pub food. You can order a steak and fries (*steack-frites*) and wash it all down with a carafe of red wine before heading back to the office.

The *Bistro*

This is generally a step up from a *brasserie* and is a smallish, informal restaurant or neighbourhood eatery. Traditionally, it is where you will find copious

Bistro Beat

A visitor to Paris can't help but feel a tinge of nostalgia for what the City of Light must have been like at the height of its café culture: back when literary giants like Ernest Hemingway, Oscar Wilde and members of the Beat Generation migrated to their favourite watering holes to scribble furiously in notepads; back when Jean-Paul Sartre and his entourage, Picasso, and others chiselled away at the concept of *le rendez-vous de l'élite intellectuelle*, back when gangs of brain boys took up residence in a given café within a distinctly delineated territory.

If you have a few hours to contemplate the pavement panorama, head to Les Deux Magots in the *6ème arrondissement* across from the Abbey of St-Germain (its rival Café de Flore, is next door). The Deux Magots (**www.lesdeuxmagots. fr**), which attracts buskers and jazz musicians from the Beaux-Arts school, has stayed in a time capsule for more than a century. The historic café gets its name thanks to the two Chinese statues (the two *magots* or 'grotesque figures') that dominate the inside room. Intellectuals have been replaced by tourists, but fragments of the café's golden era still shine bright – and you'll want to scribble something 'important' on your napkin just to say you did.

servings at reasonable prices. In recent years a glossy veneer has been applied to the concept of the *bistro*. Many have evolved into trendy joints frequented by bohemians and fashionistas. Prices have been inflated accordingly.

The *Restaurant*

A restaurant offers a more formal dining environment, usually with white linen and waiters in uniform. The top-of-the-range restaurants are those that appear in the influential *Guide Michelin*, the one with the red cover. The book is an excellent yardstick for fine dining. Of course every restaurant will tempt you with its creative cooking, and menu items usually include regional specialities (for more about the foods of France, see **France Today**, 'French Cuisine', pp.98ff).

Haute cuisine is the most expensive and usually involves heavy creams and rare ingredients, such as black truffles or morel mushrooms. *Nouvelle cuisine* is similar only the portions are smaller and more attention is paid to the design impact of the food. *Cuisine régionale* is what we all love about France and is translated as 'regional gastronomy'. The *bouillabaisse* fish soup stays in Marseille and the *baeckeoffe* meat and potato casserole stays in Alsace. A restaurant's *plat du jour* is the 'dish of the day'.

Most restaurants offer 'menus' for a fixed price. The options are more limited than ordering from the menu (*à la carte*), but your meal will be cheaper. Menus are also assembled with an eye for which appetizer goes best with which dish. You will see children's menus (*menu pour enfants*) and tourist menus (*menu touristique*), although true gourmands will implore you to avoid the latter. Watch out: in France, you eat very well generally, but a few bad apples have spoiled the bunch as far as 'tourist' restaurants are concerned.

Transport

Getting from point A to point B in France is not only about getting to your destination. It involves fashion-statement automobiles, new standards in etiquette and, unfortunately, a need for speed. Judging from the behaviour on the roads, there is no doubt that France is a hot-blooded Latin country where the lumbering foreigner is either 'flashed' back into the slow lane or risks being mown down. To keep up with traffic, you'll need to make 'adjustments' to the staid road manners you were encouraged to use back home. Or take the bus.

Public Transport

Using France's excellent network of public transport is one way to go. Although the options are more than adequate and comfortable, France suffers from debilitating strikes that can bring the whole system to a screeching halt. Industrial action is common – especially in the spring and autumn when unions are set to renegotiate their contracts – and hits airports, ferry services and the railway at random. Often the strikes are intentionally staged the week before Christmas and can turn your holiday into a nightmare.

The *Métro*

London, New York and Paris are the holy trinity of underground engineering genius. Some four million people ride the Paris *métro* each day and their numbers are rising as traffic congestion plagues the surface streets. The network counts over 300 stations and 15 lines, making it easy to reach all parts of the city. Lille, Lyon, Marseille and Toulouse also have an underground service, although not nearly as exhaustive as the Paris *métro*.

Thanks to the many Paris postcards you've encountered over the years, you already know that the *métro* station is distinguished by a big 'M' sometimes decorated in Art Deco details. You can buy a map (highly recommended, since when selecting a line you need to know the name of the train's final stop) or consult one of the many maps on the station walls. Trains run from 5am to 1am and in peak hours you wait no more than a minute for the next train to come rolling down the rack. Tickets, usually purchased in packs (*carnets*) of 10, can be bought in the station or in the nearest *tabac*. You could buy a Carte Orange, which is valid for one month of travel. You need to supply a passport-sized photo and fill out an application and will be given the pass with your photo and a handy pocket-sized map (*plan de poche*). These passes are not transferable and you are fined if you use a pass with someone else's photo.

Buses

City buses are dependable, convenient and top the list of desirable forms of public transport. But the bus service in rural areas sits glumly at the bottom of the list. The bus service (*autobus*) in Paris, for example, is complementary to the *métro* system. Where one form of transport won't get you there, the other will. You need to stamp your ticket (the same ticket as used in the *métro* is valid for buses) in the machine near the driver. If you are travelling longer distances you may need to stamp more than one ticket – a plan on the bus stop tells you whether one ticket or two is needed for the journey. Service is reduced on Sundays and after 8.30pm.

If you live in the country or a small town, the bus service (also called *autocars*) is dismal. On some routes only two buses operate per day and reflect the hours children need to get to and from school. Night-time service is sketchy at best. You will be forced to take trains or buy a car, bike or scooter.

Trains

The SNCF (Société Nationale des Chemins de Fer Français), or the national rail network, truly is a technological masterpiece. The network is the largest and most comprehensive in Europe, with 20,000 miles of tracks, spanning the breadth of the *l'hexagone*.

The fastest and most famous train in the French rail family is the TGV (*train à grande vitesse*) that speeds along at a mind-boggling 300km per hour. The French government spends more than any other European nation on its transportation infrastructure. The TGV service links Paris to major cities such as Lille, Lyon, Marseille and Bordeaux and connects the capital to Geneva, Brussels, Amsterdam and London via the Channel Tunnel. The journey from Paris to Marseille, for example, has been reduced to under three hours. More rail network is currently being installed to bring the TGV service to Nice and over international borders to Italy's Turin and Milan.

Besides the TGV, France has slower trains to other smaller cities. There are local trains and long-distance trains (*trains grandes lignes*). If you live in the south of France, a slower train runs right along the Mediterranean cost linking Menton and Monaco through Nice and Antibes to St-Raphaël and is handy for towel- and umbrella-toting beachgoers.

Otherwise, if you are travelling to France from abroad, chances are you must pass through Paris. Trains coming from southwest France, Spain and Portugal arrive at the Gare d'Austerlitz. Trains from eastern France, Luxembourg, southern Germany, northern Switzerland, Austria and Eastern Europe come in to the Gare de l'Est. The Gare de Lyon services trains from the south of France (Nice and Marseille), Italy and parts of Switzerland. Western France is plugged in to the Gare Montparnasse. Trains originating in northern France, Belgium, northern Germany, the Netherlands and the UK come into the Gare du Nord. Last, trains from northwest France and some from the UK make their final stop at the Gare St-Lazare. All these stations connect with the *métro* system.

The easiest way to buy a train ticket and check timetables and availability is to consult **www.voyages-sncf.com**. You will get an electronic confirmation number after you pay with a credit card and pick up your ticket before your train is scheduled to leave. If you are not internet-savvy, you could call SNCF (**t** 08 91 67 68 69, not a free number) and again pick up your ticket at the station. In some areas, you can arrange to have it delivered to your home for a small fee. Or, you could simply go to the nearest train station and buy your ticket there. If you travel by rail often, you should buy either the *Forfait* or the *Fréquence* rail pass that give you discounts of up to 50 per cent if you travel the same route every week. Weekend travel is often available at discounted rates and fares are reduced for families, the elderly and minors. Remember to validate your ticket before boarding, otherwise you face a fine when the ticket inspector comes along.

Air Travel

Air France (**www.airfrance.fr**) has national flights but recently a host of budget airlines has made travel within France often cheaper – and definitely faster – than the train. Some easyJet fares from Nice to Paris for example are advertised at €30. The one-way train fare between those two cities costs as much as €80.

At the time of going to press the following budget airlines offered routes within France:

- **EasyJet (www.easyjet.com)** has routes that include Marseille to Paris Orly, Nice to Paris Charles de Gaulle and Paris Orly to Nice and Toulouse.

- **Aéris (www.aeris.fr)** is France's latest budget airline (started in 2003 after the demise of Air Liberté) with routes within France, Greece and North Africa. These include Paris Orly to Nice, Lourdes, Perpignan, Toulouse, Marrakech and Dakar, Paris Charles de Gaulle to Málaga, Toulon to Brest and on to Djerba, Nantes to Marseille, Montpellier to Brest with continuing service to Athens or Ibizia, Lyon to Marrakech, Caen to Ajaccio in Corsica and Ajaccio to Brest.

- **Air Littoral (www.airlittoral.com)** still offers cheap fares from Paris Orly to Agen, Montpellier to Lille, and Nice to Lille and Strasbourg. Nice also links Rome, Venice, Naples and Florence in Italy and there is a Nice to Madrid flight. However, many of its routes have been phased out and the airline itself may not last long.

- **Ryanair** and **BMIBaby** fly to many cities within France from abroad (for more information, *see* **First Steps**, 'Getting to France', pp.112–14).
- For more airline options, go to the French airports site (**www.aeroport.fr**). It is in French, but the airports are listed on the left hand side, and the word for airline is *compagnie aérienne*.

Cars

The moment you bring your car to France, or buy one here, you cross that invisible line that separates the tourist from the traveller. An independent means of transport makes you a fully fledged traveller, a step above the lowly tourist, and if you are moving to France your car becomes a symbol of your willingness to integrate. The roads of France are like an enormous sporting field with millions of players contemplating the moves and directions they need to take. Once you join them you become part of the national team. But first, you'll need to know the rules.

The Rules of the Road

Seatbelts are obligatory in both front and back; the car on the right always has the right of way in an intersection; never pass on the right; if you are 'flashed' it means pull into the slow lane quickly; traffic on the inside of the roundabout has the right of way; try not to overshoot the dashboard-level traffic lights (otherwise you have to back-up and that is embarrassing). You must carry a red breakdown triangle in your boot and are supposed to fix an 'F' sticker to the back of your car if you have French licence plates or a 'GB' if your car is registered in Britain. If any of the above doesn't make sense, buy a copy of the French Road Code (*Code de la Route*) available at bookshops and magazines kiosks and study it carefully. Otherwise the road is clear.

France is endowed with thousands of kilometres of paved road, much of which is managed by private companies, making it of the highest standard. Repairs and maintenance are impeccable and the French are justifiably proud of

Speed Limits

Motorways: 130kph (80mph)
Urban stretches: 110kph (68mph)
Paris ring road (*périphérique*): 80kph (50mph)
Dual carriageways: 110kph (68mph)
Rural built-up areas: 90kph (55mph)
Urban built-up areas: 50kph (31mph)
Motorways when raining: 110kph (68mph)
Dual carriageways when raining: 100kph (62mph)
Rural built-up areas when raining: 80kph (50mph)

their motorways. The biggest drawback is that the *autoroutes* are expensive. One study confirmed that the 50km stretch from Nice to the Italian border was the most expensive piece of roadway, barring bridges and tunnels, in Europe. There are four tolls to pay – or an average of one every 12km.

The alternative is to stay on the *routes nationales,* which are often jammed with motorists avoiding the tolls on the *autoroutes.* The national routes function like anywhere else in the world – with the glaring exception of the many rotaries (roundabouts; *sens giratoires*). These take some getting used to and are a particularly 'French' invention (just like yellow headlights: France's memorable, albeit dubiously innovative, contribution to motorists a few decades ago). Don't go speeding into the rotary because, first, they are dangerous and, secondly, police often lurk inside.

Although you must fork out many euros for the *autoroutes* (in same places you throw coins into an automated basket so make sure to keep spare change handy), they provide an extremely comfortable drive. You will see rest areas (*aires de repos*) every 15km where you can use the toilets, the phone (also emergency phones) or picnic areas. Eating on the side of the road is another particularly 'French' passion and many families travel with their own collapsible dining table – complete with chequered tablecloth and carafes of wine – in the event, God forbid, that they should actually be on the road during peak lunching hours. Some *aires de repos* even have exercise circuits for working off the calories accrued after all those roadside banquets. Technically, you are not allowed to sleep overnight in an *aire de repos*, although many motorists do. France does have very cheap automated motels that function without human intervention. Arrive any time of night or day and insert your credit card into an automatic teller machine. Tap in for a double or single bed, smoking or non-smoking room, and a plastic room key is supplied. You can even order breakfast because the machine is stocked with stale croissants and very bad coffee. It's the *2001: A Space Odyssey* of the hotel world.

The French *autoroutes* are their own autonomous universe. Once you check in, you can drive around France for eternity keeping all of your bodily systems operational.

If you don't pay 'per section' of *autoroute* (this is usually done by dropping coins into the automated baskets described above), you pay 'per network'. That means you get a ticket at the beginning of your trip and pay the total at the *péage* of your exit. France's main motorway networks are: SAPN, Autoroute Paris, Normandie SANEF, Autoroutes du Nord et de l'Est de la France SAPRR, Autoroutes Paris, Rhin, Rhône COFIROUTE, Compagnie Financière et Industrielle des Autoroutes ASF, Autoroutes du Sud de la France ESCOTA, Autoroute Esterel, Côte d'Azur AREA, Autoroutes Rhône-Alpes STMB and Tunnel Routier sous le Mont Blanc.

If you breakdown or have an accident, there are SOS phones every two kilometres as well as in the rest areas.

Driver's Licences

To change your licence or not to change your licence is the question that vexes so many expats. We'd all do it immediately if the mere mention of 'French driver's licence' didn't immediately evoke apocalyptic images of bureaucratic hell. Of all the paperwork procedures, this is the one that poses the biggest obstacles to well-intentioned foreigners.

Thankfully, EU harmonization laws have loosened some of the bureaucratic knot. If you hold a driving licence from any EU member state, you are *not* obliged to exchange your driver's licence for a French one. For example, if you have an English licence, which is recognized by the reciprocal French licence exchange board, you can continue driving on that.

The only time it would be compulsory for you to exchange your EU member state licence into a French one is if you commit a driving offence in France. If you reside in France (are a holder of a *carte de séjour* or *carte de résident*) and get a speeding ticket or some other driving infraction, French authorities need to take 'points' from your driving record. Everybody starts off with 12 points and each infraction removes a certain number of points (one point for failing to dip your lights, two for driving and talking on your mobile phone, three for failing to wear a seatbelt, six for driving drunk). Points can only be subtracted from a French licence – which means you will be forced to exchange your licence.

Generally, long-term residents suffer the problems of obtaining a French licence because it simplifies other aspects such as insurance. A French licence is also easier to replace in the case of loss or theft because it saves you a trip back home. If you do exchange your licence, the original is withdrawn.

There are other special circumstances to look out for. For example, if you have a UK licence, you are required to inform the DVLA of your change of address. If you submit your address in France, your UK licence may become invalid and you will be obliged to get a French licence.

In order to exchange your licence you must go to the nearest *préfecture* and ask for a *demande d'échange de permis de conduire*. You will be asked for:

- **your *carte de séjour* or *carte de résident***
- **proof of address, for example, an EDF bill or a lease**
- **your original driving licence (you may be asked to provide an official translation done by a *traducteur expert-juré*; this may be required if you are a non-EU citizen)**
- **proof that you are a student (in the event that you are)**
- **two passport-sized photographs**
- **photocopies of all the above documents.**

If you are not a citizen of the EU you may be required to exchange your licence. (Note: holders of South African and Australian licences are treated like EU licence-holders and you are not required to exchange them.) Non-EU licence carriers (who live in France and have a *carte de séjour*) are allowed to drive in France for one year. After 12 months, you are required to obtain a French licence.

One year from the date marked on your *carte de séjour,* your non-EU licence is invalid and you are uninsured to drive. You have two options. You may be able to exchange your licence for a French one provided you do so before the one-year period is up (this depends on the agreement your country has with France). If you are denied this, your second option is to apply for a French licence, which means taking the theoretical and practical driving exams.

For Canadians: if your licence is from Quebec or Newfoundland you may exchange your licence within your first year of residency in France. Otherwise you must apply to take the French driving tests (the Canadian Embassy has more information).

If you are from the USA, you may drive with your US licence for the first year of residency in France. If you have a temporary visa to be in France three months or less, you can easily drive on your US licence.

If your licence comes from any of the following states – Colorado, Connecticut, Delaware, Florida, Illinois, Kansas, Kentucky, Michigan, Ohio, Pennsylvania, South Carolina or Virginia – you can change your licence into a French one just like a EU citizen, provided you do so within the first year of your *carte de séjour*. If your licence is not from one of those states, you must take the French drivers' exam otherwise your licence is illegal after one year and you are uninsured to drive.

The minimum driving age in France is 18. If you are a 17-year-old British driver with a valid licence, you may not drive in France. You may face fines and the impounding of your vehicle.

Importing a Car

If you have a summer home in France and just visit for a few months each year, there is no reason for you officially to import your car. But if you reside permanently in France, you will need to register your car within three months (although many foreigners are relaxed about the timing since it is almost impossible to prove when you brought the car over in the first place).

If you have already paid the VAT on your vehicle, you can import your car into France without additional VAT charges. If you did not pay VAT, you will need to pay it when you import it. VAT is reduced according to the age of the car, boat or motorcycle. Some savvy foreigners manage to keep their new cars abroad long enough to import them to France as 'used', thus hitting a lower VAT bracket. If you need to pay the VAT on your car, you should do so at the Hôtel/Recette des Impôts where you live.

The next step is to have your car checked to make sure it meets French safety standards. This is called a *contrôle technique* (equivalent to a UK MOT) and amounts to a little sticker that you fix to your window, next to your proof of insurance, that proves your car is in good health. Any qualified mechanic can issue it after a complete testing of your vehicle (brakes, lights, tyres, steering, suspension, bodywork, seatbelts, mirrors, windscreen wipers and horn). Warning: if your car does not conform to these standards, you must make the necessary adjustments and this can be costly. There are also smaller adjustments to make. For example, it is compulsory to place converters on your headlights to ensure that your dipped headlights point to the correct side and won't blind oncoming traffic.

After this, you need a customs certificate (*certificat de douane*) that permits you to register the vehicle in France. This is obtained at the local customs office (Direction des Douanes) – every town has one.

The DRIRE (Direction Régionale de l'Industrie, de la Recherche et de l'Environnement) will require the following:

- **the customs certificate (*certificat de douane*)**
- **a manufacturers' certificate of construction, which can be obtained at a car dealer (this is not required for new cars made in the EU but is for older models)**
- **a completed application for vehicle registration (*demande de certificat d'immatriculation d'un véhicule*), which you can get at your local *préfecture***
- **vehicle registration (*titre de circulation*)**
- **contrôle technique to prove the car meets French safety standards**
- **fee and applicable tax stamp**
- **your *carte de séjour* or *carte de résident*.**

Once the DRIRE office has that, you get a French registration certificate (*certificat d'immatriculation* or *carte grise*) at the local *préfecture*. The final two digits of the car's registration number reflect the *département* where the car is registered. For example, cars registered in central Paris end in '75' (*see* **Reference**, '*Départements*', pp.277–8 for a complete list). Once you have your *carte grise*, you are required to order French licence plates. Hardware stores and supermarkets can do this and you need two: one for the front and one for the rear of the car. French licence plates are now white but in the past were an assortment of different colours. If you lose your *carte grise*, or if it is stolen, you must ask for a duplicate copy at the *préfecture* and you will need a police report.

Buying a Car

Depending on the current exchange rate, cars in France can be cheaper than in the UK. Even British cars may be cheaper in France. So if you're looking to buy a new car, it makes sense to do so in France and avoid the import hassles. You'll probably also want a car with left-hand drive in the long term. A diesel is also an interesting option since your fuel bill will be about a third less.

If you are interested in a new car (note: most French buy French), your local dealer will point you in the right direction in terms of price and financing options. You'll need to apply for a *carte grise* at the *préfecture*, arrange for your licence plates to be made, and get insurance.

All cars over four years old are required to have a *contrôle technique* (or MOT) every two years. Antique or collectors' cars (over 25 years old) are exempt from the *contrôle technique* – and, as the owner of a 1976 Mini Minor, I can assure you they wouldn't pass anyway.

If you are buying a used car, you should ask the seller for a *lettre de non-gage* (issued by the *département*) declaring that the vehicle is debt-free (unpaid financing would be passed on to you). Make sure the chassis number matches the one listed on the *carte grise*. Never, never buy a car that doesn't have a *carte grise* or that has one that doesn't match the vehicle: it means the car was stolen. France has a huge underground market of stolen cars. You can also request the owner to write a letter confirming that the car has not been involved in any collisions. Last, and just as important, make sure that the *contrôle technique* sticker is current and valid.

Car Insurance

All cars in France and cars coming into France must at least be insured for third-party risk. If your insurance was issued in another EU country, Switzerland, the Czech Republic, Hungary, Liechtenstein, Norway or the Slovak Republic your insurance automatically has third-party coverage. If it was not, you can buy additional insurance (valid for a set period). If your car is insured in France, you will automatically be give the 'Green Card' or international insurance that in France is known as the *carte internationale d'assurance automobile*. These are the basic insurance packages you can purchase:

- **third party (compulsory)**
- **third party, fire and theft**
- **multi-risk collision (covers damage to your car in an accident when the third party is identified)**
- **fully comprehensive (covers all accidents even when the third party is not identified).**

Insurance premiums are very high in France. If you are in an accident, you need to fill out a *constat amiable* or the *constat européen d'accident* that goes to your insurance company in the event of a claim. The insurance company will arrange for an inspection of the damage.

Proof of insurance must be kept with the car at all times. In addition, an insurance stub is fixed to the windscreen (lower right corner facing the passenger seat). Make sure your stub is valid and current as this is the first thing a police officer will check. Driving without insurance could lead to imprisonment.

Macabre Motoring

In response to France's tragically high mortality rate due to drunk and careless drivers, authorities have cracked down with severe – some would say 'grotesque' – measures. In the 1970s, an average of 14,000 people lost their lives on French roads each year and even President Jacques Chirac broke a leg in a 1978 car accident. In 2002, that number was halved to 7,000 and in 2003 it went down to 5,000 – still one-third more than in Britain. Transport officials put more police on the roads, lowered speed limits and imposed stiffer fines for driving under the influence of drink (the blood alcohol limit is 0.05 per cent). But the number of road deaths is still too high.

Something drastic had to be done and the French did it. Besides putting up signs reminding drivers to wear their seat belts, the authorities installed flashing signs on motorways that ominously warn: 'too fast, too close, too late' and even fitted mechanical mannequins made to look like police officers ready to write out speeding tickets.

The next move was to put huge yellow signs at the start of a road that list the number of people who have died or were injured on it. In an even more sinister touch (that borders on extremely bad taste) they mounted metal cut-out forms that look like human bodies on the exact spot where a life was lost. Driving down a particular road, you might see dozens of them: four 'bodies' dead here probably representing a family, two 'bodies' there that may have been a husband and wife, or six 'bodies' there representing a collision between two vehicles. You often see bouquets of flowers by their feet left by a grieving family. Some of the 'bodies' have long hair to indicate a woman and others have a red 'X' across their chests to hammer the point home harder. You bet: road mortality rates have came down. Seeing all those 'bodies' certainly does direct your foot away from the accelerator.

The overall sensation you get from driving on French roads is that same sense of foreboding that hits your gut when you see cowboys stepping into sacred Indian burial grounds in films. You just know something bad is going to happen. It is the same in France and only the ominous drumbeat is missing. That could be next.

A few years ago, French motorists had to pay a mandatory 'road tax' and display a *vignette* (yet another sticker fixed to a windscreen already jam-packed with a colourful patchwork of adhesives). As of 2001, this no longer exists.

Crime and the Police

At the beginning of the millennium new crime statistics were compiled and French lawmakers were faced with the startling realization that the crime problem had grown out of control. The most shocking poll came from the Sorbonne University. It indicated that violent crime had quadrupled in the eight years ending in 2002. Even President Jacques Chirac was the target of a failed shooting attempt in Paris. Previously, financial crimes and property theft were a primary concern, but the attention shifted to rapes, armed robberies and murders. In 2000–2001 alone, armed robberies in Paris alone had increased by 50 per cent.

With the pending crisis, violent crime moved to the forefront of the political agenda and government officials adopted a staunch 'zero-tolerance' policy. New laws came into effect including ones in which squatters occupying private land can go to jail, 'passive soliciting' by prostitutes is a crime and people begging for money are forbidden to work in groups. The sweeping anti-crime bills have helped, and crime figures – especially violent crimes – are decreasing.

But don't be too comforted by the good news. Foreigners should be especially careful of not becoming the target of two all-too-common types of crimes. The first is pick-pocketing. Pick-pocketing rates in Marseille and Paris are high enough to merit a very firm warning.

The second kind of crime that you should be concerned with is house-burglary. House robberies have reached epidemic levels especially in the south of France in the area spanning Marseille to Nice, where many foreigners have summer homes. (The very same morning I wrote this section I was awakened by police because my British neighbour had been robbed the night before. This is the second time he was hit in less than a year.) Be on guard with your home, your purse and your car. (Last week the British Jaguar next to my car in the long-term Nice Airport parking was smashed open with rocks.)

There are basic precautions to take – identical to the ones available to you back home – to keep criminals and other morally challenged types at bay. You can install iron bars on your window or fit metal curtains on your doors. These make your home almost impenetrable. You can fit electric alarms or hire the services of a private patrol or guardian. Some owners install fake security cameras as a deterrent. The best strategy is to know your neighbours and local shopkeepers and stay active in your community. Don't leave obvious signs that your home is empty. A pile of unopened mail or an overgrown garden could attract unwanted attention. The majority of home robberies occur in summer months when most home-owners are on vacation.

Many reasons have been suggested for the crime wave. Immigration has led to higher unemployment figures (although it would be irresponsible to jump to conclusions), poor suburbs are growing, jails are overcrowded and the police can't recruit new officers fast enough. Most importantly, the media devotes more time and space to crime-reporting, fanning an overall sense of panic.

There are four primary kinds of police. The first is the *police nationale*, under the control of the Interior Ministry, which is responsible for policing Paris and provincial urban jurisdictions with populations of more than 10,000. The jurisdiction is the area around the police station or *commissariat de police*, and the officers often wear white caps.

The *gendarmerie nationale* are controlled by the Defence Ministry and wear blue uniforms and patrol rural areas and small towns. During the Middle Ages, a band of aristocrats took on policing duties and called themselves the *gens d'armes* (or 'gentlemen at arms'). Today, they can be seen in patrol cars on the motorway, or as paired motorcyclists (*motards*). They are looking out for serious criminal offenders and have national jurisdiction.

The *Compagnie Républicaine de Sécurité* (CRS) is generally the most disliked branch of police since controlling riots and public spectacles is among their primary activities (not that any of them enjoys an overwhelmingly rosy reception by the general population). Some are also beach lifeguards. Nonetheless, they have earned a reputation for intolerance and violence.

The last branch of police is the municipal police (*corps urbain* or *police municipale*) – with flat caps – who are hired by the local town hall of medium-sized municipalities. They deal with petty crimes and road offences.

In an emergency, dial 17 to speak with the police. Be advised that the police can stop you on the road for a random control (*contrôle*) (usually to check against drunk driving and to make sure your vehicle registration and insurance is in order). If you are arrested, call your embassy first and ask for a list of English-speaking lawyers. It is inadvisable to sign any statements or paperwork until you have legal representation.

If you are the victim of a robbery, contact the nearest *commissariat de police* or *gendarmerie*. You will be asked to file a report of what was stolen (*déclaration de vol*) that can be used in an insurance claim. You must do so within 24 hours of the robbery – and don't expect a sympathetic shoulder to cry on.

Taking your Pet

Man's best friends have reason to rejoice now that England's 100-year-old pet quarantine system has been supplemented by the Pet Travel Scheme (PETS for short), in which the pet receives its own British 'Pet Passport'. The final scheme was in place by 2001 and makes it much easier to bring Fido and Felix to and from England and France (French Guyana, St Pierre and Miquelon are excluded from the scheme).

To qualify for the PETS programme, you must ensure your pet meets the following criteria:

- **it must be microchipped (a chip is implanted under the skin by a vet)**
- **it must be vaccinated against rabies**
- **you should arrange for a blood test that confirms a satisfactory level of protection against rabies. (If you pet is qualifying for PETS for the first**

time, it must undergo a test to confirm the presence of rabies antibodies in its blood after the vaccination – sometimes this requires a delay of 30 days. Pets that have already qualified for PETS must have documents showing it received its booster vaccinations. Blood samples must be analysed at a DEFRA-approved laboratory. Please note that there is a compulsory waiting period after the blood test. Animals may not enter the UK under the Pet Travel Scheme until six months after the date on which the blood sample was taken.)

- when the successful test results are ready, you will receive a PETS certificate from your vet.

When you are ready to bring your pet back to the UK, you must:

- check your pet for ticks and tapeworms (*echinococcus multilocularis*) 24–48hrs before its journey back to the UK. A qualified vet can carry out the test and will issue an official certificate giving your pet a clean bill of health
- sign a declaration in which you state that your pet has not been outside any PETS qualifying countries within the previous six months.

Not doing the above will leave you in the doghouse. Remember that the PETS scheme is limited to cats and dogs and only operates on certain sea, air and rail routes between England and France. If your pet does not meet the PETS requirements, it is subject to the old quarantine system.

Once your pet has lived in France for three months, it is considered 'French' and is therefore subject to French laws governing pets. For example, puppies and kittens are given identifying tattoos on their ears and are registered in a national pet database and you will be notified when its annual vaccinations are due. Some pets were both microchipped and tattooed, giving rise to the so-called 'French protocol'. Both the identifying English and French numbers were listed on the pet's official registration card (the equivalent of a human with dual nationality). Now, under French law, a pet that is microchipped does not need to be tattooed.

If your pet is qualifying for PETS in France, you need to take it to a veterinary surgeon (for the microchipping) who holds a *mandat sanitaire* from French authorities. A list of qualifying vets is available at your local town hall (*mairie*).

In general, there is not a more pet-friendly country on the planet than France and your four-legged friend will soon learn that a belly-scratch is always a nose-nudge away. Dogs are unofficially tolerated in shops, cafés and even restaurants to a far greater extent than in the UK or North America. If only someone would clean up the mess on the streets.

If you want to bring something more exotic into France, you will have to check first with the French authorities. Some South American birds and African reptiles, snakes and turtles require special importation certificates from the

Foofy

Among the most peculiar and misunderstood stages in the evolution between man and beast was when the French befriended the poodle. Why would a people of such stoic pride and flawless composure choose as a mascot a whiny, odorous (especially oral cavity emanations) canine cotton ball? Why not a less vulnerable symbol of virility and moxie along the lines of the German shepherd or the American bald eagle?

Truth is, the French and the poodle live a perfectly symbiotic existence, like the water buffalo and those little birds that pick fleas off its back. In this case, the poodle helps lick *béarnaise* sauce off its owner's plate. The French and their fluffy pets also share a common affinity when it comes to avoiding the fashion *faux pas*. When seen in public, little jackets, skullcaps and diamond-studded collars are *de rigueur*. Other cultures might consider the permanent union between two such different organisms an affront – or an embarrassment – to civic pride. Not here.

The poodle is a dog of antiquity and in fact ancient Egyptian and Roman artwork depict the animals retrieving game fowl and herding. Over the course of time, it was bred as a water dog and its name 'poodle' is a derivative of the archaic German word *pudeln*, which means 'to splash around'. The dog travelled across Europe with German tribes such as the Goths and Ostrogoths and eventually reached France.

French nobility during the Renaissance used poodles as hand mittens and special compartments were sewn into the sleeves of a woman's gown so that she could insert a warm dog inside. Thanks to their intelligence and athletic agility they also became a standard feature of carnivals and travelling circuses. But the poodle's unique fur also caught the attention of wig-wearing nobility at about the same time the *coiffeur* industry reached its zenith. A poodle's hair could be shaved, clipped, dyed and decorated with ribbons in an infinite range of styles. A veritable artistic movement ensued. Today poodles remain a hobby and an accessory and have been honoured as the 'national dog of France'.

France's *Ministère de l'Agriculture et de la Pêche*, which may have a long list of conditions attached to it. In an effort to protect endangered species, many rare animals are simply not allowed to travel across borders.

For more information on bringing your pet to France, you should consult the UK's Department for Environment, Food and Rural Affairs (**www.defra.gov.uk**) or the French Agriculture Ministry (**www.agriculture.gouv.fr**).

Health and Emergencies

The French might be proudest of two things – cheese and their excellent healthcare system – and of course the two are not mutually exclusive. Both play a role in France's high quality of life, and living easier is the pot of gold we all seek at the end of the rainbow.

France's healthcare system is rated among the best in the world. Waiting times are minimal, treatments are affordable and available to the poor, facilities and equipment are of the highest standards and the services and staff are excellent. France pays a high price to make the cushiony national health system available to all those who contribute to the social security scheme. Becoming a contributor will give you enormous security under the umbrella of protection so carefully designed by the French government. Someone will have to deal with the public deficit it is creating, but that's a problem for another day.

The generous nature of the system has shaped a nation that believes strongly in healthcare. To the cynical eye, this is also called 'hypochondria'. The French do love to see doctors and an overall emphasis is put on preventative medicine – which tallies up to more time in the clinic. But something must be working because, overall, the French are a healthy bunch. The incidence of heart disease is among the lowest in the word and the French are rarely overweight. A lot of the credit goes to the local diet, which despite its large quantities of wine, cheese and fatty meat is one of the healthiest in the world. Herein lies the famous 'French paradox' so often discussed in international media. How can the French be so gluttonous and stay so healthy at the same time? We'd all like to know.

If you contribute to French *sécurité sociale* (if you are under contract to work in France), you and your family will receive subsidized or free medical care (visits with specialists, hospitalization, medicines, maternity care and dental care). You go to a doctor and pay for the services. Then, *sécurité sociale* will reimburse you. Some expenses are reimbursed fully and others in part. Here is a general run-down of coverage:

- **maternity expenses: 100 per cent**
- **general hospitalization: 80 per cent**
- **doctors' and dentists' bills: 70 per cent**
- **ambulances, laboratories, and spectacles: 65 per cent**
- **medical auxiliaries (nurses, chiropodists, etc.): 60 per cent**
- **essential daily medication (like insulin or heart pills): 100 per cent**
- **other medicines: 65 per cent**
- **minor medicines: 35 per cent.**

Certain people are exempt from paying any charges, including the disabled and mentally ill. Those covered under *sécurité sociale* can also take out low-cost private insurance (known as a *mutuelle*) to cover the other 20–30 per cent not covered by *sécurité sociale*. For example, if *sécurité sociale* pays 65 per cent of the cost of your new pair of reading glasses, your *mutuelle* might cover another 20 per cent, leaving you responsible only for 15 per cent of the total cost.

Emergencies

As soon as you move to France you should compile a list of emergency numbers and the address of the nearest hospital and tape it to your refrigerator door. Check for the numbers in the phone book under *services médicaux*.

In case of a medical emergency, such as a heart attack, call the SAMU (*Service d'Aide Médicale d'Urgence*). They will send an ambulance. The number to dial is 15.

For the fire brigade (*pompiers*) call 18.

For the police, look for *commissariat de police* in the phonebook or dial 17.

You will be charged for SAMU services and the ambulance fee but you can deduct these expenses later with your insurance scheme.

The French have recently introduced the *carte vitale*, which looks like a credit card but is embedded with a microchip and has your personal information and medical history. The new card makes getting medical reimbursements from *sécurité sociale* very easy as the doctor just swipes your card and the amount due is immediately calculated and eventually credited to you bank account via wire transfer.

Entitlements

• **EU visitors up to 90 days**: To qualify for medical treatment as a tourist from a EU country you should ask for a form E111 before leaving home (in the UK this is available from post offices). Although the E111 is valid indefinitely, it only provides coverage for three months at a time. If you have the form E111 you are entitled to French medical treatments and must pay the same contribution to charges as a French person. Without the form, you will be responsible for the full charges and then must request a reimbursement when you get back to the UK. EU pensioners enjoy special status that grants them any medical treatment necessary while in another EU country.

• **EU visitors for over 90 days**: The form E111 will not protect you after three months and you will need an alternative. If you hold a *carte de séjour* or *carte de résident*, you can apply to be covered by Universal Health Cover (*Couverture Maladie Universelle* or CMU). The CMU is a medical health scheme designed to ensure that everyone (including people on low income, and the unemployed) is covered for basic medical costs. It is not available to people already insured under another scheme.

• **Non-EU visitors**: Non-EU citizens have no automatic entitlements, although some nations have bilateral agreements with France that offer limited benefits. Otherwise, you must take out private insurance. For example the USA has no agreement with France, and American students are required to prove they have private insurance before moving to France for study.

• **Residents and people entitled to state medical assistance**: Those entitled to state medical care include qualifying workers (workers paying *sécurité sociale* contributions who have worked, generally, 100hrs per month) and retired people from other EU countries and their respective dependants. Workers may also be entitled to sick-leave allowances, similar to UK incapacity benefits. Your contributions to the UK national insurance scheme are taken into account when calculating your entitlements in France. Thus, you may be entitled in France on the basis of your UK contributions (ask the DDS for a form E104). If you are a pensioner, ask for form E121 that confirms your status and is your passport to the special benefits you are entitled to.

People not entitled are:

- **the economically inactive (those who 'retired' below retirement age)**
- **students who are no longer dependent on of a EU worker**
- **non-EU nationals**
- **civil servants covered by special schemes.**

For more information for British nationals, look at the website of the Department of Health (**www.doh.gov.uk/traveladvice**).

The vast majority of people in France are covered by *sécurité sociale* and also subscribe to complementary insurance (*mutuelle*). Almost every professional trade has its own *mutuelle* for its employees to join. Each *mutuelle* is different – some cover almost all the additional costs and others pay in full for items not covered in full by *sécurité sociale*.

Social Services and Welfare Benefits

Healthcare is just one component of the all-embracing *sécurité sociale* system in France that offers welfare benefits such as sickness and maternity benefits, entitlements following an accident at work or occupational diseases, invalidity benefits, old-age pensions, widower's or other survivors' benefits, death grants, unemployment benefits and family benefits.

Welfare benefits in EU countries are governed by a simple idea: a person exercising his right to move from one EU state to another should not lose welfare benefit rights. People covered include:

- **employed and self-employed nationals of EU states**
- **pensioners who are nationals of EU states**
- **civil servants of EU states and members of their families provided they are not covered by an enhanced scheme for civil servants in their own country. This is generally not a problem for UK civil servants.**

Note that the EU rules do not cover the economically inactive (people retired early, students, etc.).

EU rules do not replace the national benefits to which you may be entitled. Rather, they coordinate varying national schemes and dictate in which of several possible countries a person should make a claim and which country should pay the cost. Apart from the basic principle that you should not lose out on benefits simply by moving to another EU country, such as France, the other basic principle to keep in mind is you should only be subject to the rules of one country at a time. To make this clearer: the laws of one EU member state cannot – except in the case of unemployment benefits – take away or reduce your entitlement to benefit just because you live in another member state.

If you remain entitled to a UK benefit while living in France, payment of that benefit can be made in different ways, depending on the benefit in question. It can be made by authorities in France on behalf of the authorities in the UK. Or, it can be paid to you directly in France from the UK.

How do you decide which rules apply to you? There are two main considerations. Which country insures you? Which country do you live in?

You are insured in the country where you work. If you work regularly in more than one EU member state you are insured in the country where you live. (A short-term posting of less than one year to another country is ignored.) Retired people who have only worked in one EU member state will remain 'attached' to that country for pension and other purposes for the rest of their lives. People who have worked in several states will have built up pension entitlements in each member state in which they worked for more than one year. Otherwise, some benefits stem from your presence in a country. Each potential benefit, both in Britain and in France, has restrictions stipulating which categories of people are entitled to it.

French Benefits

If you need to claim *sécurité sociale* benefits in France, your entitlement will be determined by the contributions you have made in France as well as any relevant contributions made in the UK.

Social security contributions account for a very large part of the income generated by the French government; they are only paid by people who are tax-resident in France. There is a General Social Contribution (*contribution sociale généralisée* – **CSG**) payable on most types of income. There is also the **CRDS** (*contribution au reimboursement de la dette sociale*), and the **PS** (*prélèvement sociale*). CSG and CRDS are not payable on salaries, self-employed earnings or foreign pensions if you are over retirement age. If you are tax-resident you also have to pay a **CMU** (healthcare) contributon on income over a certain level. These contributions should not be underestimated, and can easily add 10 per cent to your overall tax bill.

• **Health benefits**: See the health care section above.

Facts on File

According to a study conducted in 2002 by the Centre for Economics and Business Research (CEBR) for MarketPlace at Bradford & Bingley, people in the UK may earn more than people in France, but are missing out in terms of 'quality of life'.

Cost of living: The cost of living is 13 per cent lower in France than in the UK.

Disposable income per household: In the UK: £24,407; in France: £22,668.

Percentage of disposable income put into savings: In the UK: 5 per cent; in France: 15.8 per cent.

Paying taxes: It takes a UK household from 1 January to 15 April to pay their gross income tax bill. In France, households have fulfilled their tax obligation almost four weeks earlier on 22 March.

Working hours: The average working day in the UK is 8.7hrs. In France, the average person works one hour less.

Holidays: In the UK a worker can expect 28 days off between holidays and bank holidays. In France, workers get 47 days off per year.

• **Accidents at work, occupational sickness and invalidity and disability benefits**: Only available, logically, to those working in France. You should continue receiving UK benefits if you are entitled to them.

• **Pensions**: Unless you have worked in France most of your professional life you are not likely to receive a French pension. But you will continue to receive your UK pension. Pensions in EU countries are paid on the basis of 'totalization'. This means if you have lived in various countries all of your contributions in any EU country will be added together to calculate your entitlement. For example, if France pays a minimum pension after 20 years' contributions and a full pension after 40 years and if you have paid enough contributions to qualify anywhere in the EU, you get the pension. If you have worked for five years out of 40 in France and the balance elsewhere, the French government will pay 5/40ths of your pension at the rates applicable in France. If you had worked for 15 years in the UK the British government would pay 15/40ths, and so on.

• **Unemployment benefits**: If you lose your job, the French unemployment benefit authority must take into account any periods of employment or NI contributions paid in other EU countries when calculating your entitlement to benefits in France. You must, however, have paid at least some sécurité sociale payments in France prior to claiming unemployment benefits here. That means you cannot go to France for the purpose of claiming benefit. You should obtain form E301 from the UK benefit authorities. If you travel to France to seek employment there are restrictions on your entitlement to benefit and you must comply with all French procedural requirements. (You must have been unemployed and available for work in your home country for at least four weeks before going to France. You must contact your home unemployment benefit

Case Study: From the Blog of Oblique Opinions

Martyn Horner has lived outside England for 12 years and has spent the last three in the south of France. When science park Sophia-Antipolis – France's own Silicon Valley – was going ahead at full steam, thousands of international computer programmers and technology specialists were recruited to work at the dozens of companies headquartered here. Martyn was one of these. Shortly afterwards, the area was hit by the glum global economy and the demise of the high-tech start-up. Heavily state-subsidized, Sophia-Antipolis was proclaimed a disappointment. Hundreds of employees lost their jobs, including Martyn.

With more time on his hands and unemployment benefits to live on, he launched a web page to put his French sojourn into perspective. He fills it with little vignettes and observations on England and France.

On the weather: 'A British body is only just partially adaptable to this sort of climate. Every now and then your body's tolerance of this incessant heat gives up and it fitfully perspires: you can never explain it. Keeping dry is everything.'

On driving: 'The French still drive … er … quickly. On the whole French drivers are not reckless. That is a vicious slander perpetrated by English and Swiss drivers over for their holidays. Look more closely and for longer and you'll notice that the French style of driving is more, shall we say, negotiative. They do not give way naturally.'

On food: 'The French still have more respect for food and more love for it than any other nation. Well, certainly the British. As Jonathan Meade recently said in one of his excellent TV programmes, only the British use the word "wicked" when referring to food. The French would never. There are bad meals. I've eaten badly here. But this is more to do with statistics than attitude. There is a joy in preparing food, in presenting it and serving it that transmits itself to the consumer and to the consumer's digestive system.'

On losing your job in France: 'The French social system is incredibly supportive of the working man and woman. Incredibly. If you come to France to start a small company, you will find that the social charges above and beyond what you pay to the employee are huge, indeed so often crippling. The upshot is that if you come to France, as I did this time, as an employee, you are amazingly cushioned against the natural result of this exorbitance, the demise of your employer.'

Now Martyn is contemplating leaving France to find work elsewhere. If he does, he says, he is delighted to leave behind **www.mhorner.net** and his colourful literary snippets, so that a small piece of himself stays in France.

authority and obtain a form E303 before leaving. You must register for work in France within seven days of arrival. You will be entitled to benefit for a maximum of three months. If you cannot find a job during that period you will only be entitled to continuing unemployment benefit in your home country if you return within the three-month period. If you do not you can lose all entitlement to benefits. You are only entitled to one three-month payment between two periods of employment.)

• **Family benefits**: If the members of your family live in France with you and you pay *sécurité sociale*, they are entitled to the same benefits as a French national. If your family does not live in France, and if you are entitled to benefits under the rules of more than one country, they will receive the highest amount to which they would have been entitled in any of the relevant states. Pensioners normally receive family benefits from the EU state that pays their pension.

Retirement and Pensions

A large number of the foreigners who move to France do so in their 'golden years'. The section above describes French social security benefits, including French pensions. The following section, on the other hand, highlights some of the other questions a pensioner might face when retiring in France.

• **How do you receive your pension payments?** If you have a company pension it will be paid wherever the pension scheme rules dictate. Some plans allow the administrators to pay the money into any bank in the world and others, ostensibly for security reasons, insist the money be paid into a UK bank account. Of course, if your plan will pay into your French bank, this is the most convenient option. Keep in mind that bank transfers are costly and are best done no more

---

British Pensions

If you are already retired and you only ever paid national insurance contributions in the UK, you will receive your UK retirement pension in France. You will be paid without deduction (except remittance charges) and your pension will be updated whenever the pensions in the UK are updated. If you have established an entitlement to a retirement pension in several EU countries by virtue of working in them all, your pension will be paid to you in France without deduction (except remittance charges) and your pension will be updated whenever the pensions in those countries are updated. If you have not yet retired and moved to France (whether you intend to work in France or not) your entitlement to your UK pension will be frozen and the pension to which you are entitled will be paid to you at UK retirement age. This freezing of your pension can be a disadvantage, especially if you are still relatively young when you move to France. This is because you need to have made a minimum number of NI contributions in order to qualify for a full UK state pension. If you have not yet done this but are close to retiring, it may be worth making additional payments while you are resident overseas.

than four times per year. You should also keep an eye on fluctuating exchange rates. Some pensioners make arrangements with currency dealers who send the money at an exchange rate that applies for the whole year. If you have a government pension (army, civil service, police, etc.) your pension will still be taxed in the UK. Otherwise the pension should be paid gross (i.e. tax-free) and it will be taxed in France.

• **What to do to make burial and cremation arrangements?** Deaths must be registered within 24hrs at the town hall (*mairie*). You must also record the death with the British consulate. Burial is much more common in France than cremation. Funerals are as exceedingly expensive as they are in the UK, and taking a body home is also costly.

• **What are the inheritance rules in France?** French inheritance law is much more restrictive than UK law and does apply to people who own property in France (yes, you!). Certain groups of people have almost automatic rights to inherit all or a part of your property, such as spouses and offspring. French inheritance law does not apply to the property you own outside France.

• **How do I make a will?** It is always best to make a French will to supplement your English one. If you do not, your English will should be treated as valid in France and will be used to distribute your estate. The cost of implementing the English will is much higher than the cost of implementing the French one. Always use a lawyer to advise you on the contents of your will. If you fail to draft a will of any kind, your heirs will be left with a complex and costly liability. Untangling which assets are covered by which country is done on a case-by-case basis and requires many hours of debate among expensive lawyers.

• **When is the retirement age?** In France, it is possible to retire at the age of 60 (for both men and women), after working in the private sector for 40 years and in the public sector for 37.5 years. Early retirement (*retraite*) does apply to particularly burdensome professions. In many European countries, the retirement age is 65 and France is taking controversial steps to standardize its own retirement age to the same level.

Education

The French School System

If you are moving to France with children you'll need to understand the French schooling system before you decided whether to enrol them in a private foreign-language school or a public French school. There are pros and cons to both, and your decision ultimately depends on your priorities for your child and your child's inclinations. Most importantly, you'll need to factor in your girl or boy's ability to integrate and make friends. Perhaps s/he would feel more

Case Study: A Higher Education

'I got thrown in at the deep end,' says Mike Hall, who has studied for two degrees in France. 'I didn't understand a word of French and I had to arrange for things like buying furniture for an empty apartment bottom up. But when I have kids of my own I would want them to have the same kind of experience as I did.'

Mike came to France in 1989 to participate in a two-year degree programme with the Management School of the Université de Reims in the Champagne-Ardenne area. His UK university, Middlesex University, is linked in an academic partnership with the French university. 'I didn't want to continue studying in an English-language programme,' he explains. 'I wanted to get new language skills and something even more practical than that.' Mike became a member of an international student body. In his class, totalling 120 students, 60 were French, 30 were British and the rest were divided largely between Germans and Spaniards. 'It was total immersion on every level.'

After obtaining his bachelor's degree, and years later, Mike decided to study for an MBA. Thanks to very positive impressions and memories left from his time in Reims, he decided to look for a university in France once again. This time he settled for the Theseus International Management Institute (**www.theseus. edu**), located in the high-tech science park Sophia-Antipolis near Nice. Following a one-year programme (in English) that he completed in 2001, he graduated with an MBA and a specialization in innovation strategy information technology. Now, France has become home, and his next priority is preparing for a job interview in Paris with a business software company.

comfortable with other English-speaking youngsters (*see* 'English-language schools', p.221). But if your child is outgoing, curious and responsive to a new language and culture, s/he will gain a lot more from a French school. Before long, your offspring will be more fluent than you.

The general rule of thumb is, the younger the child, the easier it will be for him or her to integrate into the French schooling system.

You'll also find that France's schooling system has built-in flexibilities that differ from what you and your child are accustomed to. At the end of the 1980s a package of wide-reaching educational reforms established schooling stages (*cycles pédagogiques*) which allow each individual student to progress at his or her speed. Instead of repeating or 'failing' an academic year, a student completes each cycle at his or her own pace with the counselling by a joint teachers' committee (*conseil des maîtres de cycles*). The objective is to rid the pupil of the pressures associated with peers and keeping pace. It also allows students who are faster learners to move forward individually.

If you have a toddler, you may want to consider the national system of **nursery schools** (*écoles maternelles*) which is subsidized by the state. There is no tuition.

The *écoles maternelles* teach pre-school-aged children basic social skills, movement and self-awareness, and provide the foundations for future instruction in reading and writing. The local town hall (*mairie*) can provide information on the *écoles maternelles* closest to where you live. Pupils usually start between the ages of two and four (one-third of French students start at age two). If you are two working parents or a single parent, there are nurseries and day-care centres (*jardin d'enfants* or a *crèche*) that will prepare a child before s/he is of age to attend an *école maternelle*. The French nursery schools are regarded as some of the best in Europe.

School hours in the *école maternelles* are usually 8.30am–12pm and 1.30–4pm. Lunch at the school cafeteria (*cantine*) and a napping period separate the two. There is no school on Wednesday and many *départements* have a morning session on Saturday. In general, the *école maternelle* is divided into three stages: the lower section (*petite*) for ages two to four; a middle section (*moyenne*) for ages four to five; and an upper section (*grande*) for ages five to six.

Children start **primary school** (*école primaire*) at the age of six and continue until age 11. It sounds confusing, but students start *école primaire* at the *onzième* level and finish at the *septième* before moving on to secondary school. There is no exam at the end of *école primaire* and schooling options are both public and private.

Primary schools, which have 26hrs of instruction per week, are the basic building block of the French schooling system. By the end of it, each child will be able to read and write in French and will have formed a solid background in other academic disciplines such as history, geography, civic studies, maths, science, computers, sports, music and arts and crafts. Teaching a foreign language is also included in the curriculum and over 80 per cent of students choose to study English. The programme is also heavily focused on field trips (*classe de découverte*) in which students might spend a week in the mountains, by the sea or sometimes in a foreign country.

Secondary school starts at age 11 when a child enters a *collège* and is compulsory until age 16. At age 15, the top students are selected following an exam to attend a *lycée* (that lasts until age 18 and ends with the gruelling *baccalauréat* exam). Students who move on to a *lycée* are completing the *cycle long*. Those who opt for the short cycle (*cycle court*) usually finish their education at a vocational school. Some schools are a *collège* and a *lycée* in one, and admission to higher education is all but guaranteed. This depends on where you live.

Collège education is divided into two two-year stages that range from the *sixième* to the *troisième* (which a child completes at age 15). The first two years include the *cycle d'observation*. There are two cycles in secondary schooling. The first or *premier cycle* (*6ème* and *5ème*), includes a common curriculum for all students covering all subjects ranging from science and maths to history and language instruction. New subjects such as economics, technology, physics, geology and chemistry are also introduced. Lessons total 24hrs per week. In the last two years, or the *cycle d'orientation* (*4ème* and *3ème*), each student is allowed increased flexibility to pursue individual interests. For example, s/he can opt to take a second foreign language or a classic language such as Greek or Latin or can choose more technology-related courses. Classes generally total 25hrs per week. At the end of the last year of *collège*, a student takes a written exam in French, maths, history and geography that earns him the *brevet des collèges*. Passing that exam guarantees admission to the *lycée*.

The **lycée** covers three years of specialized education. In chronological order they are the *seconde* (*2ème*), the *première* (*1er*) and, last, the *terminale*. The whole focus, now, of the student is deciding which *baccalauréat* exam to take, and of course, passing it. The '*bac*' is taken at age 18 or 19 and only 50 per cent of students pass it. Those who do are guaranteed admission to a French university.

There are seven *baccalauréat* exams which are divided into two principal groups – although there are some 30 individual *baccalauréat* exams to choose from. The first is the general *baccalauréat* in literature, economics and social studies, science, or medicine and social science. The second is the technical *baccalauréat* in science and tertiary technology, science and industrial technology, or science and laboratory technologies. The exams are taken in stages at the end of the *première* and the *terminale* years of *lycée*.

The science-based *baccalauréat* is the most prestigious. Sometimes the *bacs* are referred to by letters. *Bac* D is for those wanted to continue studying medicine – the high end – while *bacs* A and B – the low end – are for students interested in liberal arts professions. All those who pass the exam are known as *bacheliers*.

English-language Schools

The most authoritative source of information on English-language schools is compiled by the Education Information Service of the British Council (**www. britishcouncil.fr**) in Paris. Their list of educational facilities in France for English-speaking children (*établissements d'enseignement anglophone ou bilingue en France*) was created in collaboration with the American Embassy in Paris and is an invaluable resource for parents.

They list schools in three categories:

- **schools with tuition entirely in the English language**
- **international sections in French *lycées***
- **international/bilingual schools.**

Among the most prestigious schools in the first grouping (**private schools with an English-language curriculum**) is the British School of Paris, with both a senior and junior school (**www.ecis.org/bsp/**). Open since 1980, it focuses on a British educational philosophy and is located about 30mins from central Paris. It is co-educational, with 600 pupils aged four to 18, and boards students with

French families. Senior school prepares pupils for GCSE, AS levels, A levels and S levels. Another Paris-based school is the International School of Paris (both primary and middle school), **www.isparis.edu**. This is a co-education, multinational school where a strong emphasis is made on French language and culture. Children whose native language is not English also attend. Students are prepared in the subjects of the International GCSE as well as the International Baccalauréat.

The Dordogne has the Dordogne Study Centre that also offers GCSE. Summer courses in French and English as a foreign language are available. In Mougins, near Cannes, the Mougins School (**www.mougins-school.com**) provides an English curriculum, based on the UK National Curriculum, for 225 pupils aged 3–18 from approximately 25 countries. It has a quiet campus and excellent sports facilities.

Among the American-styled schools are the American School of Paris, which offers the International Baccalauréat diploma; the Marymount School in Neuilly-sur-Seine outside Paris; the International School of Nice that offers both the International GCSE and the International Baccalauréat certificates; and the English Language Montessori School in Chantilly.

In the second grouping of schools (**French schools with international divisions**), you can choose the Collège-Lycée International Ferney-Voltaire, which is located about 16km from Geneva. It is a co-educational day school for ages 11–18. Examinations prepared for include the French *baccalauréat*, the International Baccalauréat, GCSEs, IGSEs and AS levels. Fontainebleau has the Anglophone Section, which is integrated within three co-educational French schools situated on the same campus. Grenoble has the Cité Scolaire Internationale Stendhal in English, but includes a compulsory course of French as a foreign language. Not too far away is the Cité Scolaire Internationale de Lyon, which is a co-educational day school from ages 6–20. Instruction for the French *baccalauréat* and the International Baccalauréat, GCSEs, and the American PSAT and SAT are offered. Monaco has the international section of the posh Lycée Albert 1er.

Other options under this heading include the Collège-Lycée Honoré de Balzac in Paris; the Classes Internationales de l'Académie de Reims; the Lycée International (**www.lycee-international.net**), which is 30km from Paris and has the largest British section in a French *lycée* with 680 pupils; the Collège de Sèvres Lycée de Sèvres (a French state schools with sections for British, American and other English-speaking pupils); the Lycée-Collège International des Pontonniers in Strasbourg; and the Lycée Polyvalent International (Section Britannique) located in the Toulouse suburbs.

The third grouping (**international and bilingual schools**) is particularly rich in nursery schools. Among them are: the Lennen Bilingual School in Paris, the Bilingual Montessori School of Paris, Jardin d'Enfants Montessori d'Auteuil in

Paris, Montessori Kids in Paris, Etre et Découvrir in St-Nom la Bretèche near Paris, the United Nations Nursery School in Paris and La Petite Ecole in Paris.

The list of primary/secondary schools in the third category include: Europe: Rencontres et Echanges in Paris started in 1933, the Lennen Bilingual Primary School in Paris, the International Bilingual School of Provence (IBS) in Luynes; the Bordeaux International School, the Ombrosa Lycée Multilingue de Lyon (**www.ombrosa-education.fr**), the Association des Parents Anglophones de la Région de Chantilly (**www.aparc.com**), the Ecole Active Bilingue Jeannine Manuel/Ecole Internationale de Lille Métropole in Marcq-en-Baroeul, the Ecole Active Bilingue in Paris (**www.eab.fr**), the Ecole Active Bilingue Jeannine Manuel in Paris, the Eurécole in Paris, Hermitage in Maisons-Lafitte, the International School of Sophia Antipolis near Valbonne, the Ecole des Roches in Verneuil-sur-Avre (**www.ecoledesroches.com**), the Greenfield Ecole Bilingue in Collonges au Mont d'Or (**www.greenfield.fr**) and the Ecole Internationale de Marne-la-Vallée in Esbly.

University in France

Established in 1253, the Sorbonne University in Paris remains in our minds as one of world's finest academic institutions. Post-revolutionary French culture embraced a mantra of individual liberty and social equality, and nowhere were these tenets more firmly rooted than in the university system. The Sorbonne went through a tough spell during the turbulent 1960s, and student protests and marches in May 1968, marred with violence, remain a painful moment in the French memory bank.

There are two types of universities in France: traditional universities and *les grandes écoles*. Admission to one of the country's 72 **universities** (a large proportion of which are in Paris) is granted to any pupil who passes the French *baccalauréat* exam. More than one million students attend these schools – representing one-third of *bac*-holders – and the student body is mixed with international students and children of immigrants. These schools are funded by the state and run by the Education Ministry. They do not charge admission, although other student fees may apply. A large percentage of the students who start university don't complete their course of study and eventually drop out. The bureaucratic procedures are stifling and overcrowding is a problem. The average age of a university graduate is 29 and many of those who do graduate become frustrated when they realize their degree will not guarantee job placement.

On the other side of the academic spectrum are the lavishly funded *grandes écoles*, first founded by Napoleon. They tend to focus on specialized subjects, such as civil engineering, agriculture or political science. France has over 250 *grandes écoles.* They are run by the individual ministries that oversee their specialization, meaning that more attention is given to programmes and facilities. Fewer than 100,000 students attend these schools and the admission criteria are rigorous.

France is also home to a growing collection of excellent **international business schools** that provide top-level executive educations. Among these are INSEAD Management School, which offers an American-style MBA degree, EDHEC Business School France, ESCP-EAP Graduate School of Management and CERAM in Sophia-Antipolis.

Recreational Courses

You can come to France to enrol in a language school, but France offers foreigners wanting to put their time to good use many more learning opportunities. In recent years, a new appetite for hands-on travel experiences and niche courses has grown exponentially. More people are arriving with an interest in learning crafts and skills they can't acquire back home. Today, you can take courses on the art of painting on Limoges porcelain, embroidery, monogramming, baking, selecting wild mushrooms and much more.

This new trend is fuelled by a centuries-old tradition in which learned masters, or experts in a specified craft, passed on their experience and know-how to younger apprentices. The traditions of ironwork, masonry, glassworks and textile-manufacturing were carried on through the generations thanks to the tight bonds between masters and their pupils. Moving to France means you too can become a pupil and take part in this tradition. None of the courses listed below requires fluency in French.

If you are at a loss pairing that bottle of Syrah you've stashed away in your cellar with the right cuisine, the Ecole des Trois Ponts (Château de Matel, Roanne, **t** 04 77 71 53 00; **www.3ponts.edu/cooking/**) located near Lyon can help. There are **wine and gastronomy** pairing courses that last five days or more as well as seminars on baking, making pastries and other mouth-watering dishes.

If you are in the Auvergne region and want to learn to make oven-fresh **French bread**, you will pick up handy tips from Christian Boutonnet (Chavagnat, **t** 070 90 73 56; **www.membres.lycos.fr/chavagnat/**). He shares his 28 years of experience in two or four-day classes on all kinds of bread including rye, brioche, raisin bread and of course the *baguette*. He also specializes in *charcuterie* courses and will take you mushroom-hunting. If you've always been tempted to pick wild mushrooms but are afraid you won't distinguish the good ones from the fatal fungi, this course is for you. You'll expertly sift through giant wicker baskets and pick out the *cèpes*, chanterelles and morels and learn to prepare them in a beautiful country kitchen.

You can smell your way through Paris by browsing the many boutiques and perfume shops. Or you can train your olfactory sense at La Grande Boutique de l'Artisan Parfumeur (2 rue de l'Amiral de Coligny, 1er, **t** 01 44 88 27 50). During the three-hour lecture held weekly, the salon of the French fragrance house's Paris boutique teaches the theory and history of **perfume composition** and tests your sense of smell with hundreds of samples ranging from rose and peach to eucalyptus leaf.

But if **porcelain** catches your fancy, you'll want to enrol in Françoise Villegoureix's French porcelain courses in Limoges. This ceramicist claims three generations of porcelain-painters in her family and conducts classes on decorating soup tureens, platters, tea sets and all the other ceramic objects that go into dressing a table. The courses also cover the history of Limoges ceramics and there is a field trip to the city's Musée National de la Porcelaine.

Les Ateliers du Bégonia d'Or in Rochefort, the Poitou-Charentes region (67 av Charles de Gaulle, Rochefort, **t** 05 46 87 59 36) specialize in **embroidery and monogramming**. You'll learn to embroider household linen, napkins, table clothes and anything else you can stick a needle in. Classes are limited to a handful of people. Les Ateliers is one of the nation's most prestigious schools in this field and graduates have moved on to apply their stitch work and handicraft on some of the biggest names of *haute couture*.

If you're looking to apply your talents to an art form even more precise and defined than embroidery, you could try your steady hands on **mosaics**. Christian Sicault in Saint-Génard (Puy Berland, **t** 05 49 27 20 43; **www.christian-sicault. com**) offers six-day classes on the craft of assembling tiny shards of colourful stone, marble, glass and granite to create a bigger picture. Sicault gets inspiration from ancient Rome whose master craftsmen, or *tessellarii*, made polychrome mosaics an enduring craft. In ancient times, many *tessellarii* were trained in the North African provinces, especially Carthage, where tile layers took advantage of colourful stones, or *tesserae*, not available in Europe.

France even offers a course in an art form perfected in the Far East. Brigitte Moron (Poterie des Riailles, **t** 04 75 37 13 06; **www.moron.com.fr**) in Lagorce in the Languedoc offers *formation* courses in the ancient Japanese ceramics tradition of **raku**. Pots and vases are left with an emblematic 'crackled' or 'metallic' surface that is achieved in the ceramic-firing process.

Sports

In 1998, France made football history when the underdogs beat defending champions Brazil in a 3–0 victory to clinch an unexpected World Cup victory before a delirious crowd of 80,000 people in Paris. Striker Zinedine Zidane ('Zizou' or 'ZiZi') became a national hero and French children nationwide proudly wore number 10 shirts in honour of the Marseille native. Zizou and the other members of the beloved *Les Bleus* team parading the Cup down a jubilant Champs-Elysées are epic moments in the French national diary.

The 1998 World Cup Championship gave new meaning to the concept of the home-team advantage. Since then France has reconnected with its passion for football and athletics in general.

With alpine mountains, 3,427km of coastline including Corsica, generally good weather and a healthy populace nourished on world-class food and wine, the French are a sporty bunch. According to a recent poll, two-thirds of French men and half of the nation's women participate regularly in sporting activity. This figure has risen threefold in the last three decades and perhaps one of the reasons for the French sporting frenzy is its stellar performance in recent international athletic competitions. In addition to the 1998 World Cup, France nabbed 13 gold medals at the 2000 Sydney Olympics (and a total of 38 medals). Both the Tour de France and the French Tennis Open have matured to become sporting events of European and global scope. Skiing, sailing, judo, fencing and motorcar racing have also helped elevate France to the winner's podium.

An excellent source of information and contact information, listed per region, on the following sports is available at **www.discoverfrance.net**.

Cycling

Watching the Tour de France on television is one thing, but pedalling your way along France's kilometres of hilly roads, picturesque countryside and coastal paths is another. You can easily rent a bicycle in France or bring your own and you will be rewarded with a wealth of empty roads and friendly fellow cyclists. For more information, contact the Fédération Française de Cyclotourisme (**http://perso.wanadoo.fr/velonin/ffct/index.html**) or the Fédération Française de Cyclisme (**www.ffc.fr**).

Paris has been making huge efforts to become more biker-friendly and has recently installed some 100km of bike lanes in the city. Some of the most enjoyable are along the rue de Rivoli, the boulevard Saint-Germain, the Bois de Boulogne (where you can also rent bicycles) and the Bois de Vincennes. On Sundays, cars are banned from the banks of the Seine between the Tuileries and the Eiffel Tower 9am–6pm and along the Canal St-Martin 2–6pm.

Hiking

France has 40,000km of hiking paths (*Grandes Randonnées*, marked by red and white signs) with the most popular rolling through the hilly regions of the Alps, the Ardennes, Beaujolais, Brittany, Champagne, the Dordogne Valley, Ile-de-France, the Jura, the Massif Central, the Pyrénées and the Vosges. Among the most popular is the Gorges du Verdon in Provence, France's own Grand Canyon.

Each GR is described in a *Topoguide*, with maps and details about campsites, refuges and so on, available in area bookshops or from the Fédération Française de la Randonnée Pédestre, 14 Rue Riquet, 75019 Paris, **t** 01 44 89 93 93, **www. ffrp.asso.fr**. Otherwise, the best maps for local excursions, based on ordnance surveys, are put out by the Institut Géo-graphique National.

Of special interest are: GR5 from Holland to Nice; GR3 following the entire length of the Loire; GR65, the Chemin de St-Jacques, from Le Puy-en-Velay to Santiago de Compostela (in Spain); GR52 from Menton up to Sospel, the Vallée des Merveilles to St-Dalmas-Valdeblore (in the Provençal Alps); GR52a and GR5 through Mercantour National Park (both of which are only open end of June–beginning Oct); GR51, nicknamed 'the balcony of the Côte d'Azur', from Castellar (near Menton), taking in the Esterel and Maures before ending at Bormes-les-Mimosas; GR9, beginning in St-Tropez and crossing over the region's most famous mountains – Ste-Baume, Ste-Victoire, the Luberon and Ventoux; GR4, which crosses the Dentelles de Montmirail and Mont Ventoux en route to Grasse; and GR42, which descends the west bank of the Rhône from near Bagnols-sur-Cèze to Beaucaire.

Riding

The same areas listed in the hiking section also offer opportunities for those interested in riding horses (*équitation*).

Balls and Boules

If a sport can be an emblem of a nation, *boules* – also known as *pétanque* – is to France what pizza is to Italy. Similar to British lawn bowling and Italy's *bocce*, *boules* evokes images of amber sunshine, the sounds of crickets and the aniseed aroma of *pastis*.

The rules of the game are simple. Each *pétanqueur* must launch his balls so that they land as close as possible to the *cochonnet* (a smaller wooden ball that sets the perimeters of the game). If your opponent's ball is closer to the *cochonnet* than yours, you can attempt to hit the *cochonnet* so that it moves closer to your balls. Each player comes prepared with a set of three steel balls to the *boulodrome*, the playing field which is usually a dirt-covered plain under sycamore trees within convenient proximity of a drinking hole.

The *boules* usually weigh 650–800g and are 70.5–80mm in diameter. Choosing your balls is part of the winning strategy as a heavier *boule* is more difficult to displace and a smaller *boule* represents a more difficult target for your opponent. But, a lighter *boule* is easier to launch and it has more chance of staying put on the ground after knocking your opponent's ball away from the *cochonnet*. This ace move is known as the *carreau*. The *cochonnet* is usually a 2.5cm ball made of beech wood stained with a bright colour but often other objects are used in its place. The only other tool needed is a measuring tape for those moments when a hair's width can divide a *boule* winner from a loser.

Skiing

The winter Olympics in Grenoble in 1968 and Albertville in 1992 only made enthusiasm for winter sports explode among a populace already squarely fitted into their ski boots. France has some 100 world-class skiing facilities and excellent conditions for both downhill (*ski alpin*) and cross-country (*ski de fond*) skiing. You can even ski on the island of Corsica and in the mountains behind Nice with views of the sparkling Mediterranean below you.

The most famous winter resort is Chamonix-Mont-Blanc in the French Alps, which hosted the winter Olympics in 1924 (the first winter Olympics ever held). The area is also home to the world's highest cable car that rises 12,000ft in altitude up the Aiguille du Midi peaks and boasts breathtaking views of Mont Blanc. Other skiing resorts include L'Alpe d'Huez (near Grenoble), Briançon, Courchevel, Megève, Méribel, Serre-Chevalier and Val d'Isère, Less expensive are Pyrénées and Vosges. Nearly all these resorts also offer mountain-biking, hiking, horseback-riding, ice-skating, luge, river-rafting, rock-climbing and tobogganing. **www.skifrance.fr** has snow conditions, a list of open lifts and the locations of the skiing slopes nearest you.

Tennis

There's a little-known footnote in the history of tennis that not many people know. Although lawn tennis became popular in Great Britain in the 19th century, the sport was actually born 600 years before in France. A precursor to tennis was France's *jeu de paume* (the 'palm game') in which the ball is passed between players with a swift smack of the hand. Tennis racquets were invented later (presumably as a way of avoiding wrist injuries).

The sport evolved in France thanks to the French Open event staged in Paris' Roland-Garros stadium during May and June. There are plenty of courts (*terre battue* are clay courts) throughout the country and tennis clubs where you can buy membership. The Fédération Française de Tennis promotes tennis in France and provides information at **www.fft.fr**.

Water Sports

From the Mediterranean and Atlantic coasts to Corsica, there are infinite places for windsurfing and water-skiing. Surfing and body-surfing is popular in the Atlantic resort town of Biarritz with its world-class rollers. There are municipal swimming pools all over the country, including the Pontoise Quartier and the Piscine des Halles in Paris, for making muggy summer days bearable.

Working in France

07

Unless you've come to France to retire and enjoy blissful snippets of life involving friends, family, hobbies, food and wine, or you've come to France as the owner of a holiday home, you'll need to find a job. Those who do, become French for all practical purposes, and contributing members of an energized and proudly productive society.

Happily, there are no bureaucratic obstacles to prevent an EU national from looking for work in France. In fact, once you do find a job you can easily apply for a residence permit (*carte de séjour*) – which may be on the way to becoming unnecessary, *see* pp.122–3 – and ultimately settle permanently in the country. Non-EU citizens are forced to jump through more hoops and usually must arrange employment before moving to France. They also must arrive *with* the work permit, which can be difficult to arrange. For more detail on these areas, *see* **Red Tape**, 'Visas, Permits and other Paperwork' pp.120–26.

Many foreigners come to France with a foreign company or bank that has a branch office here. Others look for work with a French employer. But the overwhelming majority opt to go it alone either by freelancing or by starting their own business. Whichever your case, this chapter will paint a basic picture of France's labour market, work etiquette, and, more importantly, will give you ideas on how to become part of it.

Moving to France means starting a new life: the perfect opportunity for doing the things you've always dreamed of accomplishing. Some leave the rat race behind to open a pub, an English-language bookstore, or a nursery. Others come to get their creative juices flowing by dabbling in journalism or art restoration. If you work for yourself, or if you come as part of a company, one thing is certain: the more you contribute to France, the more she will give in return.

Business Etiquette

The dos and don'ts of doing business in France do not differ drastically from what you are accustomed to in the UK. In France, affairs are executed with a carefully contemplated flair for elegance. You will notice it in the formal language used and the respect paid to colleagues.

The French put much emphasis on non-verbal communication and first impressions. A firm handshake, direct eye contact and body gestures are often more revealing than words. Someone who shies away from another person's eye contact may be perceived as hiding something, and getting close to someone physically is not always an invasion of personal space. It can communicate affection and camaraderie.

Introductions

It is important to know how to present yourself, your company and your ideas in a proper way. When setting up a business meeting, remember that no matter how many e-mails and telephone calls you exchange, nothing will be more vital than the first one-on-one encounter. The French, most especially in urban settings, are very conscious of how people dress and will notice things like unpolished shoes or shirts that need ironing. Both women and men are well groomed, and women usually wear heels and light make-up. Another way to make a good first impression is to have an elegantly printed business card ready in your breast pocket or purse. Start with a handshake at the first meeting. Successive ones, depending on your work environment, can be sparked with a cheek-to-cheek kiss known as *la bise*.

It goes without saying that you should greet all new acquaintances using the formal *vouvoiement* form until the person you are addressing says it is all right for you to use the informal address and to *tutoyer* them. In many businesses, work colleagues never switch to the informal *tu*, while in others – especially when young people work together – conversations start off in the informal tense. It is always better to err on the side of being too formal.

Meetings

Conference-room conversation often doesn't cut to the chase as you'd expect, and instead becomes an opportunity for participants to expand on thoughts and opinions. To be part of the forum of ideas, prepare with research and charts and displays when necessary. Don't necessarily expect a course of action to be ironed out at the end of the meeting. Business decisions may be finalized in the future or at a second meeting.

Making the Call

The French are a chatty bunch, but not when the telephone is involved. Because local calls can be expensive, people generally do not spend hours on endless conversation. They would prefer to meet in person and that is, of course, the driving force that keeps France's lively café culture in business.

If you are calling someone for the first time, it's best to include a title: '*Bonjour, Monsieur*' for a man and '*Bonjour, Madame*' for a woman. Avoid simply saying '*Bonjour*'. You should then introduce yourself with your name and work title. For example, '*Jean-Paul Sartre, philosophe existentialiste et écrivain à l'appareil*' (it's Jean-Paul Sartre, existentialist philosopher and writer here). To end a telephone conversation, include the title once again: '*Au revoir, Madame*' or '*Au revoir, Monsieur*'.

When it comes to scheduling **business meetings**, never plan them for the week of 15 August, when going to the office is almost considered a criminal offence. In fact, cross the entire month of August off your business planner. Scheduling meetings around Christmas isn't such a good idea either, and take care to avoid the smaller holidays sprinkled throughout the year (*see* **Reference**, 'Public Holidays and Events', p.276).

In general, **business hours** are from 8.30 or 9am to 7pm. Lunch can last up to two hours (or more if you live in the hottest areas of the country). In Paris, punctuality is taken very seriously. Don't get tempted into believing that the rules are more relaxed the further south you go. Stereotypes are worth believing only if they are true.

If you have agreed to a **business lunch**, remember it is a time for eating as much as it is for negotiating. This is intended as an opportunity to get to know each other and, as a result, conversation that touches on family life or personal preferences can be expected. Getting down to the 'meat' of your business, especially where money matters are concerned, may be considered abrupt. Business lunches are usually not a quick affair. Instead, they can last hours, giving you and your guests the chance to enjoy a full meal consisting of the various tempting courses listed on the menu, and wine is always welcome. The person who organized the encounter should be the one footing the bill.

Case Study: Banking on Paris

'When I go back to London, I'm homesick for Paris,' says 32-year-old David, who calculates profit and loss for bank Société Générale. 'I've been in Paris four and a half years. I am an expat by status but have immersed myself in the French way of life so I can no longer classify myself as English either.'

David was employed by a branch of the French bank in London and was exhausted by the back-and-forth travelling and nights in hotels he spent for work. 'When the bank offered to transfer me to Paris, I jumped at the chance.' His employers took care of most of his paperwork, such as obtaining his *carte de séjour*, and he transferred his driver's licence, but had no problems in doing so. 'I was in and out in five minutes.'

David says life in Paris couldn't be better, although he has noted cultural differences in the workplace. 'In the UK the work environment is more aggressive. In London, there were people screaming and shouting in the middle of the dealing room, whereas here that's just not part of the mentality.' He has also noticed differences in the way colleagues interact. 'At the end of the work day in London everyone heads to the pub together to have a few drinks. Here, you just don't go out with people from work. You either see people outside work or go home to your family.'

Nonetheless, David has no plans to move anywhere else. No wonder. He is engaged to marry a former dancer: 'Four years at the *Moulin Rouge* and four years at the *Lido*,' he proudly points out.

The Corporate Hierarchy

The lines dividing categories of workers may be more firmly etched, especially in a corporate setting. Fraternizing with superiors or people below you on the corporate ladder may raise some eyebrows. Generally, socializing outside the office is done by employees of equal status and is virtually unheard of between bosses and their underlings. Sometimes little cliques form. Other Europeans have complained of barriers raised, and of limited communication, between different levels of management. This is further aggravated by the importance given to France's top business and engineering schools to the detriment of employees who have not had this privilege, see pp.82–4. This may lead to a feeling of frustration among foreigners, who are unsure of where they stand in the corporate hierarchy. So that you know, the president of a French company is known as the PDG, or *président directeur général*. If you work in the mailroom, you don't want to be caught sending spam e-mails to his address.

More information on the dos and don'ts of doing business is available at the excellent site **www.workinfrance.com**.

The Labour Market

France's labour force is 26 million people strong – a figure that is roughly half the nation's population. Of these, about 20 million currently earn a wage or salary. Some 2.4 million people are looking for a job. Indeed, French unemployment figures have been hovering in and about the nine per cent mark, although recent reforms in labour laws have been designed to reduce that figure.

Here is a rough breakdown of France's labour force: about three per cent are farmers or work in agriculture; about six per cent are self-employed non-professionals such as carpenters, plumbers, instructors, shopkeepers; 11 per cent are managers or classified as 'professionals'; 18 per cent are intermediate occupations, or in other words temporary jobs; 25 per cent of the labour force are white-collar workers; and 23 per cent are manual labourers. The remaining slice of the pie represents the jobless and those who have never worked.

France's healthy private sector labour force is one of the nation's strongest features for attracting foreign investment. In order to ensure that investors find the high-quality labour at the relatively competitive wages costs they require, and in order to keep the national economy in shape, the French government has implemented a package of wide-ranging reforms.

Like many other European nations, France is focused on:

- **creating more jobs in the commercial and service sectors (which have already seen a sharp increase)**
- **stimulating economic growth and a healthy economy**

- allowing for more labour flexibility in employment laws to permit manageable turnover in companies; in other words, loosening some of the restrictions that previously made it difficult or disadvantageous for employers to fire or hire employees
- setting the stage for more temporary workers as a way of fighting unemployment numbers
- creating more temporary and part-time work contracts
- creative stimuli and incentives for businesses to hire additional employees; these include tax breaks or government subsidies.
- the move towards a 35-hour working week (heated debate on the subject started in 1997 and was a major focus of the Lionel Jospin government) in order to curb joblessness. The idea is that new jobs will be created because employers will hire more people to make up for the shortened working week. Businesses with fewer than 20 employees were given until 2003 to switch to the 35-hour working week.

The results of these reforms still must be tested and more time will be needed to assess the the long-term benefits or disadvantages. So far, the news has been very good. Thanks to the reforms, the jobless rate has fallen at a rate of roughly one per cent per year since it peaked in June 1997. In the four years from 1997 to 2000, some 1.6 million new jobs were created in France, including 500,000 in 2000 alone – which makes that the best year of the entire century, according to the French Embassy's website. Of course, this ultimately creates a more favourable employment climate and increases the opportunities for foreigners looking for work in France.

Job Ideas

There is a wide range of business opportunities for foreigners with an outsider's perspective on what's missing in the French market. In fact, thanks to our bicultural outlook we are in a much better position to determine which ventures might flourish or fail. The only decision, really, is coming up with a business proposition that suits your interests and talents.

Here are a few ideas (in alphabetical order) to mull over before coming up with a list of your own:

- **Accountants or solicitors**: Few French accountants are familiar with foreign tax laws, especially when complicated situations involving both the UK and France arise. These might be inheritance laws or understanding of the treaties that govern dual taxation.

- **Art or furniture restoration**: This is an attractive option for those who adore peeling off soot to reveal hidden colour or stripping off paint to find the wood's delicate grains. Many foreigners, especially in small towns, open a laboratory where they can concentrate on these little pleasures.

• **Bars and restaurants**: This is one of the most popular small business ideas among Britons in France. English pubs are popping up across the nation from Normandy to Nice and attract a steady flow of clients looking to escape the confines of traditional wicker café chairs. The very ambitious could try opening a restaurant, borrowing from the tastes and exotic spices of home.

• **Bed & breakfast**: From the French Alps down to Cannes, the English are embracing the French high quality of life, and are making a living doing so. You really must be a 'people person' to open up a small hotel or bed & breakfast, as most of the charming people in this field are.

• **Building**: Anyone who has done construction work on their French home and who is not totally fluent in French knows that there is an enormous demand for masons, electricians and plumbers with whom they can communicate.

• **Business services**: Again, your English language skills could be put to good use by those seeking to organize conventions, seminars or logistical considerations (e.g. transport and accommodation) for businesses. This could be a thriving field for experienced consultants.

• **Computer technology**: Yes, the boom has come and gone, but there is always a need for people versed in the latest hardware and software – especially web-page-designing programmes like Dreamweaver that are sold in English. You could open a studio or consultancy for building web pages or managing a site.

• **Estate agents**: As more and more English people gobble up tasty morsels of French property, the need for qualified agents to help them through the complicated procedure will increase. The boom in this sector has been outstanding within the past five years and English-speaking estate agents with knowledge of the regions of France are always in demand.

• **Health foods**: French are increasingly attracted to 'health foods' like organic groceries, frozen yoghurt shops and vegetarian restaurants.

• **Medicine**: France lacks these specialists whether or not you have the background: English-speaking chiropractors, acupuncturists and doctors specialized in holistic or homeopathic medicines.

• **Plant nursery**: In awe of the many French microclimates and proud of your green fingers? Many foreigners come to France to start a plant business. The south of France is full of them. Some sell palm trees and others bushes with wild berries. The French love gardening and would appreciate tips from a cold-climate expert.

• **Relocation services**: Many entrepreneurs are making money out of what you are seeking to do now: working and living in France. Relocation or expatriate consultants can help foreigners wade through bureaucratic procedures, such as getting a work permit, or setting up a lease to let property. They can also help change ownership of a car and give tips on how best to save on one's electricity or gas bill.

• **Retail**: Maybe you miss certain products you associate with home like Cadbury's chocolate, McVitie's biscuits, Quaker crisps, Marmite or Colman's mustard. Many enterprising foreigners are opening boutique food or grocery stores to satisfy the cravings of epicurean nostalgics.

• **Schools:** French students may need help preparing for exams or writing CVs in English. Some foreigners open English-language kindergartens and others focus on the educational and recreational needs of adults by opening fitness, pottery or painting schools.

• **Theatres and art galleries**: France is a country with a soft spot for the arts as the large number of French musical and theatrical venues demonstrates. Why not share a new vision from afar and create a space in which non-French and French artists alike can showcase their craft?

• **Tourism**: France attracts more foreign tourists per year than any other nation on the planet, and the trade to service their needs is immense. Britons have been able to capitalize on the market by organizing walking tours, bike tours, wine-tasting trips and even hot air balloon trips over Burgundy.

• **TV services**: With the growing number of Britons who can't live without the BBC or SkyNews, many expatriates are opening small businesses to help them install television satellite services.

• **Wedding services**: The laws governing foreign weddings in France are quite complicated, yet the popularity of 'destination weddings' continues to rise. You could open a small business catering to the needs of newly-weds-to-be. They will need to locate a good wedding venue, photographer, florist, photographer, and chauffeur.

'Pocket Money' Jobs

If you are coming to France for a few months, or just for the summer, you might consider the following ways to line your pockets with extra money. Many young women are hired as nannies or au pairs in villas by the sea in the south of France. An au pair is employed for general childcare and light household work and is given board and lodging and a small allowance. Other enterprising young people have been able to get work walking other people's dogs or looking after holiday homes while their owners are away.

There are also a plethora of seasonal jobs, usually linked to the natural cycles of agriculture. Each September the same thing happens. As the sugar content in grapes rises and the growing season nears its end, vineyard managers start their mad scramble to find temporary workers to pick wine grapes. Regional officials work hard to recruit as many as 45,000 temporary workers for the harvest. The region of Burgundy, land of pinot noir and chardonnay, needs 7,400 pairs of helping hands; the prestigious Bordeaux region needs 9,000; and the land of the bubbly, Champagne, calls for half that many. Roussillon, the Rhône and Alsace also have a high demand for autumn labour. In addition, apple-pickers are needed in Limousin, Pays de la Loire, and the Var.

All you need to apply is an identity card (or passport) and a copy of your insurance card. You must be over 18 and a European Union citizen. Foreign students registered in a French school or university and people holding a French work permit may also be employed. The harvest starts in early September and usually lasts from one week to 10 days. Depending on the region, payment is usually set

Don't Mime Me

There's something intrinsically French about a mime artist. Dressed in a black and white striped shirt with suspenders and a black hat, he regularly puts in appearances all over the country: from in front of the Palais des Festivals in Cannes during the film festival to Paris's Centre Pompidou. But you may wonder, is he really French?

The art of mime, a theatrical form in which physical gestures replace verbal expression, was born in ancient Greece and flourished in the 5th and 4th centuries BC. Back then, mime performances were meant to teach a moral lesson and, it could be hypothesized, they communicated political sentiments most mortals would dare not mouth in public. The rowdy Romans were quick to appreciate the art of the silent clown. During the reign of Emperor Augustus, mime companies developed characters and storylines to fuel Rome's notorious love of spectacle. As the Roman Empire fell, and the Catholic Church rose to power, mimes were associated with pagan debauchery and forced underground. The art of mime survived and soon reappeared with religious themes. Its popularity exploded again in the 1500s when it took the form of *Commedia dell'Arte*, or theatre staged spontaneously in the streets of Italian cities by acrobatic actors wearing colourful masks.

In 1576, a troupe of Italian actors led by Flamino Scala went to Paris, and since that date mimes have enjoyed a happy existence in France. In 1811, Jean Gaspard Baptiste Deburau, a member of a travelling theatre group, stopped in Paris to give regular performances at the Funambules on the Boulevard du Temple. Over the course of the years he spent there, he created the lovesick character 'Pierrot' and made miming what it is today.

Following the Second World War, the actor Marcel Marceau created a character similar to Pierrot named 'Bip' (with a flower in his hat). Marceau's Bip was heavily influenced by silent screen mime Charlie Chaplin – who of course had been shaped by the down-trodden characters before him, like Pierrot.

French or not, miming may be the one of the world's oldest professions.

at the minimum wage per hour for eight hours a day. And, best of all, you're bound to be given a few extra bottles along with your cheque.

Other seasonal jobs could include work in a bar or restaurant that is particularly busy in the summer season. Beach areas are full of these opportunities. Another very popular source of income, especially among young people, is working on boats and private yachts. Large vessels require help on the decks, in the kitchen (galley) or cleaning.

Or, you could simply invent a job for yourself.

Being Employed in the Public or Private Sector

Before you read on, it must be stressed that getting a job in the public, and to a lesser extent the private, sector in France is not an easy task. Years of high unemployment combined with today's gloomy economic climate have slowed the job turnover rate. Few jobs come up, and people holding good jobs do not give them up easily. This is obviously true the world over, but it should be pointed out that the hardship associated with finding the job you want is more intense when you are a foreigner in France. Your main competitors for French jobs are the French themselves.

It is difficult, but not impossible. Your biggest selling point is your ability to speak and write English fluently, and that makes you attractive to businesses, especially ones involved in finance, media, technology or foreign markets. It is assumed that you will be able to understand software, internet pages, manuals and other work-related literature better than most. Your second asset is having a bi-cultural outlook, or European perspective. You may be able to bring a new attitude and valuable new ideas to the French workplace. How successfully you can use that to your advantage will depend on your ability to speak French. A solid command of the French language is paramount to most job searches.

The European Union was expected to trigger a flood of trans-continental job recruitments and cross-border job-swapping. Although this has occurred, it has not been to the extent that might have been anticipated. However, it has increased the mobility of EU nationals seeking jobs in other EU countries. In other words, it is now easier to look for a job in France.

Job-hunting

If you have no leads through university contacts, personal friends or former colleagues, you will be faced with starting your job search from scratch. British **newspapers** are a good place to start, especially publications that speak to a European audience such as the *Guardian*, the *Independent* and *The Times*, the

Economist and the *Financial Times*. All of these carry job advertisements from other European countries. Two American publications, the *Wall Street Journal* and the *International Herald Tribune*, also print job listings. National French newspapers such as *Le Figaro*, *Le Monde* and the weekly *L'Express* have ads in French and are commonly available on UK news stands.

If searching through print newspapers for employment seems a bit old-fashioned, you will be overwhelmed by the number of **online resources** to set you in the right direction. Although it would be impossible to list them all, some of the best internet sites for Britons looking for work in France are: **www.overseasjobs.com**, **www.careermosaic.com**, **www.jobware.net** and **www. monster.com** (with a whole section on France). If your French is up to par, you can log into **www.apr-job.com**, **www.emploi.com**, **www.emailjob.com** or **www. bonjour.fr**.

If you are already in France, you should explore local resources available to expatriates. In Paris, **www.parisfranceguide.com** has classified ads, as does **www.parisvoice.com**. In Monaco, Nice and the Var, Riviera Radio (**www.riviera radio.mc** or tune to 106.3 Monaco or 106.5 France) has an on-air 'Works for Me' programme in which all kinds of positions are advertised. You could become a bilingual assistant in an office in Monte Carlo or be hired as a chef on a yacht off the St-Tropez coast. The *Riviera Reporter* (**www.riviera-reporter.com**) also has an excellent database of jobs. The site **www.french-news.com** has a 'small ads' section with some job listings all over the country.

Another alternative is to go to an **agency**. The concept of a private employment agency doesn't exist in France because the government holds a monopoly on matching jobless with jobs. The state-run agency that fulfils this function is the Agence Nationale pour l'Emploi (ANPE) at **www.anpe.fr**. As a result, human resources multinationals such as Manpower (**www.manpower.fr**), which has 1,050 branches throughout France, are only allowed to focus on temporary work, not full-time contracted employment. Employment through these agencies (and many of the ones listed below) will only result in a temporary employment contract of no more than 18 months, unless the employer negotiates with you otherwise.

You might be better off contacting an agency that operates outside France and is not affected by French laws governing agencies. Good UK-based employment sites are **www.rec.uk.com**, or the Recruitment and Employment Federation, and **www.ukworksearch.com**. One recent search revealed dozens of jobs in the Ile de France/Paris area alone. Try the excellent Job Centres Plus **www.jobcentreplus.gov.uk**. Better still, you could take your job search to an agency that is neither French nor English, but European. In the UK, Ireland, and other European countries you can access the European Employment Services (EURES) network from national job centres and find out about job vacancies in other member states. The site **www.europa.eu.int/jobs/eures** answers questions about benefits, contracts, transfers and other European work issues.

If you are not interested in contacting an agency, you could try networking through the various institutes that cater to trade and business between France and England (embassies and consulates will not help you find a job.) One obvious solution is order a copy of the business directory of companies operating in France. The Chambre de Commerce Française de Grande-Bretagne in London (**www.ccfgb.co.uk**) publishes pamphlets and directories to help you make the transition abroad, as does its equivalent in France, the Franco-British Chamber of Commerce (**www.francobritishchamber.com**).

The Curriculum Vitae

English and French CVs differ only slightly in length and in content. Most French CVs are listed in reverse chronological order (with the most recent activity first) (*le CV chronologique*) or are grouped thematically (*le CV fonctionnel*). Many include a passport-size photograph and personal information like your age and marital status, which you might not have included on your English CV. Contact information should include e-mail and a telephone number with the international dialling code.

The CV is a marketing tool aimed at making the employer interested in you. It should be brief (one page or more only in certain fields like academics or entertainment), concise and direct. Shorter CVs are easier to scan and send as file attachments if you are applying from abroad.

Most importantly, it should be in French, so have a native speaker check it over. For an example, see page opposite.

Some Words to Use

Additional vocabulary in French with English translations to help you prepare your CV:

Situation personnelle et état civil (personal information), *nom de famille* (last name), *prénom* (first name), *adresse* (address), *numéro de téléphone* (telephone number; remember to include international dialling codes), *bureau* (office telephone), *domicile* (home telephone), *portable* (mobile), *adresse électronique* (e-mail), *nationalité* (nationality), *âge* (age), *situation de famille* (marital status and number of children), *célibataire* (single), *marié(e)* (married), *divorcé(e)* (divorced), *veuf* or *veuve* (widowed), *projets professionnels* or *objectifs* (objectives), *expérience professionnelle* (professional experience), *formation* (education), *connaissances linguistiques et informatiques* (language and computer skills), *langues* (languages), *bonnes connaissances* (conversant), *lu, écrit, parlé* (proficient), *courant* (fluent), *bilingue* (bilingual), *langue maternelle* (mother tongue), *informatique* (IT), *divers* (miscellaneous), *passe-temps* (interests), *loisirs* (leisure activities), *activités personnelles/extra-professionnelles* (hobbies).

Nom – Prénom
Adresse
Tél :
Adresse électronique
5 novembre 1970
Célibataire

Traductrice : Quatre ans d'expérience internationale dans la traduction français–anglais.

EXPERIENCE PROFESSIONNELLE

Depuis 2002	Traduction freelance de documents économiques et politiques. Clients choisis: Les Nations-Unies (traduction de plusieurs discours officiels), Chambre de Commerce Française de Grande-Bretagne (traduction de la présentation du budget) et Union Européenne (traduction des études sur les nouveaux membres).
2001–2002	Gouvernement français Traductrice officielle (annonces politiques, rédaction de discours officiels)
1999–2000	SuperTranslations, Londres – Traduction de documents courts – Vérification de traductions simples

ETUDES ET FORMATION

1998	Diplôme de traductrice-terminologue de l'ISIT (Institut Supérieur d'Interprétation et de Traduction), Paris
1995	Diplôme de la Chambre de Commerce Franco-Britannique, Paris
1993	Classe préparatoire littéraire, Lycée Jules Ferry, Paris
1991	Baccalauréat A2, Lycée Charles de Gaulle

COMPETENCES LINGUISTIQUES

Anglais : bilingue, langue maternelle
Français : bilingue
Espagnol : bon niveau

COMPETENCES BUREAUTIQUES

Maîtrise de Word, Windows, PowerPoint, Dreamweaver

DIVERS

Voyages, cinéma, voile, ski, natation

The Covering Letter

The rules governing the content of a good covering letter (*demande d'emploi* or *lettre de candidature*) are almost precisely the same as anywhere else in the world. The letter should be short and should state your purpose and give a general thumbnail overview of your qualifications and background. The only glaring exception in the French covering letter is that it is generally hand-written. This is because up to 80 per cent of French employers use graphology in the application process. As strange as this may sound, handwriting analysis is considered an important aid to recruitment. Even if you e-mail a covering letter, you may be asked to submit backup writing samples.

The two main types of letters are a *lettre de réponse à une annonce* (in response to a published advertisement) or a *lettre de candidature spontanée* (an 'on spec' letter to ask about possible openings).

Opposite is an example of one.

Down to the Letter

Here are some basic phrases in French, with English translations, to help you draft application covering letters, or *lettres d'emploi*:

Je me réfère à votre annonce (with reference to your advertisement).

Je me permets de poser ma candidature au poste de ... (I wish to apply for the post of ...).

J'aimerais changer de situation (I would like to change jobs).

J'aimerais pratiquer davantage ... (I would like to make better use of ...).

Ma formation de ... (my training as ...).

Mon expérience de ... (my experience in ...).

Je vous prie de bien vouloir me faire savoir (please let me know).

Je vous serais très reconnaissant(e) (I would be very grateful).

Je vous prie de bien vouloir m'envoyer des renseignements plus complets sur le poste de ... (please send more information regarding the position of ...).

Je vous prie de bien vouloir me faire savoir s'il me serait possible d'obtenir un emploi dans votre entreprise (please let me know if there is possibility of work in your company).

Je vous prie d'avoir l'obligeance de ... (please be so kind as to ...).

Je suis au regret de vous faire savoir que ... (I'm sorry to inform you that ...).

J'ai bien reçu votre lettre du ... (I received your letter of ...).

Je vous remercie pour votre lettre du ... (thank you for your letter of ...).

Dans votre lettre, vous me demandiez ... (in your letter, you asked me ...).

En réponse à votre lettre ... (in response to your letter ...).

Je suis désireux/euse de travailler en France afin de perfectionner/d'acquérir ... (I'm interested in working in France in order to perfect/to acquire ...).

Nom – Prénom
Adresse
Tél :
Adresse électronique

Entreprise Traduction
Monsieur XX
Direction des ressources humaines
40, rue de France
75015 Paris

Paris, le 4 mars 2004

Monsieur,
A la suite de votre annonce, parue le 2 mars dans *Le Monde*, je me permets de vous proposer ma candidature à un poste de traducteur officiel.
A la lecture de mon curriculum vitae, vous pourrez constater que j'ai quatre ans d'expérience internationale dans la traduction français–anglais et que je suis spécialisé(e) en traduction économique et politique.
Bilingue, connaissant la comptabilité anglo-saxonne et française, je pense que ma bi-culturalité me permettra de bien m'intégrer dans une entreprise internationale comme la vôtre.
Je reste à votre entière disposition pour tout renseignement complémentaire et pour un éventuel entretien, au cours duquel je pourrai vous donner de plus amples informations.
Veuillez agréer, Monsieur, l'expression de mes salutations distinguées.

(Your name and signature)

Interviews

The French take interviews seriously. If you have been invited to one, it probably means your candidacy is important to the selection team and your qualifications have caught their eye. The actual interview can be a formal event – either a one-on-one encounter or an interview in front of a panel of people. That means, of course, that you should use every means in your power to make a good impression from the moment you walk through the door. The importance of dressing well, using eye contact and conveying confidence cannot be exaggerated.

If your interview is in French (and hopefully you have not stated French fluency on your CV if that is not the case) you will be expected to use the formal *vous* form of addressing your peers and should use appropriate titles. A *Monsieur* or *Madame* alone, without the name, is the correct form of address. You should offer a firm handshake at the start and end of the interview. If your French is not great, there's no harm in explaining that you are currently working on improving it and you look forward to continue doing so in the future. Another good hint is to read the French newspapers more carefully than normal a few days or weeks prior to the interview so you can offer opinions and comments on other topics should you be given the opportunity.

You may have to wait a while before an offer is made. In general, the French don't negotiate offers with the same intensity we do. Often when an offer is made, it is immediately accepted. There is nothing wrong with taking a few days to mull an offer over, and perhaps, come back with a counter-offer. In fact, that may win you points for professionalism and determination. The types of work contracts, terms of employment and salaries are discussed in detail below.

Employment Contracts

There are three basic kinds of contracts (*contrat de travail*): a temporary employment contract, a fixed-term contract (*contrat à durée déterminée* or CDD), and a permanent contract (*contrat à durée indéterminée* or CDI).

Temporary Employment Contract

In this case, the employee is usually hired and paid by a temping agency, like the ones mentioned above. Temporary employment contracts may be renewed once, on the condition that the duration of employment does not exceed 18 months. The temping agency's function is to recruit or replace an employee on a temporary basis in the event of a momentary increase in work (for example in the weeks before the Christmas season) or seasonal work.

Fixed-Term Contract (CDD)

A fixed-term contract must state in writing the duration of the contract (for example, it could be a 'one-year contract'). The probationary period, or 'trial time,' of a contract of less than six months may not exceed two weeks. For a contract of over six months, the trial time may not exceed one month. The maximum time for a CDD contract is two years, after which a second CDD contract (or a permanent contract) can be offered.

Permanent Contract (CDI)

This is the contract everyone wants because it provides enormous job security and a wide range of benefits. Basically, there is no 'end' to the contract. Both parties sign it and the contract will stipulate the date of employment, the social security information (healthcare) and other benefits. The length of the probationary period can last from one to three months.

If you are not an EU citizen (in other words, if you are an American, Canadian or Australian national) you must first obtain authorization from the French Ministry of Labour to work in France. This authorization is a prerequisite document for the visa to be issued by the French consulate in your country. You won't get the visa until you have been cleared to work by the French government. If the Ministry of Labour approves your contract, it is forwarded to the Office des Migrations Internationales (OMI). It is then forwarded to the French embassy or consulate you have been dealing with. It is the embassy or consulate's job to notify you when to proceed with the visa process. Once the visa is obtained, you may enter France and apply for a *carte de séjour* at the local police station (or *préfecture*). After all that, you can focus on your new job.

Terms of Employment

Once you start working in France, you will receive a pay slip (*bulletin de paie*) with your salary. This document keeps track of wages paid that month, social security contributions made on behalf of the employee, the amount deducted for taxes and the number of holiday days left. Here are the basic conditions for employment as established by the French Labour Code (*Code du Travail*).

Wages and Salaries

Your salary (*salaire*) is calculated according to your work category (what kind of contract you have). The main categories are manual workers, office employees and managers, and each has its own fixed salary grade. Usually, first-time employees earn the minimum wage, called the SMIC or *Salaire Minimum Interprofessionnel de Croissance*, and can expect a rise pegged to the cost-of-living index, which is reviewed every six months. When the cost of living increases by two per cent or more, the SMIC is adjusted. If a worker falls into a category protected by a national labour union, work contracts are renewed every few years. Collective bargaining (*conventions collectives de travail*) establishes new wage scales each time contracts are renewed. Most salaries are paid once a month.

According to the APEC research centre, the median starting salary in France is €26,000–29,000 per year. In general, French salaries are among the highest in Europe – especially managerial positions – but may be lower than what you are used to in England.

Working Hours

The *Code du Travail* has established a 35-hour working week. There is some built-in flexibility. For example, if a company needs more workers in the busiest weeks prior to Christmas it can increase the hours worked per week, as long as they are decreased in less busy times of the year. Companies can increase the number of hours worked per week through collective bargaining and by agreeing to pay employees overtime or giving them more time off. Office hours are usually Mon–Fri 8.30am–5.30pm with a lunch break of up to two hours.

Case Study: Working Illegally

'The temptation to buck the system and hire illegal workers is there and usually works out fine – unless you get caught.'

Mike Meade has lived in France for 32 years and since 1987 has edited the *Riviera Reporter*, the most popular English-language magazine in the south of France. 'Since I've been sitting in my editor's chair, I've seen dozens – perhaps even hundreds – of people caught, fined and even arrested for working in the black economy.' Even more terrifying are the stories he has collected of people who have hired illegal workers (many of them English who have not set themselves up properly to do business in France) and are ruined now because of it.

'A few years ago, an incident came to my attention of an English couple in their 70s who invested their savings in a house in Vence. They had taken on a young Englishman to do some gardening and the lad accidentally chopped off his thumb while pruning their trees with a chainsaw. Ambulance, hospital, surgery ... and the bill. Despite having a resident's permit, the young man had not set himself up as a registered gardener in France, nor had the couple declared him as a domestic employee. The authorities automatically considered him an *ipso facto* employee of the household who should have checked his legal status. The elderly couple faced €500,000 in fines and medical bills. Their dream retirement villa was seized and sold at auction and they were ruined.'

There are more stories. In one, the undeclared chef at a dinner party set fire to the kitchen and himself. The insurance company would not pay because he was not supposed to be cooking for money. In another, an illegal English 'painter' set up scaffolding on another Englishman's house. His scaffolding fell onto his 'client's' new Mercedes. No insurance claim could be put in and the man lost a Mercedes – thankfully the painter did not fall too, otherwise he may have lost his house.

'France is an expensive place to be in business. You can't hope to survive if your competitor is not playing on a level field. You wouldn't let a perfect stranger fill up his supermarket trolley on your credit card, so why should you pay taxes for roads, hospitals, schools and public services that hangers-on benefit from at your expense?' explains Mike. 'The bottom line is hiring workers in the black is fine until an accident happens, or there is a random tax control or work inspection. It's unlikely, but crazy things happen.'

The *Riviera Reporter* website (**www.riviera-reporter.com**) includes an online discussion forum. Mike Meade takes the time to answers many of the e-mails personally and has provided an invaluable resource with the dos and don'ts of living and working in the south.

Holidays

French law establishes that workers are entitled to five weeks (30 days in total) of paid holiday (*congés payés*) per year plus 11 public holidays (*jours fériés*) spread throughout the year. (For a list of the 11 national holidays and their descriptions, *see* **Reference**, 'Public Holidays and Events', p.276.) The general calculation is as follows: you must work one month (24 work days) to be entitled to two and a half days of holiday.

Bonuses

Most companies in France pay employees an extra month's salary known as the 13th month's pay (*13ème mois*). This bonus payment comes in December in time for the Christmas shopping season. If you don't work the entire year, the 13th month's pay is calculated to reflect the time you did work. A few companies also offer a 14th month's pay in July and a few lucky few can expect a 15th month's pay. In general, only bankers and people in finance are given the latter. In addition, senior employees may receive bonuses, anywhere from 10 to 25 per cent of their annual salary, that may or may not be linked to the company's financial performance (as with profit-sharing schemes – *participation des salariés aux résultats de l'entreprise*). An employee can be invited to participate in a company savings plan or stock options. Salespeople are often given commissions of three to six per cent of sales.

Different forms of bonuses are becoming common. Employee 'packages' may be offered which include a car, telephone, laptop computer, reimbursement of expenses and professional training. Bonus 'benefits' offered could include favourable interest rates for financing a car or mortgage.

Health Insurance

All employees, including foreigners working for French companies and the self-employed, must contribute to the social security fund (*Sécurité Sociale*) which covers healthcare. The amount you contribute depends on your income but can be as much as a quarter or a fifth of your gross pay. Some companies offer supplementary health insurances, called the *mutuelle*, to cover a portion of the medical expenses or hospitalization charges not covered by social security. The employer may cover those contributions. Some also companies offer private health insurance as part of a larger package of benefits. (For more information on healthcare and social security, *see* **Living in France**).

Maternity Leave

A new mother is entitled to 16 weeks of paid maternity leave (*congé de maternité*) if she is covered by French social security – generally six weeks before giving birth and 10 weeks after. She gets up to 26 weeks if she is having her third child. She earns her full salary during this time and can take additional time off with a doctor's note. Maternity leave is granted to all women no matter how long they have been employed and a mother is guaranteed her job back at the same or higher salary. New fathers in France receive 11 consecutive days of leave at full pay. Both parents can take up to three years of unpaid parental leave (*congé parental*) and expect to come back to the same job and salary (with the mandatory increases that may have occurred in the meantime). All of these rights apply to parents with adopted children.

Sickness Leave and Disability

Employees unable to work due to an illness are compensated according to their number of years in service. An employee with more than 10 years in service is entitled to two months of full salary, then two months at 75 per cent salary, and two months at half salary. An employee with between one and five years in service is entitled to one month of full salary, one month at 75 per cent, and one month at half salary. If the employee is still sick after that time, they may be considered disabled.

If an accident occurs in the workplace, injured employees receive full salary for the first three months. If they are permanently injured, they receive a pension. Many of the *mutuelle*, or health insurance supplements, include both temporary and permanent disability coverage.

If there is a death in the family or some other reason for an employee to need additional time off from work, employees can ask for a special leave of absence (*congé spécial*).

Pensions and Retirement

In France it is possible for both men and women to retire at the age of 60, after working in the private sector for 40 years and in the public sector for 37.5 years. Early retirement (*retraite*) does apply to particularly burdensome professions. In many European countries, the retirement age is 65 and France is taking controversial steps to raise their retirement age to 65. A retiree earns a pension of about half his average salary for the last 20 years of employment. Proposed pension reform has led to massive protests in Paris and other big cities and because this is a very sensitive subject it is constantly under scrutiny.

Firing Policies

An employee can be fired only if the employer can prove 'just cause' or a 'justified motive'. Just cause (*faute grave*) means the employee is found guilty of a major offence, such as stealing or unexplained absenteeism (*cause réelle et sérieuse*). This is difficult to prove and even harder to execute because it involves an official summons and a hearing. A justified motive includes corporate downsizing, or *pour faute du salarié ou pour raison économique.* Justified-motive firings must include advance notice and are usually negotiated with labour unions, making them also difficult to carry out. If the employee is fired unlawfully, he can claim his job and salary back with compensation for back wages. If an employee is fired because of downsizing, he will be the first one back on the payroll should the company have an opening in the future.

Termination Indemnity and Unemployment Benefits

Whether or not an employee resigns or is fired (except where there has been a case of serious misconduct) he gets a severance payment (*indemnité de licenciement*) which usually comes to 10 per cent of the employee's average salary during his last three months for each year in service. Payment must also be made if there is outstanding paid holiday (*indemnité compensatrice de congés payés*). Employees can leave their jobs at any time without justification as long as they notify the employer in writing by registered letter. Those who have lost a contracted position are paid unemployment benefits.

If you have any questions regarding the French Labour Code, or the terms of employment, there are two excellent legal pages available on the internet. If you speak French, go to **www.journal-officiel.gouv.fr**. A similar site in English is the excellent **www.paris-law.com**.

Teaching English

There is one job English mother-tongue speakers can count on to pay the bills. For some, teaching English is a safety net – a temporary source of income for living in France while they search for a different job. For others, teaching English is their chosen vocation. Many teachers get certificates and complete training courses to assure they keep their professional edge. How deeply you develop your teaching skills depends fundamentally on whether you see yourself as an English teacher or not. If you do, you'll want to collect the various teaching certificates available to assure a higher income potential. Ultimately, in France, teaching English can be a full-time job at a private school or university with a salary and benefits package.

If you are starting at the low end of the teaching spectrum – if, for example, you are looking to earn extra pocket money while on your gap year in France – start by rounding up some private students. You could place a classified ad (*petites annonces*) in a local newspaper or post online ads in the various internet teaching-English-abroad chat rooms. Sign on pupils through the help of friends or leave flyers at the local university. Decide whether to meet the student at his house for one-on-one private lessons. Or, arrange to meet a group of students for an English-language movie with one hour of discussion to follow. Other enterprising teachers structure their language classes in the kitchen as they prepare an elaborate dinner, or in the park for a day of sports and English conversation. Some arrange to match one hour of English with one hour of French. Teaching privately is an excellent way to fine-tune your skills. In terms of your hourly fee, experienced teachers (or simply the more confident) ask for €20–30 per hour.

If you want to take teaching to the next step, you'll have to learn a whole set of confusing acronyms. There are two kinds of English taught in France: English and ESL/EFL. When you teach 'English' your students are other native English-speakers or foreigners fluent in the language who might be getting a degree in English literature, for example. When you teach ESL (English as a Second Language) or EFL (English as a Foreign Language), your students are French who may be encountering the English language for the first time. EFL and ESL are pretty much interchangeable, although British teachers tend instinctively to use EFL, whereas American teachers use the term ESL. A third, more 'politically correct', term is EAL (English as an Additional Language) because it omits the word 'foreign' and because it implies the student may be learning a third or fourth language.

There are six basic levels of ESL/EFL teaching: conversation, reading, grammar, listening comprehension, vocabulary and writing. Books, with varying degrees of fluency, are available for students and teachers. If you want to get a job with one of the more prominent language schools (like Berlitz) you'll need some kind of teacher certification that shows you are familiar with ESL/EFL methods, especially if you don't already have a university degree (if you have a master's degree in English, for example, this requirement is often waived).

The most generic certificate is the TEFL/TESL (again there are two interchangeable acronyms for Teaching English as a Foreign Language and Teaching English as a Second Language). You'll also see TEAL (Teaching English as an Additional Language) and TESOL (Teaching English to Speakers of Other Languages). The three most widely recognized certificates are the Cambridge CELTA, the Trinity Certificate TESOL and the SIT TESOL Certificate. The Cambridge CELTA offers an intenive four-week course. There are some 300 centres offering CELTA courses in 40 countries and the costs vary from £500 to £1,000. Cambridge/Royal Society of Arts also offers a job placement service to qualifying candidates. Most Trinity Centres are in the UK and courses cost about the same. Before signing up for any certification programme, make sure it is validated by the UCLES (University of Cambridge Local Examinations Syndicate).

If this sounds all too confusing to you, there is an excellent website (**www.englishclub.com**) which explains the various acronyms in detail and has links to various teaching programmes. It also offers information on taxation, accommodation, age requirements and salaries.

You could also consult **www.tesol-france.org** and **www.volterre-fr.com** for more France-specific information.

Besides the various private language schools (consult **www.pagesjaunes.fr** to find the ones nearest you), you might also look for a teaching job with the British Council. For example, in France, it has a programme called EYL (English for Young Learners) for teaching English to children aged four and up at public and private primary schools. To find out about EYL methodology or about open positions, go to **www.britishcouncil.org**.

'Freelancing' or Part-Time Work

Unfortunately for the many thousands of people who come to France to work for themselves or freelance, they face what will seem like a daunting wrangle with French bureaucracy. In many cases it is just that. But ask many of the people who are successfully self-employed in France and they will tell you that once the process is done, it wasn't all that bad.

It should be said that there are many 'freelancers' in France, many indeed, who do not declare their status to French authorities. Perhaps they write magazine travel articles on France for UK publications out of their French summerhouse. In that case, they probably pay taxes on their income back home and don't expect or want French social security benefits or any of the other 'perks' of paying taxes in France. Rather than being 'illegal', you could say these people were on a very productive 'holiday'.

The moment a self-employed person or freelancer begins to do business in France, and earn an income in the country, they need to make their status known to the French government (remember, having a *carte de séjour* is not enough). This includes people selling 'junk' (*brocante*) at a travelling antiques fair, official translators, people installing satellite service to foreigners, builders, repair service people and artisans. Too often foreigners – especially those who work for other foreigners – opt not to set themselves up for business in France. For example, a satellite service technician specialized in setting up an English-language satellite service for people in the south of France might think it's all right to register his business in the UK, thus avoiding French hassles altogether. This is not the case. If he is caught he faces fines and could have his equipment and van confiscated. He could face time in prison.

Here are the basic things you need to know.

In France, the term 'freelancer' refers to any individual who is responsible for his income and for generating business and clients. A freelancer operates under the independent worker status (*travailleur indépendant*). That means if you are currently a salaried foreigner in France, you are required to change the status of your *carte de séjour* to *travailleur indépendant* status. If you hold a *carte de séjour, visiteur*, you are not allowed to work in France. You will need to apply for a change of residency status and become a *travailleur indépendant* with a *carte de séjour indépendant*.

As a *travailleur indépendant*, you are responsible for all social charges and benefits associated with your income. That means you will have to make contributions to France's social security system, retirement funds and health coverage. You also need to keep the following in mind:

- **You need to make a net annual income of at least €12,500 which is the equivalent of the minimum wage (this number does change each year) in order for your** *carte de séjour* **to be renewed.**
- **Your sales figure is your gross income. You will end up with roughly 30–40 per cent of that figure as your personal income or 'salary'.**
- **As a** *travailleur indépendant*, **the contributions you make to social security will equal roughly 40 per cent of your total net income before income tax.**
- **You will pay income tax as well as the social charges.**
- **You are responsible for compensating yourself for any vacation you take.**
- **Although you will not have access to many of the benefits offers to salaried employees, you be able to write off business-related expenses such as business lunches, equipment such as computers, and additional health insurance payments to a** *mutuelle* **you might make. In addition, you may be able to write off your rent (or a portion of it) if you work from home.**
- **Sick leave and maternity leave are very poorly covered, although new laws are slowly changing this.**
- **If your business fails, you will not receive unemployment benefits (although there is insurance for failed businesses).**
- **You will be responsible for your own professional development such as paying for training courses.**

Income tax must be paid if you are salaried on your net income. For a *travailleur indépendant*, income tax is paid on your profit. Value added tax (*taxe sur la valeur ajoutée* – TVA) is currently 19.6 per cent and must be added to all your bills. TVA on your expenses is deductible from TVA billed and you must pay the difference to the tax authorities. If you are billing less than €27,000 for the year, you may be exempt from TVA but you will not be able to make deductions.

Next, a self-employed person must decide the type of business structure he wants. For the basic business structures, *see* 'Starting your Own Business', below. Also all self-employed people opt for sole proprietorship (*entreprise individuelle*).

Before finishing the section on freelancing, there is one last question to address. What happens when a UK freelancer works for a UK company while living in France? The short answer is that the freelancer could keep a UK bank account and arrange for his or her income to be paid into that account. The UK and France have reciprocal tax agreements so the income will be taxed by one country, in this case the UK. But if the freelancer wants to enjoy the benefits of the French social security system he will have to pay French income taxes. That means the UK would have to pay the French social security system on your behalf. Your status would probably have to change from 'freelancer' to 'employee' of the UK company.

Starting Your Own Business

This section merits a book of its own. Along with buying property in France, one of the most common reasons for Britons to move to France is because they want to start their own business, be it a bed & breakfast or vineyard. The first thing you'll need to decide is the type of business structure you want. There are various business structures to choose from that depend on your professional activity and desired tax liability. They range from small businesses for self-employed people (as described in the section above) to large businesses with plans to be publicly listed.

Before you start, consult your local *Chambre de Commerce et d'Industrie* (CCI) and *Chambre des Métiers* (also called the *Maison des Entreprises*) or Artisans' Registry. They offer literature and courses on how to start your own business. The CCI even published a guide in English, *Setting up a Business in France for non-French Nationals,* which costs €7.

Sole Proprietorship (*Entreprise Individuelle*)

As mentioned in the 'Freelancing' section, this is the business structure most foreigners choose. Sole proprietorships are businesses in which the operation is under the control of a single individual who has total liability for its operations. This business does not have the formal structure of a corporation and therefore the assets and liabilities of the company are of the individual owner. If you start a sole proprietorship, you report all profits and losses on your personal French income tax return. Artisans, tradesmen and small shops prefer this flexible business structure. A version of the *entreprise individuelle* is the *profession libérale,* for architects, doctors and lawyers.

Partnership

There are four types of partnerships in France. As in the case of a sole proprietorship, there is no capital requirement and profits and losses are passed on to the partners, who are also responsible for debts incurred. In a general partnership (*société en non collectif* – SNC) all partners are liable without limit for the debts of their business. Each partner can report the losses or profits of their share on their individual tax return. It must have at least two members. In a limited liability partnership (*société en commandité simple* – SCS) the liability of each partner is determined by his original investment (it has at least one unlimited general partner, and one or more partners with limited liability). The *société en commandité par actions* (SCA) is a joint-stock company whose active partners have unlimited liability. The last kind is a *société civile* (SC) that deals in civil matters such as building and agriculture (commonly used by estate agencies).

Corporations

By forming a corporation you are protected against liabilities incurred by the enterprise, except where the original investment is concerned. If the corporation goes bankrupt, shareholders' personal effects cannot be taken to pay off debts. There are different kinds of corporations and each has its own set of capital requirements. All can be managed by a single director or board of directors, and all can be fully foreign-owned. They are subject to income tax, TVA and corporation tax.

The most popular is the **limited liability company** (*société à responsibilité limitée* – SARL). It is privately owned and ideal for small businesses or shops. An SARL must be formed with from two to 50 shareholders and a managing director (*gérant*) must be appointed and is held financially accountable if managerial fault is found (the other shareholders are only responsible for the value of their shares). He is usually paid a salary. At the time of going to press the SARL requires a minimum capital of €7,620. If the SARL has employees, the costs associated with their social security payments and taxes are very high. A yearly audit is not required unless profits exceed certain pre-established limits.

A variant of the SARL is the **EURL** (*entreprise unipersonelle à responsabilité limitée*). This structure is held by one person (one shareholder).

A **larger corporation** is a *société anonyme* (SA), which is comparable to the British plc. The minimum number of shareholders is seven and there is no maximum. It is run by a board of directors (*conseil d'administration*) and a *président directeur général* (PDG), who is the equivalent of a chief executive officer.

In 1994 a new structure which combines the legal status of a corporation and the flexibility of a partnership was introduced. The *société anonyme simplifiée* (SAS) must have corporate capital of at least €23,000 and cannot issue publicly traded shares.

The last business structure is the representative or **branch office** (*succursale*). This is ideal for a UK newspaper, for example, that wants to open a news bureau in France; or a software company promoting a brand in France. The branch office is considered part of the parent company and head office is responsible for its liability.

Let's say you are ready to open a small business in France. You love antiques and spend a good portion of your free time going to antiques fairs, travelling from town to town. You have a good eye for furniture and decided you want to open your own table at the next antiques (*brocante*) fair. Here's what you'd do.

- The first step is to apply officially for the right kind of *carte de séjour* at the local police office (*prefecture*). In this case, you want a *carte commerçant étranger*. In order to get it, you must fill out a 15-page questionnaire (*dossier de carte commerçant étranger*). With that document, you must submit a business plan complete with financial statements. The Chambre de Commerce et d'Industrie (CCI) offers a five-day course called '*Cinq Jours Pour Entreprendre*' which explains how to fill in the various forms and the questionnaire.

- Once you get your *carte commerçant étranger* (it takes about four to six weeks after you apply), you must apply for the special permits and licences needed to do your business. To sell *brocante*, for example, you need two separate licences. The first is to sell used furniture and the second is to sell from a movable stand (as opposed to a store in a fixed location). There is a special office at the *préfecture* that issues these licences.

- The next step is to call the Centre de Formalités des Entreprises (CFE) to set up your business. This is the same as your local Chamber of Commerce. Before you make the appointment, make sure your paperwork is in order and that you have copies of your provisional licences. At the appointment, you must choose the business structure you want (*entreprise individuelle*, SARL, EURL or whatever). You must deposit an amount of money equal to the amount of your liability (€7,620 was the minimum at the time of going to press). Bring other documents to the appointment such as your marriage licence, divorce or widowed documents.

- You will leave the CFE meeting with provisional papers allowing you to start your business and a week or two later you should receive confirmation by post that your business has been registered.

It goes without saying that to set up a more complicated business, you will need to seek professional help from an accountant or solicitor.

Volunteering

Anyone who has dedicated time to volunteer or charity work knows what the payoffs are. In addition to the philanthropic rewards, there is an added benefit to doing volunteer work abroad. Volunteers enjoy a more direct and immediate entrée into the French language and culture. Some volunteers come specifically to brush up on language skills and to make French friends. Some come as short-term helpers and use the experience as a stepping-stone for establishing a long-term life in France. All are able to fulfil an altruistic need. The best way to

Case Study: On Top of the World

Where does a man who has lived in Rhodesia (now Zimbabwe), Mozambique, Kenya, South Africa, New York, the west coast of the USA, and who has spent a fair amount of time in Tahiti, New Zealand, the Cook Islands Australia, Hong Kong, Europe and Italy, call home? For this Englishman, home is the top of the world in the beautiful French Alps. 'Actually, you could say, my home is all over the world.'

Roger Farrell-Cook and his wife, Suzanne, live full-time in Aviernoz, Haute-Savoie. Fifteen years ago they bought a house here, with a characteristic slanted Alpine roof and thick walls set against the snow-capped peaks of the Parmelan mountains and surrounded by meadows and wild flowers. 'The idea was to have a *pied-à-terre* but the house was too big so we decided to open a hotel.' Now the couple – and playful canine mascot Alpha Tango – run Hotel Camelia (**www.hotelcamelia.com**) with 12 guestrooms. 'We love it here and are near everything. Geneva is 45 minutes away and we are close to the Rhône, Chamonix, Mont Blanc and the Italian border.'

Roger and Suzanne had no major problems starting their own business in France. 'We decided we wanted to welcome people to this beautiful part of the world and the rest was easy. Maybe the bureaucracy and paperwork were a bit more than I expected,' he explains. 'But there are no major difficulties provided you accept the norm.' The process, he adds, was made easier thanks to Suzanne's excellent French. Over the years, this successful business has grown to include a restaurant and space for seminars thanks to the friendly and hospitable nature of its owners – and their dog that has become somewhat of a local celebrity. He takes guests for walks, rather than the other way around.

After so many years abroad, does this globetrotter in France still feel English? 'We live in France and we are international, but I am born in England and relate to English culture,' says Roger. In fact, Roger celebrates his native roots when Hotel Camelia throws what he calls English Theme Night. 'We sit around and drink English beer and eat English food and, then, I start singing English songs – but none that I'd care for you to hear right now.'

live in France is by understanding the country's complexities, recognizing the marginalized parts of society and comprehending its basic woes.

If you read through the personal testimonials listed on the many websites that detail volunteer opportunities in France, you will note the calibre of the language used to describe the experience. 'Mind-blowing', 'amazing', 'changed my life', 'fulfilling' and 'rewarding' give the idea. If you want to find out about volunteering in France, here's how it works. There are dozens of French and international organizations that oversee volunteer programmes. Some are linked to religious groups and others are non-denominational. Others receive public funding or are affiliated with local universities. They operate in diverse sectors but the main ones are art restoration and archaeology, environmental and animal rights issues, human rights, social services, and working with people with disabilities.

In some cases, albeit rare, a volunteer will receive a small allowance. More realistically, you will be asked to pay a registration fee, ranging from €20 for two weeks to €150 for one month, to cover food, lodging, transport and insurance. Many groups operate in summer only. Each organization sets its own limits on age, but most do not accept volunteers under 16.

Two good resources, with bulletin boards and 'want ads' from individual organizations, are **www.responsibletravel.com** and **www.volunteerabroad.com**.

For example, **BTCV**, formerly known as the British Trust for Conservation Volunteers (**www.btcv.org**), operates in the Ravin de Valbois natural reserve in the Jura region. Near the Swiss border, the area is home to massive canyons and is rich with wildlife including wild boar, lynx, honey buzzards and falcons. The organization is looking for international volunteers to work with French students to help build dry stone walls, fences and keep scrub under control. In exchange, volunteers live on the grounds of the ancient Château de Cleron and can dedicate their free time to rock-climbing, canoeing and mountain-biking.

The Association **CHAM**, Chantiers Histoire & Architecture Médiévales (**www.cham.asso.fr**), headquartered in Paris, runs youth volunteer camps to preserve and restore historical monuments – mainly medieval castles and churches. No specific skills are required but volunteers work six hours per day, six days per week, for a minimum of 10 days. Under the guidance of a technical director, they work in masonry, move earth, clear vegetation and do stone-cutting and carpentry. Volunteers pay for their travel and a small daily registration fee and are given 'basic and correct' lodging.

Another popular group for those who like to work with historic buildings is the Paris-based **Rempart** (**www.rempart.com**). They run some two hundred archaeological and heritage sites in France (castles, chapels, abbeys and villages) and need people to work 35 hours per week. There is a small registration fee. Rempart is part of the European Forum Heritage Association and the *Comité de Coordination du Service Volontaire International*. Also in the art and archaeology sector is **La Sabranenque** (**www.sabranenque.com**) that operates during the summer and needs volunteers to work on masonry, tiling and paving. What sets this organization apart is the fact it operates in Provence and is focused on preserving the typical architecture and building techniques of this sunny region. **APARE**, or Association pour la Participation et l'Action Régionale (**www.apare-gec.org**), is another large umbrella group that organizes volunteer work in historic heritage sites.

L'Arche les Sapins (**www.archesapins.org**) is part of a network of 117 Christian communities worldwide for people with learning disabilities. The Les Sapins community is located in idyllic vineyard country in southwest France. There are four houses (seven people with learning disabilities in each) and four workshops focused on gardening, landscaping and vineyard work. Volunteers live and work with people with disabilities, help with housework and organize leisure activities. No specific skills or languages are required (volunteers receive about €250 a month plus room and board and basic health insurance).

The **Association des Paralysés de France (www.unat.asso.fr)** needs volunteers to work with adults with physical disabilities for about two weeks each summer. Pocket money and basic accommodation is provided.

The umbrella organization **Concordia International Volunteer Projects (www. concordia-iye.org.uk)**, based in England, requires volunteers (from 16–30) who are UK residents. This small non-profit charity group needs volunteers for community-based projects in more than 40 countries including France. Projects range from nature conservation, restoration, archaeology, construction, and working with children and adults with special needs. Projects last from two to four weeks and volunteers must pay a registration fee and fund their own travel and accommodation.

A similar umbrella organization in France is **Jeunesse et Reconstruction (www. volontariat.org)** (also in English), which is widely respected and very popular. They need young volunteers for work all over France to clear brush and dig drains or do any other number of tasks. This is one of the best organizations for meeting young French people and costs less than Concordia.

If you are interested in social programmes, you should look at **Solidarités Jeunesse (www.solidaritesjeunesses.org)**. This group organizes long-term (of up to one year) work programmes for volunteers to work with disadvantaged and disabled people. Young volunteers (aged 18–25) are needed for gardening, working with animals and organizing free-time activities. Travel, food and lodging are paid for.

If you decide to look for volunteer work outside some of the organizations listed above, the opportunities are limitless. You could volunteer to work in a vineyard during the harvest season in the autumn, or work with a local church to collect clothing for the poor. Or you could put your English-language skills to use at a local school, library or learning centre.

Reference

08

France at a Glance

Official name of country: *République Française*

Capital city: Paris

Type of government: Republic

Head of government: Prime Minister

Chief of State: President

Area: 547,030 sq km

Coastline: 3,427km

Location: Western Europe, bordering the Bay of Biscay and English Channel, between Belgium and Spain, southeast of the UK; bordering the Mediterranean Sea, between Italy and Spain

Climate: Generally cool winters and mild summers, but mild winters and hot summers along the Mediterranean; occasional strong, cold, dry, north-to-northwesterly wind known as mistral

Terrain: Mostly flat plains or gently rolling hills in north and west; remainder is mountainous, especially Pyrenees in south, Alps in east

Border countries: Andorra 56.6km, Belgium 620km, Germany 451km, Italy 488km, Luxembourg 73km, Monaco 4.4km, Spain 623km, Switzerland 573km

Languages and dialects: French 100 per cent, rapidly declining regional dialects and languages (Provençal, Breton, Alsatian, Corsican, Catalan, Basque, Flemish)

Ethnic groups: Celtic and Latin with Teutonic, Slavic, North African, Indochinese, Basque minorities

Population: 59,765,983 (July 2002)

Religion: Roman Catholic 83–88 per cent, Protestant 2 per cent, Jewish 1 per cent, Muslim 5–10 per cent, unaffiliated 4 per cent

Administrative divisions (22 regions): Alsace, Aquitaine, Auvergne, Basse-Normandie, Bourgogne, Bretagne, Centre, Champagne-Ardenne, Corse, Franche-Comté, Haute-Normandie, Ile-de-France, Languedoc-Roussillon, Limousin, Lorraine, Midi-Pyrénées, Nord-Pas-de-Calais, Pays de la Loire, Picardie, Poitou-Charentes, Provence-Alpes-Côte d'Azur, Rhône-Alpes

France is subdivided into 96 *départements* (*see* '*Départements*'), pp.277–8)

Overseas departments: French Guiana, Guadeloupe, Martinique, Réunion. Overseas territorial collectivities: Mayotte, Saint Pierre and Miquelon

Dependent areas: Bassas da India, Clipperton Island, Europa Island, French Polynesia, French Southern and Antarctic Lands, Glorioso Islands, Juan de Nova Island, New Caledonia, Tromelin Island, Wallis and Futuna

Constitution: 28 September 1958, amended concerning election of president in 1962, amended to comply with provisions of EC Maastricht Treaty in 1992, Amsterdam Treaty in 1996, Treaty of Nice in 2000; amended to tighten immigration laws 1993

Legal system: Civil law system with indigenous concepts; review of administrative but not legislative acts

Elections: President elected by popular vote for a five-year term (changed from seven-year term in 2001); prime minister nominated by the National Assembly majority and appointed by the president

Cabinet: Council of Ministers appointed by the president on the suggestion of the prime minister

Legislative branch: Bicameral Parliament, or *Parlement,* consists of the Senate (*Sénat*) (321 seats – 296 for metropolitan France, 13 for overseas departments and territories, and 12 for French nationals abroad; members are indirectly elected by an electoral college to serve nine-year terms; elected by thirds every three years) and the National Assembly (*Assemblée Nationale*) (577 seats; members are elected by popular vote under a single-member majoritarian system to serve five-year terms)

(*Source: CIA World Fact Book* 2002)

Further Reading

Reference

Applefield, David, *Paris Inside Out*
Barbour, Philippe, Dana Facaros and Michael Pauls, *France*
Hampshire, David, *Living and Working in France*
Igoe, Mark, and John Howell, *Buying a Property: France*
Link, Terry, *Adapter Kit France*
Platt, Polly, *French or Foe?*
Pybus, Victoria, *Live & Work in France*
Reilly, Saskia, and Lorin David Kalisky, *Living, Studying, and Working in France*
Steele, Ross, *The French Way*
Welty Rochefort, Harriet, *French Toast*

History

Ardagh, John, *France in the New Century*
Ardagh, John, *Cultural Atlas of France*
Barzini, Luigi, *The Europeans*
Braudel, Fernand, *The Identity of France*
Briggs, Robin, *Early Modern France: 1560–1715*
Buisseret, D. J., *Henry IV*
Cézanne, Paul, *Letters*
Cobb, Richard, *The French and their Revolution*
Cronin, Vincent, *Louis XIV*
Cronin, Vincent, *Napoleon*
Gilot, Françoise, *Life with Picasso*
Gramont, Sanche de, *The French: Portrait of a People*
Gregory of Tours, *The History of the Franks*
Hibbert, Christopher, *The French Revolution*
Keegan, John, *The First World War* and *The Second World War*
Knecht, R. J., *Catherine de' Medici*
Knecht, R. J., *The Rise and Fall of Renaissance France*
Mitford, Nancy, *The Sun King*

Pope Hennessy, James, *Aspects of Provence*
Price, Roger, *A Concise History of France*
Schama, Simon, *Citizens*
Madame de Sévigné, *Selected Letters*
Seward, Desmond, *The Hundred Years War*
Tapié, V. L., *France in the Age of Louis XIII and Richelieu*
Todd, Emmanuel, *The Making of Modern France*
Van Gogh, Vincent, *Collected Letters of Vincent Van Gogh*
Warner, Marina, *Joan of Arc: The Image of Female Heroism*
Weber, Eugene, *Paris 1900*
Weir, Alison, *Eleanor of Aquitaine*
Whitfield, Sarah, *Fauvism*
Wright, Gordon, *France in Modern Times*
Zeldin, Theodore, *France 1845–1945*
Zeldin, Theodore, *The French*

Literature and Travel

Balzac, Honoré de, *Lost Illusions*
Barnes, Julian, *Cross-Channel*
Camus, Albert, *L'Etranger*
Camus, Albert, *La Peste*
Daudet, Alphonse, *Letters from my Windmill*
Dickens, Charles, *A Tale of Two Cities*
Dumas, Alexandre, *The Count of Monte-Cristo*
Dumas, Alexandre, *The Man in the Iron Mask*
Dumas, Alexandre, *The Three Musketeers*
Faulks, Sebastian, *Birdsong*
Fitzgerald, F. Scott, *Tender is the Night*
Flaubert, Gustave, *Madame Bovary*
Giono, Jean, *To the Slaughterhouse, Two Riders of the Storm*
Hemingway, Ernest, *A Moveable Feast*
Hugo, Victor, *The Hunchback of Notre-Dame*
Hugo, Victor, *Les Misérables*
Ionesco, Eugène, *La Leçon*
James, Henry, *Collected Travel Writings*
Lamorisse, Albert, *The Red Balloon*
Leroux, Gaston, *The Phantom of the Opera*
Maupassant, Guy de, *Selected Short Stories*
Mayle, Peter, *Hotel Pastis*
Mayle, Peter, *Toujours Provence*
Mayle, Peter, *A Year in Provence*
Pagnol, Marcel, *Jean de Florette* and *Manon of the Springs*
Proust, Marcel, *Remembrance of Things Past*
Rosenblum, Mort, *The Secret Life of the Seine*
Rostand, Edmond, *Cyrano de Bergerac*
Royle, Nicholas (editor), *The Time Out Book of Paris Short Stories*

Saint-Exupéry, Antoine de, *Le Petit Prince*
Sartre, Jean-Paul, *Essays in Existentialism*
Sartre, Jean-Paul, *Truth and Existence*
Smollett, Tobias, *Travels through France and Italy*
Steel, Danielle, *Five Days in Paris*
Verne, Jules, *Around the World in 80 Days*
Verne, Jules, *Paris in the 20th Century*
Wharton, Edith, *A Motor-Flight Through France*
Wylie, Laurence, *Village in the Vaucluse*
Zola, Émile, *Germinal*

Dictionary of Useful and Technical Terms

A

abîmer	deteriorate
abonnement	standing charge
abri	shelter
acajou	mahogany
accueil	reception
acompte	deposit
acquérir	to buy
acte authentique	legal paper drawn up (with all due formalities), by a public officer empowered by law (e.g. a *notaire*) in the place where he officiates
acte de commerce	commercial act
acte de vente	a conveyance or transfer of land (sometimes referred to as *acte d'achat*)
acte sous seing privé	private agreement in writing with no witnesses (the pre-sale agreement)
actuellement	currently
affaire	bargain/business
agence immobilière	estate agent
Agence Nationale Pour l'Emploi (ANPE)	French National Employment Office
agence	agency
agrandissement	extension
agréé	registered
alimentation	supply (water, electricity, etc.)
aménagé	converted
amiante	asbestos
ancien	old
antenne	aerial
antenne parabolique	satellite dish
ardoise	slate

arrhes	sum paid in advance by the purchaser, forfeited if purchaser withdraws or double the amount refunded if the vendor withdraws
arrière-pays	hinterland
artisan maçon	expert builder
assurance complémentaire maladie	independent health insurance
atelier	workshop
attestation	certificate
attestation d'acquisition	a notarial certificate that the property purchase has been completed
avocat	solicitor

B

baguette	beading
bail	lease to tenant
balcon	balcony
banque	bank
bâtiment	building
béton	concrete
bois	wood
bon état	good condition
bord de mer/rivière	beside the sea/river
bouche d'aération	air vent
bouchon	stopper
boulon	bolt
bureau	office

C

cabinet	small room
cadastre	local town planning register
cadenas	padlock
cadre	frame
caisse des dépôts et consignations	deposits and consignment office
Caisse d'Epargne	savings bank
Caisse des Allocations Familiales	child benefit office
Caisse Nationale d'Assurance Vieillesse ou de Retraite	pensions office
Caisse Primaire d'Assurance Maladie	medical expenses office
cale	wedge, doorstop
campagne	country

caoutchouc	rubber
carillon	doorbell
carrelage	ceramic tiles
carreleur	tiler
carte de paiement	payment card
carte de résident	resident's card
carte de santé	medical record book
carte de séjour	government permit to reside in France (also called *permis de séjour*)
carte grise	car registration
carte professionnelle	granted by the *Préfecture* to estate agents to carry out business
carte verte	car insurance
carte vitale	health card
cause réelle et sérieuse	legitimate cause
caution solidaire	guarantor
cave	cellar
centre commercial	shopping centre
centre des impôts	tax office
certificat de ramonage	certificate of chimney sweeping
certificat d'urbanisme	zoning certificate (equivalent to a local authority search)
cession	sale
chambre	bedroom
chambre des métiers	chamber of trades
charges	maintenance charges on a property
charges comprises	service charges included
charges sociales	social charges
charnière	hinge
charpentier	carpenter
chasse	hunting
chaudière	water heater/boiler
chauffage	heating
chauffe eau	hot water tank
chaumière	thatched cottage
chaux	carbonate of lime
cheminée	chimney/fireplace
chêne	oak
chèque de banque	banker's draft
cheville	expanding wall lug (mawl lug)
chiffre d'affaire	turnover
clause d'accroissement	(also see *tontine*) agreement that purchase is made for the benefit of the last surviving purchaser
clause pénale	penalty clause governing performance of an agreement
climatisation	air-conditioning

cloison	partition
clôture	fence
clou	nail
code du travail	labour code
commerçant	commercial trader
commissariat de police	police station
comptabilité	accounting, book-keeping
compensable	the clearing of a cheque
comprenant	including
compromis de vente	contract for sale and purchase of land
compte à terme	deposit account
compte courant	current account
Compte d'Epargne Logement	home-buyers saving scheme
compte titre	shares account
concessionnaire	distributor
concours	selective entrance exam
condition suspensive	conditional terms stated in the pre-sale agreement (e.g. the acquiring of a loan, the gaining of a positive zoning certificate)
Conseil de Prud'homme	labour court
conservation des hypothèques	mortgage/land registry
constat amiable	accident report form
constat de dégat des eaux	water damage form
constructible	land which is designated for building under local planning scheme
contrat à durée déterminée	fixed-term contract
contrat de réservation	the purchase contract used for purchase 'on plan' (sometimes called contract *préliminaire*)
contrat multirisques habitation	all risks household policy
contrôle technique	MOT
conventionné (médecin)	doctor working in the health service
conventions collectives	collective agreements
copie exécutoire	enforceable copy
copropriété	co-ownership
couloir	corridor
courtier	broker
cuisine	kitchen
cuivre	copper

D

dale	flagstone
dallage	paving
débarras	box room
déclaration de sincérité	compulsory formula providing that the purchase price has not been increased by a counter-deed

dépendance	outbuilding
dépôt de vente	sale room
détendeur	gas pressure regulator
devis	estimate
disjoncteur	electric trip switch
distributeur automatique de billets	cash machine, ATM
domicile fiscal	tax address
droit au bail	right to a lease
droit de préemption	pre-emptive right to acquire the property instead of purchaser
droit de succession/donation	inheritance/gift tax

E

ébéniste	cabinet maker
échafaudage	scaffolding
échelle	ladder
éclairage	lighting
écurie	stable
EDF/GDF	the state utilities: *Electricité de France, Gaz de France*
émoluments	the scale of charges of the notaire
emplacement	site
emprunt	loan
encadrement	framing
enduit	filler
enregistrement (droits d')	registration of the title of ownership (following which are the payment of transfer duties)
entreprise individuelle	one-person business
entreprise unipersonnelle	one-person limited company
entretien	maintenance
épaisseur	thickness
équipé	equipped
escabeau	step ladder
escalier	stair
espace	space
espèces	cash
espagnolette	shutter/window fastening
établi	work bench
Etablissement Public de Communes	planning agency for a group of Coopération Intercommunale
étage	storey, floor
étagère	shelf
étanche	watertight

état des lieux	schedule of condition or schedule of dilapidation depending on whether it applies to the beginning or end of a lease
expédition	the certified copy of a notarial document showing the date of its registration and the registration duty paid
expert comptable	chartered accountant
expert foncier	professional to check on the state and value of the property (usually an architect)
expertiser	to value a property

F

facture	invoice/bill
faillite	bankruptcy
faute grave	serious fault
fer	iron
ferme	farm
ferraillage	ironwork
fibre dure	hardboard
finitions	finishings
FNAIM – Fédération Nationale des Agents Immobiliers	national association of estate agents, providing a compensation fund for compensation fund for defaulting agents
Fonds Commun de Placement	unit trusts
fonds de commerce	business plus goodwill
fonds de roulement	capital supplied by all flat-owners, in an apartment block, on top of service charges to meet unexpected liabilities
forfait	fixed amount
fosse septique	septic tank
foyer	fireplace
frais de dossier	arrangement fee
frais de notaire	notary's fee
franchisé	franchisee
franchiseur	franchisor

G

garantie d'achèvement	guarantee of completion
garde-corps	railings
gardien	caretaker
gazon	turf
Gendarmerie Nationale	police

géomètre	surveyor appointed by the *notaire* to certify the dimensions of the property according to the *cadastre*
gérant	legal manager
gond	shutter hinge pin
gouttière	gutter
grange	barn
gravier	gravel
Greffe du Tribunal de Commerce	clerk of the commercial court
grenier	attic
guichet	counter, ticket office

H

haie	hedge
honoraires libres	any amount above the recommended social security fee
HT – hors-taxe	not including sales tax
huissier	has many official duties, including bailiff and process server; is used to record evidence (for example on the state of property) where legal proceedings are considered
hypothèque	mortgage – where the property is used as security for the loan

I

impôt foncier	land tax
indemnité d'éviction	compensation for eviction
indivision	joint ownership
interrupteur	switch
isolation	insulation

J

jardin	garden
joint	grouting
jouissance	right of possession which must occur simultaneously with the transfer of ownership

L

laiton	brass
lambris	grooved wood panelling
lavabo	wash basin

laverie	laundry
lettre de change	bill of exchange
lettre de non-gage	letter showing there are no outstanding debts attached
liège	cork
lime	file
lingerie	washing room/airing cupboard
linteau	lintel
lisse	smooth
livraison	delivery
livret A, B jeune or CODEVI	savings accounts
location	renting (tenancy)
logement	accommodation
loi Carrez	law by which property measurements are certified
loi Scrivener	the law protecting borrowers from French lenders and sellers on French property purchases in all cases other than a purchase on plan
longueur	length
loquet/loqueteau	door catch
lotissement	housing estate
lots	land registry plots applied in apartment blocks

M

maçon	builder
mairie	town hall
maison de campagne	country house
maison de maître	gentleman's house
maison mère	parent company
mandat	power of attorney, proxy
mandat de recherche	private agreement giving power to estate agent to look for property
manoir	manor house
marchand de biens	property dealer
marquise	porch
mas	farmhouse
mazout	heating oil (domestic use)
médecines douces	alternative medicine
médecin généraliste	GP
médecin spécialiste	specialist
menuiserie	woodwork factory
meubles	furniture
meuleuse	angle grindstone, millstone
minuteur	time switch
monuments historiques	listed buildings

moquette	fitted carpet
mortier	mortar
moulure	moulding
mur	wall
mutuelle (complémentaire santé)	top-up health cover

N

niveau	level
notaire	notary
notaire public	notary public
nue-propriété	reversionary interest where the purchaser has no occupational rights over the property until the death or prior surrender of the life tenant

O

occupation	occupant of the premises (either tenant or occupant without good title)
offre d'achat/de vente	an offer to buy or sell property which is not itself a binding contract
ordonnance	prescription
Organismes de Placement de Capital en Valeurs Mobilières	unit trusts

P

pacte civil de solidarité (PACS)	tax application to non-marital relationships
paiement comptant	cash payment
paiement de notes de frais	benefit in kind
paillasson	door mat
papier peint	wall paper
parc	park
parquet	wood floor
participation aux résultants	profit sharing
parties communes	common parts of buildings
parties privatives	parts of the building restricted to the private use of the owner
peinture	paint
pelle	shovel
pelouse	lawn
pépinière	garden centre
perceuse	drill
permis de construire	planning permission
pharmacie de garde	chemist on duty
pièce	room

pierre	stone
pilier	pillar
pin	pine
pinceau	paint brush
pince universelle	pliers
piquet de terre	earthing pin
piscine	swimming pool
placard	cabinet
plafond	ceiling
plain pied	single storey
planche	plank
plan de financement	financing scheme
plan d'occupation des sols	zoning document
plâtre	plaster
plomberie	plumbing
plus-value	capital gain realized on the sale of the property
poignée	handle
portail	garden gate
porte coulissante	sliding door
potager	kitchen garden
poteau	post
poussière	dust
poutre	wooden beam
poutre apparente	exposed beam
poutrelle	girder, RSJ
Préfecture de Police	police headquarters
prélèvement	direct debit
prieuré	priory
prime à l'aménagement du territoire	regional selective assistance
prime de frais d'installation	settling in funds
prise	electric socket
prise de terre	earth socket
privilège de prêteur de deniers	mortgage
prolongateur	extension lead
promesse de vente	unilateral agreement to sell
promoteur immobilier	property developer
propriétaire	owner
propriété	property

Q

quincaillerie	hardware shop
quotient familial	family quota (insurance)

R

rage	rabies
ramoneur	chimney sweep
rangements	storage space
redevance TV	TV licence
refait	restored
registre du commerce et des sociétés	registrar of companies
règlement national d'urbanisme	national town planning rules
rejeter	to bounce a cheque
relevé d'identité bancaire (RIB)	bank account details
rénové	renovated
répertoire des métiers	register of trade
réservation	the deposit paid in a *contrat de réservation*
réservation, contrat de	type of contract for the purchase of property *état d'achèvement futur*
réservoir	cistern
résiliation	cancellation of a contract
responsabilité civile	public liability cover
restauré	renovated
retraite	retirement
revenu minimum d'insertion	income support
revêtement	surface
rez-de-chaussée	ground floor
robinet	tap
roche	rock

S

sable	sand
SAFER	local government organization supposed to ensure the proper use of agricultural land; sometimes they will hold pre-emptive rights to buy land
salle de bains	bathroom
salle de séjour	living room
salon	drawing room
SAMU (Service d'Aide Médicale d'Urgence)	emergency medical service
Sapeurs-Pompiers	fire brigade
scie	saw
seau	bucket
sécurité sociale	social security
séjour (salle de)	living room
serre joint	clamp

Service Mobile d'Urgence et de Réanimation	emergency medical unit
société	legally registered company
société à responsabilité limitée (SARL)	limited liability company
société anonyme (SA)	company with limited shares
société civile (SC)	non-trading company
société civile immobilière	non-trading property company
société commerciale	commercial company
Société d'Investissement à Capital Variable	unit trust
société de fait	de facto company
société en commandite (SEC)	joint stock company
société en nom collectif (SNC)	general partnership company
sol	ground
sous-couche	undercoat
sous seing privé	non registered deed
sous-sol	underground, basement
store	roller blind
store vénitien	Venetian blinds
surface commerciale	commercial premises
syndicat de copropriétaires	assembly of co-owners

T

tacite reconduction	automatic renewal (of a contract)
tantième	proportion of the common parts of a *copropriété* owned jointly with other apartment owners
tartre	lime deposit
taxe d'habitation	rate levied on the occupation of property
taxe foncière	local tax on the ownership of property
taxe nationale	state tax
taxe professionnelle	business licence fee
teck	teak
terrain	grounds
terre cuite	terracotta
testament	will
timbre fiscal	revenue stamp
titre de propriété	title deeds
toit	roof
toiture	roofing
tontine	joint ownership
tournevis	screwdriver
tout à l'égout	main drainage system
tribunal administratif	civil service court
tribunal de commerce	commercial court

troisième âge	senior citizens (old age pensioners)
tronçonneuse	chain saw
truelle	trowel
TTC – toutes taxes comprises	including sales tax
tuile	roof tile
tuile à canal	roman tile (curved)
tuile de rive	edge tile
TVA – taxe sur la valeur ajoutée	value added tax (VAT)

U

urgences	emergency units
usufruit	usufruct (right to use an asset)

V

vanne	heavy duty tap
variateur	dimmer switch
vente en l'état futur d'achèvement	purchase of an un-built property
verger	orchard
vernis	varnish
vestibule	entrance hall
vignette	fiscal stamp
virement bancaire	credit transfer
vitre	window pane
volet	shutter
vue	view

Internet Vocabulary

adresse électronique	e-mail address
annexe	attachment
arobas	at sign (@)
courriel	e-mail
deux points	colon (:)
groupe de discussion	newsgroup, chat group
imprimer	to print
lien/hyperlien	link
messagerie/courrier électronique	e-mail
mot de passe	password
moteur de recherche	search engine
navigateur/explorateur	browser
naviguer/fureter	browse, navigate

page d'accueil	home page
page web	web page
point (point-com)	dot (dotcom)
rafraîchir	refresh, reload
redémarrer	reboot
se loguer	to log on
signet	bookmark
site web/site Internet	website
slash	/
télécharger	download
tiret	hyphen
tout attaché/en un seul mot	all one word
tout en minuscules	all in lower case
www (trois double-vé)	World Wide Web

Public Holidays and Events

1 January — *Nouvel An* or *Jour de l'An*. Latenight revelling on 31 December (*Saint-Sylvestre*) is usually followed by a family gathering around the dinner table on New Year's Day. Relatives and friends call and small gifts may be exchanged. If you have a doorman (*concierge*) this is a good time to give him a tip (*étrennes*).

Easter Monday — *Lundi de Pâques*. Good Friday is not a national holiday but Easter Monday is. This is another excuse for family reunions and the consumption of huge amounts of food.

1 May — *Fête du Travail*. International Labour Day in France is closely associated with the traditional exchange of lilies of the valley (*muguet*). The delicate spring flowers are sold in bunches or in small terracotta pots and given as a symbol of good luck, happiness and friendship.

8 May — *Fête de la Libération* or *Victoire* (French Liberation Day 1945). Elaborate street parades are staged throughout France with the largest and most impressive on the Champs-Elysées in Paris.

Ascension Day — *L'Ascension*. Christian holiday.

Whitsun or Pentecost — *La Pentecôte*. Christian holiday.

14 July — *Le Quatorze Juillet* (Bastille Day). The mother of all French holidays (Fête Nationale) ends with a spectacular firework display. Parties and parades start the night before in order to build momentum before the Bastille Day pyrotechnic bonanza, which usually starts at midnight. Don't miss the fireworks high above Trocadéro in Paris.

15 August	*L'Assomption* (Assumption). This Christian holiday is otherwise known as the beginning of the end of summer. Offices are closed and people head to the beaches or the mountains to escape the heat – working is considered criminal.
1 November	*La Toussaint* (All Saints' Day). Today, this holiday has been overshadowed by America's Hallowen celebrated the night before. French children dress up in scary costumes and carve pumpkins into jack-o'-lanterns. On 2 November (All Souls' Day) it is customary to visit the graves of dead relatives.
11 November	*Fête de l'Armistice* (Armistice Day). The equivalent of US Veterans' Day.
25 December	*Noël* (Christmas). *Le Réveillon*, or the traditional Christmas dinner, may include white sausage (*boudin blanc*), *foie gras*, smoked salmon, or oysters. The classic Christmas dessert is a chocolate cake shaped like a log known as the *bûche de Noël*.

In addition to these 11 national holidays, most cities and towns celebrate their own special saint day in which local banks, schools and public offices are closed. There are other odd holidays such as *la Sainte Catherine* on 25 November when 25-year-old single women are given funny hats to wear and are invited to dances. April Fool's Day is celebrated with practical jokes known as *poisson d'avril* (traditionally, pranksters make paper fish and stick them on the backs of unsuspecting friends).

When a holiday is tagged on to a weekend (Monday or Friday) the three-day block is known as *le pont*, or the 'bridge'.

France hosts many international events, the most notable of which is the Cannes Film Festival in May. Billed as the biggest film festival in the world, it is regarded as the definitive showcase for quality cinema.

In nearby Monaco (in May or early June) sporting fans flock to hear the moaning of engines at the Formula One Grand Prix event. The Tour de France cycling race is held in stages throughout the country in late July and fans line country roads with banners and signs to cheer on their favourite athletes. Tennis fans won't want to miss the French Tennis Open in Paris.

Wine and food fairs are also held in various regions especially around the grape harvest time in the autumn. For example, the Great Vintages of Burgundy Festival is split between five locations – Noyers-sur-Serein, Meursault, Chablis, Cluny and Gevrey-Chambertin – and is held in September.

Départements

France is divided into 22 regions and 95 *départements*. Departments 91–95 are part of the Ile-de-France regions that also includes metropolitan Paris (75), Seine-et-Marne (77) and Yvelines (78).

01	Ain	04	Alpes-de-Haute-Provence
02	Aisne	05	Hautes-Alpes
03	Allier	06	Alpes-Maritimes

07	Ardèche	52	Haute-Marne
08	Ardennes	53	Mayenne
09	Ariège	54	Meurthe-et-Moselle
10	Aube	55	Meuse
11	Aude	56	Morbihan
12	Aveyron	57	Moselle
13	Bouches-du-Rhône	58	Nièvre
14	Calvados	59	Nord
15	Cantal	60	Oise
16	Charente	61	Orne
17	Charente-Maritime	62	Pas-de-Calais
18	Cher	63	Puy-de-Dôme
19	Corrèze	64	Pyrénées-Atlantiques
20	Corse	65	Hautes-Pyrénées
21	Côte-d'Or	66	Pyrénées-Orientales
22	Côtes-d'Armor	67	Bas-Rhin
23	Creuse	68	Haut-Rhin
23	Dordogne	69	Rhône
25	Doubs	70	Haute-Saône
26	Drôme	71	Saône-et-Loire
27	Eure	72	Sarthe
28	Eure-et-Loir	73	Savoie
29	Finistère	74	Haute-Savoie
30	Gard	75	Paris
31	Haute-Garonne	76	Seine-Maritime
32	Gers	77	Seine-et-Marne
33	Gironde	78	Yvelines
34	Hérault	79	Deux-Sèvres
35	Ille-et-Vilaine	80	Somme
36	Indre	81	Tarn
37	Indre-et-Loire	82	Tarn-et-Garonne
38	Isère	83	Var
39	Jura	84	Vaucluse
40	Landes	85	Vendée
41	Loir-et-Cher	86	Vienne
42	Loire	87	Haute-Vienne
43	Haute-Loire	88	Vosges
44	Loire-Atlantique	89	Yonne
45	Loiret	90	Territoire de Belfort
46	Lot	91	Essonne
47	Lot-et-Garonne	92	Hauts-de-Seine
48	Lozère	93	Seine-Saint-Denis
49	Maine-et-Loire	94	Val-de-Marne
50	Manche	95	Val-d'Oise
51	Marne		

Regional Climate and Rainfall Chart

Average monthly temperatures, °Centigrade (daily maximum and minimum), and rain (monthly mm)
(Source: USA Today/US Met Office)

	Jan	Feb	Mar	Apr	May	June	July	Aug	Sept	Oct	Nov	Dec
Le Havre												
max	6	6	8	10	13	16	18	19	17	14	9	7
min	4	3	6	7	11	13	16	16	14	11	7	5
rain	14	10	12	11	11	9	9	9	11	12	12	13
Carcassonne												
max	9	11	14	16	19	24	28	28	24	18	13	10
min	2	3	4	6	10	13	15	15	12	9	5	3
rain	76	64	66	66	71	66	53	58	71	86	89	86
Lyon												
max	6	8	12	14	19	23	27	26	22	16	10	7
min	1	1	3	6	10	14	16	16	12	8	4	2
rain	43	41	51	61	76	79	66	79	76	86	69	51
Corsica												
max	13	13	14	17	21	24	27	28	26	22	17	14
min	4	4	6	7	11	14	17	17	15	12	8	5
rain	74	64	61	53	41	23	8	15	43	91	102	84
Nice												
max	13	13	14	16	19	23	26	27	24	20	16	13
min	6	6	8	9	13	17	19	20	17	13	9	6
rain	76	74	74	64	48	38	18	30	66	112	117	89
Paris												
max	6	7	11	14	18	21	24	24	21	15	9	7
min	1	1	3	6	9	12	14	14	11	8	4	2
rain	20	16	18	17	16	14	13	12	14	17	17	19
Strasbourg												
max	4	6	11	14	19	22	24	24	21	14	8	5
min	−1	−1	2	4	9	12	14	13	11	7	2	0
rain	36	33	36	46	66	74	76	71	61	51	48	3

Chronology

BC
c. 1,000,000: Arrival of first people in France
35,000–9,000: Palaeolithic cave painting
c. 4500: Beginnings of Neolithic civilization
c. 1000: Beginnings of Celtic migration
c. 600: Marseille founded as a Greek colony
121: Roman conquest of Provence
58: Julius Caesar begins the conquest of Gaul

AD
260–76: Incursions of Alemanni and Franks
c. 397: Death of St Martin of Tours
406: Germanic tribes breach the Rhine
c. 450: Celtic refugees from Britain begin to settle in Brittany
455: Visigothic kingdom established in Aquitaine, Franks occupy much of northern Gaul, Burgundians the Rhône Valley
475: Formal end of the Western Roman Empire
Clovis (482–511) Merovingian Frank rules most of Gaul
511: Division of Frankish kingdom between Clovis' four sons
578: Gascons (Basques) begin to settle what is now Gascony
687: Pepin of Herstal reunites the three Merovingian kingdoms
732: Charles Martel stops the Arab invasion at the Battle of Poitiers
Pepin the Short (751–68)
754–6: Frankish invasions of Italy in support of the Pope
Charles Ier (Charlemagne, 768–814)
800: Charlemagne crowned Emperor in Rome
Louis Ier (the Pious, 814–40)
843: Treaty of Verdun, division of the Carolingian Empire into three parts
845: First Viking raid on Paris
Charles II (the Bald, 843–77)
885: Count Eudes repels Vikings from Paris
Eudes (888–98)
896: Vikings begin to settle in Normandy
911: Duchy of Normandy created under Norman Duke Rollo
Hugues Capet (987–96)
1066: Duke William of Normandy conquers England
1095: First Crusade proclaimed at Clermont

1115: Foundation of the first Cistercian abbey at Clairvaux, by St Bernard
Louis VII (1137–80)
1140: St-Denis begun, first Gothic church
1142: Death of Peter Abelard
1152: Louis divorces Eleanor of Aquitaine, who in turn marries Henry II of England
Philippe II Auguste (1180–1223)
1190: Building of the original Louvre
1204–8: Philippe Auguste wrests control of Normandy, Anjou and the Touraine from the English
1209: Albigensian Crusade begins
1214: French victory at the Battle of Bouvines
1218: Death of Simon de Montfort at the Siege of Toulouse
Louis VIII (1223–6)
Louis IX (St Louis, 1226–70)
1249: Louis's crusade to Egypt results in his capture in battle
Philippe IV (the Fair, 1285–1314)
1302: First meeting of the Estates-General
1305: Papacy moves to Avignon
Louis X (1314–16)
Philippe V (1316–22)
Charles IV (the Fair, 1322–28)
Philippe VI (1328–50)
1328: Edward III of England proclaims himself King of France; Hundred Years' War begins
1346: Battle of Crécy
1347–9: The Black Plague
Jean II (the Good, 1350–64)
1358: Revolt of Etienne Marcel
Charles V (1364–80)
Charles VI (1380–1422)
1392: Beginnings of the factional strife of Armagnacs and Bourguignons
1420: English occupy Paris
Charles VII (1422–61)
1438: Pragmatic Sanction places the French Church under royal control
1453: English chased out of France
Louis XI (1461–83)
1482: Burgundy becomes part of France
Charles VIII (1483–98)
1494: First invasion of Italy
Louis XII (1498–1515)
François Ier (1515–47)

1515–47: Wars in Italy
1525: François Ier captured in battle by imperial forces at Pavia
     Henri II (1547–59)
1559: Treaty of Cateau-Cambrésis; end of French designs in Italy
     François II (1559–60)
     Charles IX (1560–74)
1562: Beginning of the Wars of Religion
1572: St Bartholomew's Day massacre of Protestants
     Henri III (1574–89)
1589: Assassinations of the Duc de Guise and the King
     Henri IV (1589–1610)
1594: Henri IV converts to Catholicism, enters Paris
1598: Edict of Nantes proclaimed; end of religious wars
     Louis XIII (1610–43)
1610–24: Regency of Marie de' Medici
1624: Cardinal Richelieu becomes minister
1627–8: Siege of Huguenot La Rochelle
     Louis XIV (1643–1715)
1643: Cardinal Mazarin becomes minister
1659: Treaty of the Pyrenees with Spain; France gains Roussillon
1682: King abandons Paris for newly built Palace of Versailles
1685: Revocation of the Edict of Nantes
1701–19: War of the Spanish Succession
     Louis XV (1715–74)
1715–23: Regency of Philippe d'Orléans
1720: Bursting of John Law's 'Mississippi Bubble'
1756–63: Seven Years' War; France loses most of its American possessions to Britain
     Louis XVI (1774–92)
1789: Beginning of Revolution; convocation of the Estates-General, storming of the Bastille
1791: Old provinces abolished; France divided into *départements*
1792: First Republic proclaimed
1793: The Terror; execution of Louis XVI
1795–9: Rule of the Directoire
1799: 'Coup de Brumaire'; Napoleon seizes power
     Napoleon Ier (Emperor, 1804–15)

1814: Allies enter Paris; Napoleon sent to Elba
     Louis XVIII (1814–24)
1815: The Hundred Days; Battle of Waterloo
     Charles X (1824–30)
1830: Revolt of the 'Trois Glorieuses' overthrows Charles X
     Louis-Philippe (1830–48)
1848: 'Revolution of contempt'; Second Republic formed
1851: Coup of Louis-Napoleon
     Napoleon III (Emperor, 1852–70)
1870: Franco-Prussian War; disaster at Sedan, siege of Paris
1871: Paris Commune; Third Republic proclaimed at Versailles
1889: Paris Exposition, opening of Eiffel Tower
1894: 'Dreyfus Affair' begins
1914–18: First World War; France loses 10 per cent of its population
1919: Treaty of Versailles
1920: Newly elected President Paul Deschanel goes mad, falls off a train in the middle of the night and wanders through France in his pyjamas
1927: Construction starts on the Maginot Line
1934: Stavisky scandals: demonstrations and riots
1936: Election of Popular Front government
1940: Defeat by the Nazis; 'French State' government set up at Vichy in the unoccupied zone under Marshal Pétain
1943: Germans occupy all of France
1944: Normandy landings
1946: Fourth Republic; De Gaulle in power 1946–8
1954: Defeat in Vietnam at Dienbienphu
1958: Return of De Gaulle to power
1962: Retreat from Algeria, followed by the migration of a million *pied noirs* into France
1968: Students' revolt; De Gaulle resigns the following year
1968: Opening of space port at Kourou, French Guiana
1981: Election of first Socialist President, François Mitterrand
1995: Jacques Chirac elected president
1996: Death of François Mitterrand

Index

rooster symbol 67
Rouen 29
Rousillon 47

St-Emilion 35
St-Jean-de-Luz 37
St-Malo 30
St-Nazaire 30, 31
St-Omer 38
St-Pol-de-Leon 31
St-Raphaël 46
St-Rémy-de-Provence 44
St-Tropez 46
salaries and bonuses 245
sales 190
Sancerre 31
SARL 254
satellite TV 76, 185–6, 236
savings rate 215
Savoy 43
schools *see* education
seasonal employment
    236–8
seatbelts 200
Second World War 18–19
secondary schools 220
self-employment 111, 251–5
Senate 67, 68
Sens 40
septic tanks 181
services sector 81, 235
shopping 188–94
    clothes shops 193
    DIY shops 194
    markets 193–4
    opening hours 189, 276–7
    retail employment 236
    returning goods 190
    sales 190
    supermarkets 189, 194
    types of shops 190–3
short-term loans 153
sickness leave 248
signing contracts 169
sirocco 10
skiing 228
social services 82, 213–17, 253
Socialist Party 68
sole ownership of property
    154
sole proprietorships 253

solicitors (*avocat*) 138, 140–1,
    142, 234
Sologne 32
    food and drink 101
Somme 38
Sophia-Antipolis 45, 216
Southwest France 33–6
speed limits 200
sports 225–8
starting a business 111,
    253–5, 256
statement of sincerity 172–3
Strasbourg 39
Sully, Duc de 15
Sun King 15
supermarkets 189, 194
surveys 145–8
swimming pools 145, 181

tabac 192
take-away food 195
Tapie, Bernard 84
Tarbes 37
taxation 127–8, 175, 215
    income tax 252
    TVA (value added tax) 81,
        174, 252
    under-declaring purchase
        price 159–60
tea 195
teaching English 249–51
telephones 178, 181–3, 231
television 75–7, 185–6, 236
temperature chart 279
temporary employment
    contracts 244
tennis 228
termination of employment
    249
terms of employment 245–9
theatres 93–4, 236
Toulon 46
Toulouse 36
Touraine, food and drink 100
tourism 236
Tours 32
trains 80–1, 116, 117, 198–9
travel 111–18, 197–206
    airlines 112–14, 199–200
    buses 198
    coaches 116

ferries 118
Paris *métro* 197–8
road network 80–1, 115
trains 80–1, 116, 117, 198–9
see also cars
tricolour flag 67
Troyes 39
TVA (value added tax) 81, 174,
    252

under-declaring purchase
    price 159–60
unemployment 82, 233
    benefits 215–17, 249
Union for French Democracy
    (UDF) 69
union membership 82
universities 223
utilities 177–83
    electricity 178, 179–80
    gas 178, 180
    payment options 178–9
    telephones 178, 181–3, 231
    water 178, 181

Vaison-la-Romaine 45
value added tax (TVA) 81, 174,
    252
Van Gogh, Vincent 9
Vascones 11
Vaucluse 44–5
Vendée 33
Verdun 39
Vézelay 40
Vichy 18–19, 40
viewing a property 138–9
Villeneuve lez Avignon 44
visas 121–2
visual arts 9, 10, 95–7
volunteer work 255–8
Vosges 39

wages, salaries and bonuses
    245
walking 226–7
Wanadoo 181, 183–4
water 178, 181, 195
water sports 228
weather 9, 10, 279
wedding services 236